BEYOND EGOTISM

BEYOND EGOTISM

The Fiction of James Joyce,
Virginia Woolf,
and D. H. Lawrence

ROBERT KIELY

Harvard University Press

Cambridge, Massachusetts
and London, England
1980

Publication of this book has been aided by a grant
from the Hyder Edward Rollins Fund

Library of Congress Cataloging in Publication Data

Kiely, Robert.
  Beyond egotism.

  Includes bibliographical references and index.
    1. English fiction—20th century—History and criticism. 2. Joyce, James,
1882–1941—Criticism and interpretation. 3. Woolf, Virginia Stephen,
1882–1941—Criticism and interpretation. 4. Lawrence, David Herbert,
1885–1930—Criticism and interpretation. I. Title.
PR881.K5   823′.912′093   80-14231
ISBN 0-674-06896-3

For
Anne, Jan, Christina, and Maria

ACKNOWLEDGMENTS

It is impossible to study Joyce, Woolf, and Lawrence without being continually aware of and grateful to the scholars and critics who have interpreted their lives and works and edited their letters, essays, and fiction. Some of them are mentioned in the notes, but I would like to express particular indebtedness to Richard Ellmann, S. L. Goldberg, Harry Levin, F. R. Leavis, Harry T. Moore, George Ford, Frank Kermode, Quentin Bell, and Nigel Nicholson. My project would have been all but inconceivable without their work.

More personally, I recall with increasing admiration the inspired teachers of the Amherst College English Department during my undergradute career twenty-five years ago. However I may have changed since that time, my approach to literature has been indelibly marked by the influence of Theodore Baird, Reuben Brower, Armour Craig, and, most of all, C. L. Barber, who endured with saintly patience my senior thesis on *Finnegans Wake*.

My own students at Harvard have been such a consistent source of encouragement and learning that to single out a few is a symbolic way of thanking many. Three former graduate students, Bridget Puzon, Penelope Laurans, and Bruce Robbins, and two of the more than fifty undergraduates I have tutored, Cass Sunstein and Daniel O'Neill, represent to me that combination of literary intelligence, moral commitment, and curiosity that has been a delight and refreshment to me as a teacher.

My wife and children have put up with much—sudden shifts in mood, prolonged absences of mind and body—but they have never been far from me, nor I from them.

Finally, this book was written in three places that I love very much. It was begun in The Old Vicarage, Grantchester; it was continued at Musterfield Farm, New Ipswich, New Hampshire; and it was finished in my fifth-floor study in Widener Library at Harvard. I did not change locations to accommodate each of my authors. All three seemed to be at home wherever I went.

R.K.
Cambridge, Massachusetts

Contents

BEYOND EGOTISM

Introduction

I read the first 2 pages of the usual sloppy English and . . . a lyrical bit about nudism in a wood and the end which is a piece of propaganda in favour of something which, outside of D.H.L.'s country at any rate, makes all the propaganda for itself.

JAMES JOYCE on *Lady Chatterley's Lover*

My God, what a clumsy *olla putrida* James Joyce is! Nothing but old fags and cabbage-stumps of quotations from the Bible and the rest, stewed in the juice of deliberate, journalistic dirty-mindedness.

D. H. LAWRENCE on *Ulysses*

I reflected how what I'm doing is probably being better done by Mr. Joyce.

I am also reading D.H.L. . . . he and I have too much in common—the same pressure to be ourselves.

VIRGINIA WOOLF, *A Writer's Diary*

〄

THIS IS A BOOK about the fiction of James Joyce, D. H. Lawrence, and Virginia Woolf. It is based on the premise that, despite major differences, much can be learned from thinking about these writers in reference to one another and, more particularly, by trying to be responsive to resemblances among them. In part, this premise is derived from my inability to choose. Since I was a student, I have been enchanted, instructed, and moved by all three. To join a critical camp in favor of one has too often seemed to require a betrayal of the other two, an act in which my imagination perhaps more than my conscience prevented me from engaging.[1] There is no doubt that the dialectic implied by a "battle of the books" has been a useful instrument of critical inquiry into the work of these authors and a partially accurate descriptive structure of cultural complexity for centuries. But it is worthwhile from time to time for critics to remember that their approaches to literature, much like the works of art with which they deal, are strongly influenced, if not governed, by metaphor. The imagery of conflict is not intrinsically superior as a categorical construct to that evoked by phrases like "schools of thought" or "the republic of letters."

Such constructs can be useful, like any other metaphor, so long as their limits are not mistaken for the boundaries of reality. To pit great writers in deadly warfare against one another can yield insights into their originality, but it is unlikely to exhaust the possibilities of responsiveness to their works. Contemporary critics have shied away from the old-fashioned anthology tactic of grouping authors according to "schools" for the very good reason that it too often has led to rigid simplifications—Blake, Keats, and Coleridge lined up like good children in neat rows. They have also rejected the bland alternative of a literary democracy in which every book has one vote. Yet even these tattered metaphors contain the fragments of an important truth. The literary works of a given period and culture tend to sustain, reflect upon, and, in some ways, resemble one another. To speak of Metaphysical poets, Augustan essayists, or Victorian novelists is not to be satisfied that the last word has been said about particular groups of writers or to deny important differences among them; but it does acknowledge that they shared time and language, a sense of past and present, and inherited conventions of expression that put them in a unique relation to one another.

Reading through the letters, reviews, critical essays, and fiction of Joyce, Lawrence, and Woolf, one is, of course, struck by obvious differences in style, temperament, and background. But there are similarities that should not be ignored. They were contemporaries and, though their education and reading habits varied, the same body of literature in English, especially that written and published in the nineteenth century, was more or less familiar to all three and represented a common ancestry. For Joyce, Lawrence, and Woolf, as for their entire generation, Hardy was the most important novelist of their immediate predecessors. Scott and Dickens had established the seemingly indestructible conventions of idiomatic dialogue, intricate plot, and authorial intervention, but Hardy had shown new directions for prose fiction. Each of the three was familiar with popular Victorian poetry, especially the work of Tennyson and Browning, but the Romantic poets seemed closer to them; they provided the greater inspiration and stirred a more intense reaction. Finally, all three felt themselves to be outcasts, living on the fringes of their society: one because of his place of birth, one because of her sex, and one because of his social class. Joyce's and Lawrence's lives of self-imposed exile make the point clear. The case of Woolf is less obvious. But Bloomsbury and the Hogarth Press notwithstanding, Woolf never thought of herself as at the center of the literary or any other establishment. Had they been poets, none would have been conceivable candidates for the laureateship.

One hundred years from now it may strike readers in China and perhaps even in Britain and the United States that differences in sex, class, and nationality are no more important in trying to understand Joyce, Lawrence, and Woolf than the fact that they were contemporaries, living outside of the political and cultural mainstream of their time, writing in the English language, and choosing the novel, as it had evolved in Britain and on the Continent in the preceding century, as the vehicle for their ambition and experimentation. Monumental works of biographical scholarship and literary criticism have explored the unquestionable significance of Joyce's Irishness, Lawrence's working-class background, and Woolf's femaleness. No subsequent readings or commentaries are likely to undo this work or deny its importance. But as time passes, the test of these writers will not be what class they were born into or what their gender was. Rather, it will be to what extent they were able to transform the history of their own lives and times into the stuff of art so that it retains the authenticity of the particular and still refers to qualities and experiences that are unchangeably human.

As individuals, all three were preoccupied with themselves, with their own lives and situations. They were also guilty of some of the meanest biases of their era. But as artists, all sought ways to put their limitations to use, to acknowledge, indeed, to dramatize them, and at the same time to press beyond them. Joyce's mythologies, Lawrence's prophecies, and Woolf's androgynous dreams reflect their distinctive personalities and situations. Yet they also show something of what these writers had in common as contemporaries in the early decades of the twentieth century. Each wished to break through the confinements of time, place, and sex and to perform, in an age without faith in coherence, a unifying work of universal value.

The God in which their ancestors believed had placed the particulars of His creation in graceful relationship to one another and to Himself. He did not only make matter; He made harmony. Darkness and light, sun and moon, air and water, man and woman, were placed in a dynamic but balanced order. Rhythm and symmetry might be hidden and mysterious, or they might be upset by evil, but they were as much a part of God's original intention as were flesh and fire. Nothing preoccupied the great writers of the Modern period more than the need to do what God had either ceased doing or might never have done in the first place. They felt radically obliged to put things together. And they saw this aspect of their work less as imitation than as invention and restoration.

I N B E G I N N I N G *Finnegans Wake* with Humpty Dumpty, Joyce suggests something with which Woolf and Lawrence, in various moods, agreed: that the Creation and the Fall appear, after many centuries, to have been simultaneous events. These writers did not doubt the existence of matter. In their intuitive acceptance of material phenomena, they were novelists to the core. But they could not imagine structures without seeing shards. And egocentric though they all were, they could not turn inward and rest content in fantasy pleasure domes while real but unassimilated rubble lay about them. Their solution was an extraordinary combination of the most pessimistic realism with a daringly acrobatic striving after balance. They seem alternately to confess that the artist can do nothing with the shambles the world is in and to demonstrate that he can bring the most hopelessly disparate and inert material into vibrant magnetic tension.

Lawrence repeatedly depicts Western society and the individual psyche in ruins and frequently asserts that further shattering is necessary before true reconstruction can begin. But his most consistent metaphorical patterns are those of connectedness and balance. In *Women in Love,*

[5]

one of Birkin's most intense speeches to Ursula envisions "an equilibrium, a pure balance of two single beings:—as the stars balance each other." Later, the narrator refers to the relationship between these two characters as "a rich new circuit, a new current of passional electric energy . . . released from the darkest poles of the body."

Similarly, as the final section of *To the Lighthouse* gathers momentum through Lily Briscoe's efforts to reconcile past and present, the receding of Mrs. Ramsay in time, and that of Mr. Ramsay and the sailboat in space, she seeks "that razor edge of balance between two opposite forces." To complete the painting, she draws a line in the center, an intercession that temporarily makes symmetry out of near chaos.

At the end of the Ithaca episode of *Ulysses,* Bloom drifts off to sleep after having told Molly about his day: "In what state of rest or motion? At rest relatively to themselves and to each other. In motion being each and both carried westward, forward and rereward respectively, by the proper perpetual motion of the earth through everchanging tracks of never-changing space."

Each passage reflects a well-know voice and a highly distinctive preoccupation: passionate sexuality in Lawrence, a brooding anxiety about the worth of art in Woolf, a flair for cosmic comedy in Joyce. But in two important ways they are alike. All press through the particularities of the situations and the individuality of the characters toward an abstract, almost geometric, conception of equilibrium. And all point to an equipoise that is, at the same time, earned and given, personal and universal, tentative and absolute, potential and actual. The quest for balance is revealed to be not simply a matter of plot, a journey to be completed by fictitious characters; rather, it is the artist's own unfinished drama, his search for a relationship with his art, the world, and an unknown reader. When Joyce earlier refers to Molly and Bloom as "listener" and "narrator," he makes explicit what is implicit in Lawrence and Woolf.

In their preoccupation with equilibrium and their honest depiction of its absence, and in their habitual compounding (and confounding) of the relationship among characters with that between author and reader, Joyce, Woolf, and Lawrence are alike. Their symmetries are achieved through an elaborate collaborative process that involves reader and author in unexpected parallels with various combinations of characters. Even the relationships that do not "come off" in conventional social terms—between Mrs. Dalloway and Septimus Smith, Stephen Dedalus and Leopold Bloom, Rupert Birkin and Gerald Crich—are significant in part because the author turns each painfully imperfect pairing into an invitation to the reader to complete in imagination what the text proposes but does not fulfill. The cause of the failed connection may be moral or psychological weakness in the individual or a flaw in the society, but the author does more than reveal a disjuncture. He sets in motion a rhythm that prods the reader into a mental act of reparation.

For Joyce, Woolf, and Lawrence, equilibrium is an aesthetic quality insofar as it refers to the satisfaction felt in overcoming incoherence. In addition, by forcing the reader to extend a helping hand, each author makes a moral and psychological gesture, a demonstration rather than a mere narration of the fact that balance cannot be achieved in isolation; it requires sympathy as well as wit and is a sign of emotional as well as intellectual generosity. With the author and the characters, the reader must see and feel how and why he is needed. To ensure this, the author persists, at the risk of scaring the reader away, in showing the broken circuits, the desolate spaces between unconnected parts, and the false or atrophied joinings of the past. In the act of deciphering the text, the reader is forced to consider the ways in which the author and his characters relate to one another and the world, but also to reconsider the ways in which, by attributing meanings to them, he attaches himself to words, things, and people.

Distinctive though they were in style, temperament, and tone, Joyce, Woolf, and Lawrence were similarly struck by the need, memorably expressed by Eliot, to "escape from personality." This desire has been interpreted as an excuse for a sterile aloofness in the artist and the withdrawal of art from life, yet it can mean the very opposite. Some artists of the period, dissatisfied with the expression of mere personal emotion, would have agreed with another contemporary, Martin Buber, that "all actual life is encounter." The steadiest, most fundamental and significant movement in the works of Joyce, Woolf, and Lawrence is outward from the individual and local to the relational and universal.

Each had a rare gift for the representation of experience in a highly concentrated form, for capturing, in a suddenly illuminating moment, a complex configuration of feelings and thoughts. In their ability to endow a transitory subjective vision with the substantiality of an objectively verifiable event, all resembled to some degree their Romantic predecessors. What is so surprising is their insistence on exercising this talent not as lyrical poets (notwithstanding the fine lyrical verse of Joyce and Lawrence) but as novelists. Although the novel was irritating to all three because of its trivial materialism, it was also attractive because of its association with time and space sufficiently extended to accommodate the intersections, frictions, and spaces that exist between individual visions.

In what they did within and against the inherited framework of the novel, the three writers were often radically different. But in choosing that genre as their major literary preoccupation and vehicle, they demonstrated a common desire to overcome an overreliance on false signs of coherence and to test personal visions (including their own) against the visions of others and the intransigence of circumstance. They chose the novel in order to mock it but also to remedy its faults. Most of all, they chose it for the virtue of its ambition. Of the literary genres that had survived into the twentieth century, it alone attempted to explore, criticize, and recreate life as a whole.

F EW WRITERS of any generation have been more preoccupied with their inner lives and more inclined to use autobiographical material in their fiction than Joyce, Lawrence, and Woolf. At the same time, few have so mistrusted the artist's tendency—very strong in all three—to impose his ego on the reader in the form of what Keats called a "palpable design." They accepted with relatively little difficulty the Romantic version of the Platonic view that self-knowledge is a prerequisite for coming to know the world. But even in their earliest, most autobiographical works, they sensed the limitations and dangers of lingering too long in this stage. As introspective autobiographers, they were more modest than Wordsworth or Byron. The psychic and topographical material of their personal lives—complex, fascinating, suggestive—seemed to them nonetheless physically and emotionally confining.

The movement in *A Portrait of the Artist as a Young Man, Sons and Lovers,* and *The Voyage Out* is not merely away from family, friends, and social institutions; it is also a movement toward the death of the ego and, in the case of the protagonists of Joyce and Lawrence, the possible birth of an artist freed from a preoccupation with self. Thus, while the author's assessment of the artist as a character may be relatively modest, the view of the creative imagination is boundlessly ambitious. Though Joyce is the most explicit about it, all three were possessed by the desire to exercise the unique privilege of a God who can give himself incarnate form and still remain hidden in the clouds or, like Woolf's Miss La Trobe, behind a bush. In reading the novels of these writers, it is never really risky to think, "This character is Joyce or Lawrence or Woolf," because the author who provides the clues that tempt the reader to make such identifications also provides the material that demonstrates their radical inadequacy. The ego—including some version of the author's own— may be represented, but it is invariably sacrificed to a higher cause.

That higher cause is the author's sense of responsibility to the world beyond self and a determination, despite the recognized limits of individual perception and experience, to evoke it—if only by showing that one consciousness, like one plot, is a necessary but insufficient representation of reality. Personality, like historical time, is never altogether emptied out of the novels of these writers, nor do they wish it to be. Impersonality and an aura of timelessness are desirable goals, but they can be achieved, they believed, only in terms of their opposites.

Tension and conflict are the inevitable corollaries of representing life both as particularized experience and as universal contemplation. Joyce's most famous utterance on the subject of authorial impersonality is spoken by a character in a novel—a fact that does not detract from its seriousness as a critical theory. But that the speech is delivered at a particular time on a particular Dublin street by a character who so plainly resembles the author provides a context that is crucial to interpreting its meaning. Stephen is never so arrogant, pedantic, and pretentious— so trapped in himself—as when he is theorizing about self-detachment; and he is rarely so transparently at one with the universe as when he is walking on the strand registering the sights and sounds nearest at hand.

Authorial detachment, like the detachment of characters from one another and from themselves, is a movement, not an achieved status. It is repeatedly gained and lost, shaped and reshaped, in and through discreet and biased renditions of experience. The artist who, according to Stephen, is "like the God of creation . . . within or behind or beyond or above his handiwork," may be diffused like mist in his own world. As Stephen pauses, a "fine rain [begins] to fall from the high veiled sky."[2] But the nearly invisible particles of mist can also come together into tangible and well-shaped drops. When Lynch tosses a surly question at Stephen's theory, the rain begins to fall faster, the narrative pace quickens, and Stephen lapses back into his role as a young student wondering about a girl. The symbolism of the setting need not be pressed in order to see how the external narrative context both intrudes on abstraction and gives shape to it, providing the severely limiting emotional conditions that make its desirability so apparent. The artistic God of creation needs men and women in his own image. Their boundaries are his thresholds.

Lawrence, too, was concerned with the radical limitations of artistic expression as an extension of the ego. The self that needs purification— and here Lawrence's thinking parallels Joyce's—is not so much a core of essential being as a picture composed largely by conventions of language, family, religion, and social morality over which the true self has little control. A preoccupation with the "egocentric absolute of the individual" is in fact a form of an "idolatry of self," because the object of attention is not a genuine being but a falsely drawn picture, "a good little girl," "a brave boy," "a noble woman," "a strong man."[3] (Joyce might have added, "an Irish Catholic boy who hates the English and goes to church on Sunday to pray for his mother.")

The task of the novelist is not to eliminate these familiar images of the self, but to reveal them to the reader as images rather than idols, to show them, much as plot and language are shown, as necessary, useful approximations of reality but not replacements for it. To conceive of personality in terms of a fixed image or theory is, according to Lawrence, untrue to the actual operation of the mind, especially in relation to itself. Though every human being, through family, physical environment, education, is provided with pictures of himself that he may more or less accept, everyone also repeatedly experiences preliminary versions of death through a series of departures from these pictures. Such separations may be painful, accidental, random, and ultimately destructive of sanity and moral integrity, or they may be ecstatic, willed, progressive, and beneficial to the growth of a complex and pliable character. Whichever pattern prevails, everyone experiences his own nature through an alternating sequence of composition and disintegration, gain and loss.

This view of perception and experience affects not only how authors present characters but how they present themselves. That artist "figures" play such important roles in the novels of Joyce, Lawrence, and Woolf is not a sign of mere navel-gazing or preoccupation with craft. Rather, it is one of the many indications that making fiction and making the self are parallel operations. To the extent that each writer submits his own projected authorial persona to the process, none is wholly detached from his fictitious characters. Even allowing for a certain degree of irony, Stephen's speech about impersonality defines a tentative aspect of his own character and that of Joyce-the-author as well. The doubling is the result not of a confusion of aims, but of a fundamental seriousness about the relation between experience and artistic creation.

As famous as Stephen Dedalus's discourse on detachment and impersonality is the passage in D. H. Lawrence's letter to Edward Garnett in which he discusses the ego: "You mustn't look in my novel for the old stable *ego*—of the character. There is another *ego,* according to whose action the individual is unrecognizable, and passes through, as it were, allotropic states which it needs a deeper sense than any we've been used to exercise, to discover are states of the same single radically unchanged element."[4]

Joyce's emphasis is on the author, though the speech is delivered by a character, and Lawrence's is on characters, though what he says applies as well to the problem of authorial ego. Joyce's implied metaphor, sustained by the setting, is a fine rain or mist; Lawrence's is an element like carbon, which has the "allotropic" characteristic of being able to exist in more than one form. For both, the process is a diffusion of self that comes close to total loss and even looks like disappearance, though it is not. The self is released from the prison of "stable form"; it is projected into the environment, freed to move from shape to shape. Yet, according to Lawrence, if only we could regard it rightly, we would recognize essential qualities in it that are obscured or lost in solider, more familiar and static shapes. In part, Lawrence is trying to answer the criticisms aimed at the ideological inconsistencies of some of his characters and of his own authorial persona. But his imagery and argument work surprisingly well for Joyce, too. Whatever stunts Joyce tries, whatever voices and guises he may adopt, however feverishly he works at escaping from "the old stable *ego*" of the narrator, his controlling presence is unmistakable to the reader who approaches his books with a "deeper sense" than he may have been accustomed to exercising in the reading of fiction.

Virginia Woolf, like Joyce and Lawrence, would probably have had misgivings about the stress some readers have placed on the deatils of her private life in an effort to interpret her fiction. In an essay on "Personalities," she explored the relationship between an author's personal history and her self-revelation through her created work and concludes that the great artists are those "who manage to infuse the whole of themselves into their works, yet contrive to universalize their identity so that, though we feel Shakespeare everywhere about, we cannot catch him at the moment in any particular spot."[5] Woolf's ideal of an ego that is capable of being dispersed into the world while retaining a recognizable character is strongly reminiscent of Joyce and Lawrence. Though Shakespeare and the drama may provide the prime models, the novelist can achieve the same effect: "There is Jane Austen, thumbed, scored, annotated, magnified, living almost within the memory of man, and yet as inscrutable in her small way as Shakespeare is in his vast one. She flatters and cajoles you with the promise of intimacy and then, at the last moment, there is the same blankness . . . The people whom we admire most as writers . . . have something elusive, enigmatic, impersonal about them . . . It is the imperfect artists who never manage to say the whole thing in their books who wield the power of personality over us."[6]

The elusiveness of the artist is not, for Woolf, an escape from seriousness, not a playful evasion of moral responsibility; it is necessary to lifting literature beyond self-pity or preening into the realm of universal experience. The problems and situation explored are exposed to moral scrutiny precisely because they are shown to belong to more than the author's own life or the idiosyncratic lives of her characters. Gissing fails where Austen, Dickens, and Shakespeare succeed because his imagination is incapable of generalizing; "it becomes petty and personal" and too often limits itself "to the consideration of a particular case calling for sympathy."[7]

Woolf's reflections on the ego, like Joyce's and Lawrence's, extend beyond the author's relationship to the reader and her characters to the relationships fictional characters have with one another. It is obviously vain for an author to risk with her own ego what she cannot imagine her characters' being capable of risking with theirs. An author cannot free her own imagination while keeping those of her created characters in bondage. On this subject, Woolf often sounds as exasperated as Lawrence: "We long sometimes to escape from the incessant, the remorseless analysis of falling into love and falling out of love, of what Tom feels for Judith and Judith does or does not feel for Tom. We long for some more impersonal relationship. We long for ideas, for dreams, for imaginations, for poetry."[8] Lawrence might have added passion and philosophy, and Joyce myth and drama to the list, but all three are struck with the burden of personal history and the artist's need to transform it, since he can never hope to avoid it.

For Woolf, the underlying sense that human nature possesses certain common and generalizable traits does not necessarily restrict the artist. On the contrary, "to believe that your impressions hold good for others is to be released from the cramp and confinement of personality."[9] It is remarkable to find Woolf using a metaphor of imprisonment, a favorite among Romantic writers wishing to call attention to the limitations imposed on the creative imagination by society and cultural tradition, in order to describe the ego so "free" of others as to be confined to itself.

IRONICALLY, Woolf, Joyce, and Lawrence have often been accused (and accused one another) of authorial egotism and indifference to humanity. In their ambition as artists and in their pride in the power of the imagination, they were undoubtedly egotists. But in their preoccupation with discovering the common spirit of human experience, in their insistence on searching for general truths by means of concrete characters and situations, in their determination to break the isolating shell of personality, and in their own practice as artists as well as in the lives of their characters, they were universally generous. About most of her contemporaries, Woolf writes that "they afflict us because they have ceased to believe. The most sincere of them will only tell us what it is that happens to himself. They cannot make a world."[10] For all their differences, Joyce, Lawrence, and Woolf share a belief in their ability to tell and the readers' ability to understand a good deal more than just what has happened to themselves. Part of what makes them great novelists is that all three can make a world. Bloom's Dublin, Mrs. Dalloway's London, the Nottinghamshire of the Morels and Brangwens are highly particularized places, regional, circumscribed, unique, and, at the same time, infinitely accessible and familiar habitations of a common human spirit.

But it is not in the treatment of place alone that these writers make a world. In the very innovations—stylistic and structural—that have made their books difficult and have discouraged some readers, they have extended the domestic, bourgeois, historical conventions of the old novel to a breaking point that opens the way to a wider range of experience. Chronological time is as apparent as the landmarks of Dublin or London, but it, too, is bent and broken to let in the citizens of all epochs. Joyce's mythic cycles, Lawrence's rhythmic pulse, Woolf's elegiac refrains reach out to touch the imagination of the reader in some universal space. Indeed, the "difficulty" of their fiction is most often the result not of a wish to make their worlds inaccessible to readers, but rather of a desire to break out of the "cramp and confinement" of the aspects of personality, religion, nationality, language, and history that isolate people from one another.

The relationship between the particular and the general, the historical and the eternal, is not simple and clear in their books because they did not perceive them to be simple or clear in their time. But the wish to search out the possible links, the impulse to strain against categories, is one of the most powerful of their common traits. Furthermore, none of their theories of detachment and impersonality preclude the active participation of the reader in the effort. On the contrary, one of the reasons readers have always been so partisan in their admiration and defense of these writers is that their books demand not just intense concentration but creative intimacy. One cannot be a good reader and at the same time a passive reader of Joyce, Lawrence, or Woolf. If one is to make sense of them, one must help them make sense. Just as they are capable of dissolving themselves into their own characters and even into a reader blundering his way through their sentences, so they implicitly invite the reader to dissolve himself, not only into characters but into the persona of the author. All reading is an act of collaboration, but in the absence of ready-made and familiar connections, the reader finds himself busier and more actively involved than usual. When a coherence beyond the merely mechanical is discovered, the sense of achievement is enormous, not because it is a problem solved or a question answered, but because one recognizes with exhilaration the vital actuality of intercourse between mind and mind, imagination and imagination, spirit and spirit.

ONE

By the Beautiful Sea

Nature and the Artist

Under the upswelling tide he saw the writhing weeds lift languidly and sway reluctant arms . . . day by day: night by night: lifted, flooded, and let fall. Lord, they are weary . . . To no end gathered.

JAMES JOYCE, *Ulysses*

We are in the deep, muddy estuary of our era, and terrified of the emptiness of the sea beyond . . . the final I Don't Know of the ocean.

D. H. LAWRENCE, *The Proper Study*

To pace the beach was impossible; contemplation was unendurable; the mirror was broken.

VIRGINIA WOOLF, *To the Lighthouse*

THE CONCENTRATION on consciousness seeking contact with consciousness in Joyce, Woolf, and Lawrence is rooted in a deep skepticism about nature as a mirror of a universal intelligence. Vast landscapes, the sky, and the sea no longer seemed to lift humanity out of itself into a realm of transcendent understanding. More often, despite a sometimes awesome beauty, they cast the individual back on his own devices. They challenged his capacity to ask questions, to recall the past critically, and to invent "other worlds and other seas" while seeing those before him without the comforting and illusory resemblances of the old. For the modern writer—even one like Lawrence, for whom the encounter with nature remains a salutary, mystical experience—the natural world is, in its essence, a multiplicity of nonhuman phenomena.

The sea is such a powerful and persistent presence throughout literature that it is difficult to think of a major genre or epoch in which it has not figured in a crucial way. For England and Ireland, geography combined with demographic history and cultural tradition in making it an intersection of unavoidable fact and unbounded legend. Few generations were more captivated by seascapes than those of the late eighteenth and early nineteenth centuries. Romantic writers, doubtful of tradition and preoccupied with self, often found a more powerful revelation from "the silence of the sea" than from Scripture and a greater "rapture on the lonely shore" than in social intercourse.

In Byron's *Childe Harold,* the sea is "unchangeable"; it is the "glorious mirror where the Almighty form glasses itself"; it is "the image of eternity." Byron's conclusion is above all a claim that the artist possesses a special vision into the unchanging, universal heart of things. When, in stanza 94, he tells the sea, "I was as it were a Child of thee," he does more than express nostalgic affection; he asserts, in imitation of a pagan hero, his imagination's birthright to immortality.

In nineteenth-century poems as different in tone as Shelley's "Stanzas Written in Dejection" and Tennyson's "Break, Break, Break," the poet recalls, even in moods of near despair, divine harmonies and a mysterious intimacy with the sea. It is Matthew Arnold, in "Dover Beach," who most effectively demystifies the sea and unravels the poet's special tie to it and its symbolic associations with the supernatural. The peculiar success of the poem in dismantling a convention derives in part from Arnold's refusal to employ heightened emotion. Unlike Tennyson, he does not "rebuke" the waves and thereby fabricate one side of a dialogue he believes to be impossible. Arnold does not rail against the retreating God, long for death, or rejoice over his newfound freedom. He faces the "darkling plain," describes the bleakness he sees, and then reaches out to a fellow creature with whom to seek a shaping destiny for himself. In these gestures of stark skepticism and in a revival of interest, out of sheer self-defense, in human bonds, he anticipates a number of twentieth-century writers.

T HE MODERN writer continues to roam the edge of the sea, usually in the guise of a fictional surrogate, but he does so with a peculiarly keen sense of the literary debris awaiting him there. Symbols of divine presence or anthropomorphic congeniality are impossible to ignore, not because they are present in the sea itself but because they have become so well anchored in the human consciousness. Though the artist may acknowledge that the memory of these symbols and the desire for them remains vivid and real, however, he feels the need to express in his own literary fashion the equally powerful and affecting presence of the insensible, uncooperative, nonsignifying sea. His return to the beach has an artistic as well as a "natural" motive. He wishes, sometimes with ironic mockery, sometimes with anguish and sorrow, to confront and discredit some of the most beautiful images in the language and, in doing so, to expose a nature indifferent to and untouched by words. For some modern writers, this journey to the seashore is like a classical journey to Hades. It is an initiation, a trial of wit and courage, which may destroy the intruder or strengthen him for other, less threatening encounters to come.

The climactic scene of *A Portrait of the Artist as a Young Man* is that in which Stephen Dedalus walks alone by the sea, a setting Joyce came back to in a less emotional, more complicated manner early in *Ulysses*. An artist meditating by the sea also figures decisively in *The Trespasser* and *Kangaroo*—not among Lawrence's most successful novels, though both contain powerful and characteristic passages worthy of greater critical attention than they have received.

Portrait and *The Trespasser* are both relatively early books. Joyce worked at *Portrait* through his early and mid-twenties; Lawrence was twenty-four when he wrote the first draft of *The Trespasser* and twenty-six when he revised it. *Portrait* was serialized in 1914; *The Trespasser* was first published in 1912.[1] Though *Portrait* is more carefully constructed and more polished than *The Trespasser,* each is the product of a young, unknown writer preoccupied with the role of the artist in rebellion. Joyce's Stephen Dedalus is marked by his peculiar name, which evokes the Greek myth of Daedalus and Icarus and seems in itself to separate him from his countrymen. "Are you Irish at all?" asks his friend Davin. As he walks toward the sea, we know that Stephen has made three crucial refusals: to participate in Irish politics, to remain in his family, to enter the priesthood. His impulse is not yet toward a known goal but merely to escape the confinements of the familiar world: "The end he had been born to serve yet did not see had led him to escape by an unseen path."

Lawrence's Siegmund is a musician also set apart by his foreign name, that of the woeful semidivine hero of the German myth of the Nibelung, who rescues Sieglinde from a brutish husband and sires Siegfried. At thirty-eight, Siegmund is not a young man, but he is nonetheless seen, like Dedalus, rejecting his old life and rushing almost blindly toward a new one without knowing or caring where it will eventually lead him: "For years he had suppressed his soul, in a kind of mechanical despair doing his duty and enduring the rest. Then his soul had been softly enticed from its bondage. Now he was going to break free altogether ... This, to a man of his integrity, meant a breaking of bonds, a severing of blood-ties, a sort of new birth."[2]

The surface plot of *The Trespasser* is not distinguished or, in itself, compelling. A violinist runs away from his wife and children to spend a holiday on the Isle of Wight with his mistress. But then, the story of a proud young Irishman rejecting his family and preparing to set off on his own is not in itself what distinguishes *Portrait.* Each author must make these potentially ordinary narrative situations significant by revealing to the reader something extraordinary in the way the artist-character himself experiences them.

In bringing their rebellious, fatefully named artists to the edge of the sea, both Joyce and Lawrence were aware of the mythological and literary weight they were taking on. In the Proteus episode in *Ulysses,* Joyce takes explicit advantage of the literariness of the sea, repeatedly quoting or echoing lines from other works. In *Portrait* the difference is not merely that Joyce is more restrained, but that the Stephen he is presenting is wavering between artistic control and slackness, confidence and fear, sharp observation and vagueness, a great new vision and a confused patchwork. The danger for this defiant young artist is that he may transfer to himself and his art the sentimental and undiscriminating attachment he has refused his family, church, and nation.

The sea is an image of release and freedom, but it is also a reminder of trouble. There is literal death by drowning as well as a metaphorical "drowning" that, for the rebellious artist, can mean being overcome by the infinite possibility his defiance has won. The literary and life-giving sea also threatens language with death by cliché. The young man who is on the verge of escaping from political and religious formulas risks falling into poetic ones. In short, the escape to the sea is an automatic solution to nothing. The sea is the "sea," a word, an idea, an accumulation of images as well as a mysterious phenomenon lurking beyond or behind the pictures and sounds used to signify it. For Joyce, the innovative artist-hero becomes a prototype of modern man in that his quest for vitality and meaning requires him to steer between the death traps of prefabrication and formlessness.

THE KEY to the success of the sea passage in *Portrait* and to its modernity lies in its being what Joyce names it from the start and then goes on to demonstrate, "fitful music." Taking the convention of opera, musical theater, and possibly the accompanied silent films of his day, Joyce describes an internalized "background music" in his hero's mind. He eliminates the potential sentimentality of the convention by suggesting that the music is not all crescendo and predictable harmony: "It seemed to him that he heard notes of fitful music leaping upwards a tone and downwards a diminished fourth, upwards a tone and downwards a major third." As is so often the case in Joyce, this prelude serves as a kind of rule for the rest of the passage, a sign that can help us through the remainder of the scene. Not only is it a metaphor for Stephen's vacillating emotions; it is a description of a search for resolution and a highly concentrated illustration of Joyce's artistic method, "upwards" toward familiar literary beauty—assonance, alliteration, picturesque imagery, allusion—and "downwards" toward gross or trivial sights and blunt, prosaic sounds, or meaningless noise. These contrasting directions may, of course, undermine and mock each other. But, as in the music and poetry of the period, they may also enhance each other, allowing the reader the freedom to observe the making and breaking of particular language systems and, in doing so, to draw fresh conclusions about their relation to experience.

Throughout the passage, we are shown what Stephen sees and—they are rarely the same—what he brings to it in his imagination and makes of it verbally. The question is often asked whether Joyce is mocking Stephen's reveries or whether he so identifes himself with him as to present them without irony. The shifts from external descriptive narration through narrated monologue to interior monologue are sometimes so subtle that they make the relationship between the author-narrator and the protagonist unclear. As Wayne Booth has pointed out, there are logical inconsistencies in Joyce's presentation of Stephen.[3] But logical consistency may not have been Joyce's aim. There are, in fact, structural and tonal consistencies in Joyce's narrative movement between sympathy and detachment toward his protagonist and in Stephen's intellectual and emotional vacillation about his surroundings and his future as an artist.

Partly because of the narrator's own seeming ambivalence, some readers have doubted that Stephen is really talented enough to deserve our approval, but this is an odd, if not totally irrelevant, question. Joyce, not Stephen, is the author of the book; though some of Stephen's thoughts are florid and self-consciously literary, Joyce introduces with them those raw, "unusable" sounds and sights that give the sea episode and the book as a whole a dynamic balance. We are shown by what Joyce does with words, as well as by what he describes his protagonist doing, that trying to be an artist is not merely a matter of resting in some new ordering of experience different from that of priests and politicians; instead, it involves the risk of continually losing and rediscovering order in one's own mind. With whatever reservations we may have about Stephen's priggishness or poetic genius, we do take his *efforts* seriously. Whether he will go on to be a great artist is not what the book or this passage is about. The picture is that of a young man on the brink.

Stephen's artful reveries, even his most attractive ones, are repeatedly interrupted. He remembers a "proud cadence" of Newman's, but his lyrical sentiments are intruded upon, as he turns seaward, by a "squad of christian brothers" whose "uncouth faces passed him two by two, stained yellow or red or livid by the sea." The sound of their names is a kind of anti-poem—"Brother Hickey, Brother Quaid, Brother MacArdle, Brother Keogh"—familiar, monotonous, guttural, without meaning.

In the next paragraph, Stephen wonders whether he prefers language to the realities it supposedly reflects. He looks out to the horizon, notices a darkening squall in the distance, and realizes again "how his flesh dreaded the cold infrahuman odour of the sea." His sudden fear turns him to a highly literary transformation of the scene in which such phrases as "veiled sunlight" and "vague arras" seem to wrap the sensation in soft words.

He begins to hear a "nebulous music," but it recedes and turns into a piercing voice calling his name in Greek, mixed with screams and shouts of "Ao . . . guzzle him . . . help." He has come upon some of his young friends bathing, a scene, especially at the time Joyce was writing, ripe for stylized literary treatment evoking neopastoral innocence and manly beauty. But for Stephen the sight of the wet bodies, like the animal shouts, brings an even greater dread than the dark sea. Words like "corpsewhite" and "pitiable nakedness" betray his unease and then, as he hears again his own name in Greek, give him a sense of superiority because he begins to think he can control his fear and soar higher and farther than in his earlier, more tentative attempts. Even the cries of "look out" and "uk" seem not to stop him, though the "o, cripes, I'm drownded" reminds the reader that in his ecstatic "flying sunward" he sounds more like the impetuous Icarus who flew too close to the sun and fell into the sea than the crafty Daedalus who fashioned the wings and got home safely.

The following passage, in which Stephen imagines himself as the resurrected Christ casting off the "cerements" of his former inhibitions, is only as powerful as Joyce allows it to be by juxtaposing it with an almost dainty wading scene; Stephen is pictured with "his stockings folded in his pockets and his canvas shoes dangling by their knotted laces over his shoulders." Although we cannot always be sure which utterances are Stephen's and which the narrator's, this detail is clearly the narrator's observation. So much, he implies, for casting off "cerements." As Stephen begins to wade into the water, we are shown what *he* is thinking in a highly excited, rhetorical piece of narrated monologue: "Where was his boyhood now? Where was the soul that had hung back from her destiny?" and so on for several more lines.

Joyce's distancing himself from Stephen's enthusiasm is not a repudiation of it, but a way of bringing it back across the centuries from the Holy Land or the warm Icarian Sea to the Irish coast where the water is cold and briny and a prim young man would fold his stockings and carry his shoes over his shoulders. The flight can have no meaning at all unless we are reminded where it begins.

Stephen's vision of the young girl standing before him in midstream combines his tendency toward vague metaphor and idealization with sharp observation of concrete reality. Visible within shifting and somewhat confused images—in fact, made visible by interaction with them—is a flesh-and-blood girl with thighs, hips, drawers with white fringes, slate-blue skirts, and long, fair hair. The fathomless sea has at last yielded a gift, in the form not of a goddess, but of a mortal infused with beauty because seen without the inhibitions of an Irish Catholic boy or the selfishness of a young male animal, but with the awe of an artist who has caught a glimpse of life not yet transformed into a text. Her legs are described as "pure save where an emerald trail of seaweed had fashioned itself as a sign upon the flesh." The image is perfect. The sign is not a word or human marking by which the girl can be classified, but a fragment from the infinite, inhuman sea, highlighting, by contrast, the particular distinctiveness of her own being—what Stephen, in his later Thomistic attempts to define beauty, calls "radiance." It is as essential that no name be given to the phenomenon at this point as it is that no word should pass between Stephen and the girl. Words can suggest, guide, correct, and invigorate, but they do not, in the end, touch reality.

A necessary aspect of this vision is Stephen's ecstatic turmoil after the event and the flood of totally inadequate words that pour through his mind. After his apparent triumph over himself, his fears of the sea and of the flesh, he succumbs to a deathlike sleep in which he sees the unfolding of a luminous flower, reminiscent of Dante's paradisal rose. But Stephen's dreamt death is no more final than his imagined rebirth; nor does it negate it. He has left the world of communal and automatic experience—of family, political party, Christian brothers, and bathers—to witness and record the continual rising and falling of mood, order, and meaning in his own way.

In the two short, final paragraphs of the chapter, Joyce weaves together in tranquil unsentimental beauty the elements of his seaside scene: the young artist, his joy, his fear of barrenness, his new existence between land and sea, all wheeling in a kind of countermotion with moon and tide, which only words can arrange.

ON TURNING to the first scene in *The Trespasser* in which Siegmund goes down to the sea alone, one is immediately struck by the qualities of voice and observed detail that make it so easy to distinguish between Joyce and Lawrence. Indeed, it is tempting to sum up the two writers by pointing out that while Stephen Dedalus goes wading and playing with mental images of "profane joy," Lawrence's Siegmund throws off his clothes and plunges naked into the sea. Though this kind of impressionistic contrast does tell us something, it hardly exhausts the subject.

As in *Portrait*, a musical analogy and prelude to the episode by the sea introduces a theme of harmony and discord. During a misty night, Siegmund and his lover, Helena, hear a sound from the sea, "low, swelling, like the mooing of some great sea animal," which turns out to be a foghorn. Helena, characteristically, makes a musical allusion out of it and begins to hum "the call of the horn across the sea to Tristan."[4] For Siegmund, the sound is noise, not music, and its toneless intrusion on their idyll is a reminder that there is no shape or coherence to what they are doing, that it does not "fit" into their lives and can have no future. Lawrence prepares us, much as Joyce did with his "fitful music," for a view of experience that includes chaos, a new art that not only describes but incorporates material that is the antithesis of conventional art.

The modern writer's effort to give chaos its due is not in theory more paradoxical than other ancient, impossible aims of literature—to express the inexpressible: silence, love, the divine. What is new in Joyce and Lawrence (and in certain of their contemporaries, such as Pound and Eliot) is the tendency to keep contradiction alive rather than to present and then subdue it with words. A variety of ways in which language gives order to experience—including those that seem necessary to the progress of the novel—are subjected to negative buffetings that sometimes appear about to stop action and language altogether. In Joyce, the cold, inhuman force of the sea and its pretty, placid seductiveness—the first associated with Stephen's guilty lust, the second with his romantic sentimentality—are experienced as threats to his artistic integrity. Both are forms of death by drowning, and both have linguistic analogues: the squawks of the "corpse-white" swimmers or the literary clichés of seaside poetry. Each is unacceptable by itself, yet the artist cannot wholly escape either. He walks the shoreline, aware of and responsive to both, using each to stir meaning and order in the other.

Lawrence's Siegmund is in a similar predicament. He may plunge right into the water, but his immersion is not an unmixed pleasure and the author-narrator, if not the hero, keeps a foot on land. Siegmund is alone; he has forgotten his forebodings of the previous evening, and he races happily into the waves, personifying wind and sea into partners in a sexual frolic. "It delighted him to feel the fresh, soft fingers of the wind touching him and wandering timidly over his nakedness." But Siegmund is hardly in the water before the erotic poetry gives way to blunt prose: "It was cold, and he shrank." Siegmund tries to continue his "game with the sea," but scrapes his leg painfully on a submerged rock.

Like Stephen Dedalus's movement between linguistic control and raw sensation, Siegmund's advances and recoils in the sea are not presented in moralistic terms. The game—the creative establishment of relationship and meaning—is as inevitable and necessary as that which resists being played with. The artist, for Lawrence, does not repudiate the human need to imitate and reconstruct the world even in the face of what seems inimitable and unsusceptible to reconstruction. Human relations demand reciprocity, but in his relation to the natural universe, the artist offers a pure, unselfish love that exults in being and expects nothing in return.

Like Stephen, who casts off the "cerements" of death and undergoes a rebirth, Siegmund experiences a sacred baptism in the sea. The rocks resemble "square altars"; he "tastes" the sea and "offers his body to the morning." In *Portrait* the revelation is objectified in the wading girl, but it is obviously Stephen's way of seeing the girl that is important: without fear or desire, intensely but unegotistically conscious, "touched with the wonder of mortal beauty." We learn not about the girl but, as always, about the young artist. Siegmund's exultation comes from a fresh awareness of his own physical beauty: "He delighted in himself." But though he admires his "handsome, white maturity" in a pool of clear water, the scene is no more a straight repetition of the Narcissus myth than Joyce's is of the Resurrection or of the legend of Dedalus and Icarus. In fact, as is almost always the case when Lawrence uses myth, he reverses its traditional sense and makes the episode the beginning of Siegmund's detachment from self. Seeing his beauty in the pool does not make Siegmund cling to himself. On the contrary, as he identifies his own physical being with that of his surroundings he is filled with a kind of wonder that frees his will and loosens his hold on life.

The pool in which he sees himself contains "one rose anemone" and lies within a rock that is "white and wet, like himself." This image has much the same function as the seaweed Stephen sees as a "sign upon the flesh" of the young girl. It is the blemish that brings out the marvel but also the vulnerability of beauty. Siegmund notices in his reflection "an insidious creeping of blood down his thigh," and later on, when walking through a Catholic churchyard, he associates his whiteness and his wound with the body of Christ on the cross. Siegmund sees himself as a victim, but the imagery associated with him throughout the novel, especially in the scenes by the sea, suggests that the impossibility of his love for Helena, like the rough implacability of the rock that wounds him, coincides with a godlike glimpse of a beauty of which his mortal self is part but not center.

Though Siegmund, like Stephen, has played with the sea and indulged in "poetic" thoughts about it, he rejects the tendency of art to reduce, harmonize, and soften reality. He is repelled by Helena's view of the sea as all "fairy horns" and "Rhine maidens." When they come upon a monument to Tennyson, who lived on the Isle of Wight, he shocks Helena by saying that the railing around the stone is appropriate since Tennyson "did belittle great things."

For Lawrence, as for Joyce, art is one of the central subjects of the novel, even at this early stage. And despite important differences in method, he, like Joyce, searches with his artist-hero among the ruins of traditions that have lost their potency but cannot be forgotten. Moreover, much of his power, like Joyce's, derives from the violence with which he rejects certain aesthetic as well as social conventions. The hope for a new kind of being and a new kind of art—even if they can only be momentarily realized by the protagonists in these early novels—hinges on a sustained, radical "no."

Like Stephen Dedalus, Siegmund is irrevocably changed by his revelation from the sea. He can no more conform to Helena's poetic fantasies than he can to the lifeless routine of his family existence. When he returns to bathe again in his cove, his thoughts are already drifting toward death. Once again, he feels an "intimacy with things," he plays with the sea, is scraped by a rock, admires his own beauty, but then he lies down in the sand imagining his death. This kind of replaying of a scene with variations is much more characteristic of Lawrence than of Joyce, in whose treatment recurrence is more likely to take place within a character's memory. In both cases, however, the repetition of details from a particular episode suggests a life pattern, as well as a narrative one, that is more cyclical than progressive. Change does occur, but the altered and continually altering self returns again and again to the past even as it moves toward its end.

J U S T as in both books order is glimpsed through disorder and disorder through order, time is seen through and in terms of a negation of time. When Stephen Dedalus hears his name called out in Greek by the swimmers, his mind is lifted out of time: "So timeless seemed the grey warm air, so fluid and impersonal his own mood, that all ages were as one to him." Stephen's momentary joining with ancient poets, prophets, and gods in an epiphanic encounter with the sea and the wading girl, regarded by some readers as the height of his insufferable egotism, is the antithesis of the egotistical. He is seeing for the first time without immediate concern for the way in which what he sees will contribute to or detract from his well-being. He is seeing as an artist.

The fact that the chapter following Stephen's vision by the sea begins with a discussion of time does not undercut the value of his "eternal" moment. What it does, in characteristic Joycean fashion, is to show how the experience of timelessness affects clock-time for Stephen and, through him, for the reader. The "eternal" for Joyce is not a plateau or a fixed state in which one rests after a long ascent; it is a way of seeing that comes and goes with the imaginative struggle against received ways of measuring and parceling out life. The morning after Stephen's walk by the sea, he asks his mother: "—How much is the clock fast now? His mother straightened the battered alarm clock that was lying on its side in the middle of the kitchen mantelpiece until its dial showed a quarter to twelve ... —An hour and twentyfive minutes, she said. The right time is twenty past ten" (174).

Stephen sets off for his classes, knowing but not particularly caring that he is late. He notices clocks, fast and slow, but continually drifts into a realm in which the obligations they remind him of seem trivial and unreal. *Portrait* ends with another strong reminder of time—Stephen's diary from 20 March to 27 April—juxtaposed with its author's efforts, expressed in entries, to participate in eternity: "I go to encounter for the millionth time the reality of experience." Like the movement between form and formlessness, that between one time and the millionth is not a matter of ultimate victory or defeat for one or the other but a matter of continual winning and losing for both.

If Stephen Dedalus's moment of eternal vision seems to him a rebirth, the beginning of a great adventure, an entry into a new life, Siegmund's love affair with and by the sea is presented by Lawrence as a gradual giving in to death. The impersonal beauty and attraction of the sea— including the dangerous rocks beneath the surface—make a life divided into weeks, days, and hours of routine obligation seem worse than no life at all. The lovers are constantly forgetting and then remembering time, how long they have been on the island, when the train leaves, when they will meet again.

When they return to the mainland and separate, the narrative is filled, almost cluttered, with references to timetables, schedules, dinner hours, bedtime, breakfast time, a constant series of markings in the day which determine automatic action. Siegmund's return to his family is presented as a strange still point, "a slow bullet," in the midst of hurried movement. In the morning, his daughter shouts the hour to him through his locked bedroom door. As he prepares, in a kind of stupor, to take his life, he asks himself, "Is there no more time for me?" Later, not knowing what her husband has done, his wife fumes over his wasting time and, in doing so, sums up the life he has chosen to relinquish: "Siegmund's lying late in bed made Beatrice very angry."

If the novel is thought of as a linear, naturalistic narrative with a clear beginning, middle, and end, the consequences of Stephen's and Siegmund's epiphanies by the sea could hardly be more dissimilar, since one leads to a second birth and the other to suicide. But if we recognize the ways in which both authors superimpose on the linear narrative an impersonal cycle of events that involve the protagonists but do not begin and end with them, the difference seems less great. Stephen's rebirth is seeded with thoughts of death, not only the obvious loss of friends and family, but the fears, symbolized by his dream of death by drowning, of being overwhelmed by his new vision or being defeated by his own provincial ignorance. These and the fast and slow clocks, the days of the month being ticked off as Stephen prepares his flight, maintain a powerful, unsentimental balance in the book. They, like the "sign" of seaweed on the girl's otherwise pure flesh, are the necessary blemish.

The blemish or wound in Siegmund's case becomes the dominant factor as Lawrence's novel draws to a close. In describing Siegmund's suicidal mood, the narrator returns to musical analogy: "The discord of his immediate situation overcame every harmony." Nevertheless, the harmony, the order made by the musician as an act of adoring an unresponding universe, remains a permanent reality in the book. Even when there is nothing left in it for him, perhaps especially when there is nothing left in it for him, Siegmund is able, with a detachment not unlike Stephen's, to see and realize in a new way the beauty of the world. Knowing everything is lost, he stops in London on his way home from the Isle of Wight; as he pauses by the Thames he is filled with exaltation. "As he leaned on the Embankment parapet the wonder did not fade, but rather increased."

Joyce does not show us Stephen's family and friends after his departure, but Lawrence casts a cold eye on Siegmund's survivors, and it is clear that their arrangements and plans, even their grief, are like a living death when contrasted with the intensities recalled by the memory of Siegmund and even the sight of his violin. There is a lack of finality in both novels that is essential to the views of art and life they reflect. Stephen is poised for flight, but whether he will live up to his name and become a successful Daedalus or plunge, like Icarus, into the sea is not certain. Siegmund's name also evokes a legend of immortal fatherhood and impetuous sonship. He is already dead when the narrative begins, but his presence is more strongly felt throughout than that of any of the other characters. It is misleading—though literally accurate—to say that the two novels have opposite conclusions. Neither is really conclusive. They leave their "newborn" heroes at different points on a cycle that continues with or without them, one their vision has enabled us to see.

In important ways the two books are distinctive and incomparable. Joyce's *Portrait* is a masterpiece of control and careful construction, a modern *Bildungsroman*. Lawrence's *Trespasser* is an uneven, sometimes overwritten love story. Yet the encounter of the artist with the sea is a situation of analogous importance to both, a paradigm of the dilemma of the artist at the beginning of the twentieth century. The artist-hero, suffocating from the constraints of society, turns to the sea in an instinctive desire for freedom only to find that generations of myth and poetry have preceded him there and are ready to reecho in his own humanizing imagery and rhythmic language. In startling contrast with the literary experience of the "sea" is a kind of preverbal sensation of fear or pain associated with the formless depth and breadth that correspond to nothing human, freedom discovered in terms not of moral liberation or religious salvation but of chaos. This aspect of the sea offers up no gods or words of wisdom, yet it is through the paradoxical effort to "keep it in the picture" that the modern artist tries to avoid falsehood and transmit the persistent and precarious beauty of the human version of things.

Both Joyce and Lawrence were concerned with form, and though Joyce's structures were more ingenious than Lawrence's, they were not more complex nor more resistant to emanations of disorder. Neither was content, as Milton had been in *Paradise Lost,* to "behold the Throne / Of Chaos, and his dark pavilion spread / Wide on the wasteful deep," containing disorder between hell and earth. Joyce and Lawrence allow the "wasteful deep" to impinge on their artist-heroes' poetic inclinations as well as on the coherence and meaning of their own language. They also see human experience as much in terms of recurrence as in terms of progressive development. Joyce's protagonist is compared with Christ resurrected and Lawrence's with Christ crucified, a choice that may reflect their Catholic and Calvinist backgrounds (though Lawrence later devoted an entire book to the theme of the risen Christ). But despite the obvious ways in which the references are peculiar to each passage and author, they have in common the modern tendency to return to ancient symbols of suffering and survival, not for the sake of individual redemption in heaven but in order to restore to man his living relationship with earth. It is on this shore that the authors of *Finnegans Wake* and *Phoenix* meet.

T H E S E A is such a pervasive presence in a number of Virginia Woolf's novels that it is difficult to single out one or two crucial encounters with it. In *Portrait* and *The Trespasser,* the hero's approach to the sea requires decision and preparation; it signifies the rejection of an old life and a desire to embrace a new, unknown, mysterious, even dangerous one. *The Voyage Out, Jacob's Room, To the Lighthouse,* and *The Waves* open at the edge of the sea; that is where the reader begins. All else that happens refers back to it. Furthermore, Woolf's presentation of the sea is never so concentrated within the perceptions and experience of a single character as is the case in Joyce and Lawrence. All of her novels contain artists of one kind or another, but their ways of seeing cannot be said to dominate in the same sense that Stephen Dedalus's or Siegmund's does. It is characteristic that *Jacob's Room* begins with Betty Flanders's view of the sea and moves only secondly to that of the painter Charles Steele—a view that is "spoiled" as soon as Mrs. Flanders gets up, brushes off the sand, and takes her children away. Lily Briscoe, the painter in *To the Lighthouse,* is a more important character than Charles Steele, but the internal drama of her scene at the end of the novel derives from her effort to incorporate into her "view" the ways of acting and seeing of Mr. Ramsay and especially of Mrs. Ramsay. Lily's "success" as a painter momentarily leaves her, to an almost Keatsian degree, with no personality of her own.

While Joyce and Lawrence, in their early works, send their artist-heroes to the sea in a gesture of release, to confront the formless unknown rather than continue with stale patterns, Woolf takes that kind of liberation for granted. There is little exhilaration or sense of discovery at her seaside. Her characters seem always to have known about the beauties and treacheries of the sea. Its presence does not knock them into a new relation with life; it heaves and sighs like some vast mystery within them, which they must acknowledge but at the same time protect themselves from in order to live. For Joyce and Lawrence, the encounter with the sea, however dangerous, provides an opportunity for renewal; for Woolf, the familiar unknown sea is a continual challenge to survival.

In Woolf's first novel, *The Voyage Out,* a young pianist, Rachel Vinrace, sets out on a sea journey to the coast of South America with her aunt and uncle.[5] Rachel is the central character, but she is impressionable and passive, and her way of seeing by no means dominates the narrative. Woolf's shifting viewpoint may not be as subtle in *The Voyage Out* as it became in her later novels, but the refusal to fasten onto a particular mentality is characteristic of all of her fiction. It is also strikingly revealing of her attitude toward art and individual perception. On the one hand, she doubts the reliability of the omniscient artist; on the other, she distrusts the narrow egotism of the individual witness. Her "solution" to this problem in *The Voyage Out* is to employ the impersonal "omniscient" voice, not in order to provide an overarching moral design, but to point out the inadequacy of the personal view of things. As the ship moves out to sea, Woolf presents a meditation on land and sea from an almost ethereal distance:

> Great tracts of the earth lay now beneath the autumn sun, and the whole of England, from the bald moors to the Cornish rocks, was lit up from dawn to sunset . . . But . . . very few people thought about the sea. They took it for granted that the sea was calm. . . . The grown-up view, indeed, was not much clearer than the view of the little creatures in bathing drawers . . . The people in ships, however, took an equally singular view of England . . . It was a shrinking island in which people were imprisoned. One figured them first

swarming about like aimless ants ... and then, as the ship withdrew, one figured them making a vain clamour, which, being unheard, either ceased, or rose into a brawl. Finally, when the ship was out of sight of land, it became plain that the people of England were completely mute. (31–32)

The function of the distancing in this passage is unusual largely because the narrator does not pretend to have a clear view of what is really happening. No pattern emerges to correct the self-deceiving and childish views of those on the shore or on the deck of a ship. Distance exposes the radical limits of particular ways of seeing and the illusion of the continuity of space. For the moment, it provides negative information but not wisdom. The sea is not always calm, and the people of England obviously do not turn into ants or mutes everytime a ship sets sail. Individual perceptions of this order cannot be trusted, but then what can? Certainly not the airborne observer who points to anomalies and raises possibilities, but resolves nothing. In reference to the ship, for example, this voice observes that she "*might* be likened to all beautiful things, worshipped and felt as a symbol." The mood is characteristically conditional and the meaning of the symbol undisclosed.

Although the voice of the distant observer clarifies nothing, it serves to alter the reader's view of the passengers on the ship, who appear smaller and more trivial than when the book began. There is much discussion of the weather and the ocean, and Mrs. Dalloway, who is regarded by the others as superficial, seems no more so than most of the rest in their various ways. When she meets the steward one morning, she tells him that "to be a sailor must be the finest thing in the world." He answers her gruffly, "And what d'you know about it? ... What does any man or woman brought up in England know about the sea?" But this man of the sea has no particular wisdom to share with his passengers. He takes Mrs. Dalloway to his cabin to show her the "secrets" of the ocean:

As he talked he kept opening drawers and moving little glass jars. Here were the treasures which the great ocean had bestowed upon him—pale fish in greenish liquids, blobs of jelly with streaming tresses, fish with lights in their heads, they lived so deep.
"They have swum about among bones," Clarissa sighed.
"You're thinking of Shakespeare," said Mr. Grice, and taking down a copy from a shelf well-lined with books, recited in an emphatic nasal voice:
    Full fathom five thy father lies,
"A grand fellow, Shakespeare," he said, replacing the volume. (54)

The exchange does not succeed in exposing Shakespeare as a humbug, but it does trivialize his words and, by juxtaposing them with Mr.

Grice's bottled specimens, show them as pathetically inadequate human tokens in contrast with the inhuman power and vastness of the sea. Mrs. Dalloway, with her ringed fingers, her courtesy, and her interest in the "arts," skims the surface of things; but that, in a variety of ways, is what all the passengers are shown to do. The ship itself carries them over the sea, and any effort to "penetrate" it would seem the psychological equivalent of suicide.

Rachel's innocent determination to avoid superficiality and "get to the bottom" of things is treated by the others as an aspect of her youthfulness and her artistic temperament. It is assumed by her aunt to be a passing phase, though in fact it turns out to be fatal. The superficiality of the other characters gives their personalities a distinct, clear outline, whereas Rachel's pensive seriousness blurs her identity. Indeed, the more she tries to concentrate her attention the more her mind "sinks" into the object of her contemplation and loses definition. The metaphor of "depth" suggests an alternative for the individual, especially the artist, dissatisfied with surface views and incapable of celestial detachment. But depth of vision is fraught with dangers of its own, as is evident when Rachel looks over the side of the ship: "Down she looked into the depth of the sea. While it was slightly disturbed on the surface by the passage of the *Euphrosyne*, beneath it was green and dim ... One could scarcely see the black ribs of wrecked ships, or the spiral towers made by the burrowings of great eels, or the smooth green-sided monsters who came by flickering this way and that" (27–28).

The sea experienced as depth rather than surface succeeds in absorbing Rachel's attention and, as the pronoun shift from "she" to "one" suggests, it also absorbs something of her particularity. But it gives nothing in return. The view grows dimmer and dimmer and what is "seen" is the product of a blurred literary imagination rather than of clear-sightedness. The "depths" take away egocentricity, but they yield nothing new in its place. The more profound the vision that Rachel seeks, the more fragmented and vague she becomes as a person among others.

Art, for Rachel, is not a means of mediating her introspection with external consciousness, but another element in which she loses herself and which obscures her view of the world. Unlike Mr. Grice, whose books are neatly lined in shelves above his specimens, Rachel lives in a tiny cabin strewn with musical scores and open books. Art in itself is no assurance of order or communication. Rachel's cabin is something of a mess and the "art" documents have no apparent relation to one another. When Rachel feels impatient with the other passengers' conversation, she closes herself in her cabin and seeks in music an experience not unlike that of staring into the sea: "In three minutes she was deep in a very difficult, very classical fugue in A, and over her face came a queer remote impersonal expression of complete absorption and anxious satisfaction" (57).

Art can be viewed from a distance or from within, alone or with others, but it has no single or absolute significance of its own. For Mrs. Dalloway (and Mr. Grice) literature makes for good conversation, and for most of the characters, music provides the occasion for great social gatherings.

The sea is similarly equivocal. One can brood over it or drown in it, but it, too, has social and linguistic possibilities. Even its great silence can be a conversation piece. Deep and dangerous though it may be, to most people the sea is for sailing over, for bathing parties, or for hikes with splendid views, like the one arranged by the young writer, Terence Hewet, after the ship arrives in South America. On the way up the mountain, Hewet has misgivings about the purpose of "bunching human beings together in a crowd": "But why do we do it?—is it to prevent ourselves from seeing to the bottom of things ... or do we really love each other, or do we, on the other hand, live in a state of perpetual uncertainty, knowing nothing, leaping from moment to moment as from world to world?" (127).

The ship crosses the sea and Hewet jumps over a stream, but, like Rachel, he has a tendency to let his mind fall to the bottom of things. He is planning a novel but he cannot get it written because fiction seems to him, like picnics and cities, a falsehood, a denial of that "perpetual uncertainty which is most real." Rachel and Hewet become engaged, but their "love" scenes and marriage plans are awkward formalities that neither understands. Their attachment is genuine, yet each seems to view it as a frail invention in a void. Rachel grows more and more vague and there are frequent intimations that she is "drowning," seeing the world, including her fiancé, as indistinct and inconsequential particles beyond her reach.

Just before the onset of her fatal illness, Hewet reads Milton to Rachel. The episode once again shows art as unable to rescue her from her own depth and therefore, for her, from the death of communicable experience, or meaning. That the lines are about Sabrina, who dwells "under the glassy, cool, translucent wave," gives them an ironic significance to the reader utterly different from what can be understood by the characters. Hewet intends the words to be cooling and pleasant sounds for a hot day. "He said the words of Milton had substance and shape, so that it was not necessary to understand what he was saying." Rachel, already feverish, finds herself attaching odd and disconnected meanings to Milton's words: "The words, in spite of what Terence had said, seemed to be laden with meaning, and perhaps it was for this reason that it was painful to listen to them; they sounded strange; they meant different things from what they usually meant. Rachel at any rate could not keep her attention fixed upon them, but went off upon curious trains of thought suggested by words such as 'curb' and 'Locrine' and 'Brute,' which brought unpleasant sights before her eyes, independently of their meaning" (327).

For the reader, too, Milton's words do not "mean" quite what they seem to. That is, the narrative legend of the nymph Sabrina has no relevance to the context of Woolf's chapter except in the single sign of the "woman under water"; the reader sees this as part of the system of "depth" and "underwater" signs that have recurred throughout the novel, especially in reference to Rachel. Even the greatest poetry, with its familiar and classical narrative structure, is shown to be subject to multiple interpretations that are so discrepant as to have little claim on stability or continuity of meaning.

Woolf's narrative of a young woman setting forth on her first and last voyage is not quite a portrait of an artist or of a lover. Neither Rachel's imagination nor her feelings are sufficiently capable of concentration to determine an identity for her in relation to which the phenomenal world can be given even imperfect shape. The formless sea is not, as it was for Stephen Dedalus, an object of contemplation or, as for Siegmund, a divine mistress to be adored. The sea is Rachel's medium. Its presence does not release her from confining loyalties and obligations; its vastness does not startle or inspire her or awaken her into new life. Her voyage is not out but under. Once she begins to sink, no music and no lover and no poet can bring her back to the surface.

It is in her last illness that the reader is given the most sustained expression of Rachel's view of things. It is a world without sharpness of line, without purposeful movement, and most important, without language: "At last the faces went further away; she fell into a deep pool of sticky water, which eventually closed over her head . . . There she lay, sometimes seeing darkness, sometimes light, while every now and then someone turned her over at the bottom of the sea" (341).

IN THESE encounters with the sea the three writers approach similar fictional material in distinctive ways. The "stories" differ greatly as histories—Joyce's artist wades, Lawrence's swims, and Woolf's "drowns." But the questions raised are remarkably similar, and the signs of artistic ambition and consternation in the context of an overlong literary tradition and an alarmingly unliterary sea are nearly identical. A single question joins a broad human need with an artistic dilemma: How does one look at the natural universe without being blinded by convention or overwhelmed by a mystery? It is a problem of perspective, of the observer's position relative to what is being observed; to answer it, one must bring realities into view without doctrines to accompany them and look not in order to find out something but in order to *see*. The effort made by all three writers is to represent the sea without imposed meanings, but each is keenly aware that representation is an act of the mind and that the mind itself must be located before the deed can be accomplished.

None of the three writers represents the sea directly; rather, each shows it through the eyes of various characters, particularly artists. In this way, the omissions, distortions, excesses of the viewers, even when not pointed out by the author, are presented to the reader as part of the unrevealed reality of the sea. Even in cases where the protagonist has the narrator's sympathy, his or her inadequacies need not be attributed to the author. Silences link reader and writer almost as much as words. In a certain sense each author leaves the sea unmarked and unmentioned. The reader's attention is turned to someone looking rather than directly to the object itself. Though only Joyce creates a world that is partly comic, all three present a view that is ironic because it is at several removes from its ostensible object. We are called on to look at ourselves looking at a writer looking at a character looking at the sea. Though this is an exercise which sounds absurd, it is akin to what Northrop Frye calls "perhaps the most distinctively human of all acts": "Science is based on a withdrawal of consciousness from existence, a capacity to turn around and look at one's environment . . . It is the act which turns the experiencing being into a subject, confronting an objective world from which it has separated itself. The ironic vision is, so to speak, a detachment from detachment: it recognizes the emotional factors of alienation, loneliness, and meaninglessness lurking in the subject-object relationship which the activity of science ignores."[6]

The separation of man from the objective world, lamented in Judeo-Christian mythology as the result of original sin, is welcomed by scientists as the condition of man's biological superiority, his peculiar capacity to know. The artist, particularly the modern artist, as Frye suggests, is caught between the two attitudes. He recognizes, indeed, often attempts to imitate, the impersonal detachment of the scientist registering without prejudice what he observes. At the same time, he experiences the equally human need to participate in what he sees, the need for understanding as well as information.

After their initial narratives of youthful encounters with the sea, Joyce, Lawrence, and Woolf return to the shore in later works, with less melodrama and more control but with the same determination to do justice both to man's alienation from his environment and his attachment to it. Since simultaneity of impression is all but impossible in language, even for Joyce, who goes furthest in attempting it, each writer develops ways of using words against words and undermining the myth of the transparency of language. Even metaphor is liable to be translated in one direction, whereas the object of these writers is a double movement, a repeated swing back and forth from union to separation, unconsciousness to consciousness, peace to anxiety. In their later books, the passages by the sea are marked by the same use and rejection of literary language, the same deliberate juxtapositions of form and apparent formlessness, but there is a new and insistent rhythm, a preoccupation with alternation, a heavier reliance on the sounds and shapes of words—not so much in rejection of their utility as signs but in harmonious counterbalance with it.

O F T H E three writers, Joyce showed the most radical change in his use of language as his career progressed. The Proteus episode in *Ulysses,* in which Stephen Dedalus is once again shown walking by the sea, is emotionally less significant than the parallel scene in *Portrait.*[7] Indeed, in the most obvious ways, it seems an altogether less eventful episode than the earlier one, yet the language is some of the most complicated in the book. It is not enough to say that the words are difficult because Stephen's thoughts are difficult. Abstract and academic as Stephen's thoughts may be, they alone do not justify the peculiarities of phrasing in the section. In fact, Joyce is presenting Stephen as a character detached from himself and his environment (thinking) and simultaneously attached to it (acting, sensing, being). If one looks at a passage in which the actual thoughts are not particularly complicated, it becomes plain that the intricacies of language express a great deal more than intellectual activity:

Am I walking into eternity along Sandymount strand? Crush, crack, crick, crick. Wild sea money. Dominie Deasy kens them a'.
Won't you come to Sandymount,
Madeline the mare?
Rhythm begins, you see. I hear. A catalectic tetrameter of iambs marching. No, agallop: *deline the mare.*
Open your eyes now. I will. One moment. Has all vanished since?

If I open and am for ever in the black adiaphane. *Basta!* I will see if I can see.

See now. There all the time without you: and ever shall be, world without end. (37)

Stephen is walking along the beach with his eyes closed thinking about eternity and Aristotle's theory of vision. In a way, what he is thinking is much less important than the demonstrated fact that he is thinking, that his mind is making abstract connections from which his individual being is removed. But while this is happening, Stephen is also functioning as a body, moving and making sounds as well as hearing and interpreting them. Indeed, the relations suggested by the words are not exclusively conceptual but visual and aural. Stephen is seen not only as a thinker who reads "meanings" in the "signatures of all things," but as a creature occupying space himself and, like the dog he sees later, "sniffing" at his own words—as he does at other curious objects that litter the strand. The dichotomy is not simply one between mind and body, but of Stephen *in* the seascape and Stephen outside it (and himself), observing. The linguistic analogue to this distinction is the use of words that call no particular attention to themselves and appear to function in direct relation to meaning, and words that call so much attention to themselves that they multiply or obscure meaning.

The opening question—"Am I walking . . . ?"—is philosophically tantalizing but verbally and grammatically straightforward. The sequence of the onomatopoetic "crush, crack, . . ." and "wild sea money" introduces considerations of aural and visual metaphor that, at the same time, extend the philosophical question and call attention away from it to the sensuous appeal of language. The coinlike shells remind Stephen of Mr. Deasy who knows all the answers, but the interplay of "sea money," "Dominie Deasy," and "Sandymount" contains its own poetry, a correlation of sounds that require no supportive meaning. The rhythm of these words and that of the jingle about "Madeline the mare" exists before it is identified as rhythm. Indeed, when the fact of the "rhythm" occurs to Stephen as "you see" (with "see" used as "understand"), the response is, "I hear." Rhythm is not a matter of understanding first, but of hearing. Rhythm does not depend on meaning, but meaning does depend on rhythm, as is shown by the scansion of the second line of the jingle in such a way as to group "deline the mare," which in an unexpected Anglo-Latin returns the reader to the sea and the philosophical question of delineation.

Stephen decides to open his eyes and "see" (find out) if he can "see" (visually perceive). The result—"see now"—combines, since the reader has been made peculiarly aware of sound, the act of seeing with its ob-

ject, the sea. But this verbal union of the witness and his world is immediately contradicted by the language with which Stephen returns to his
philosophical inquiry—"there all the time without you"—and then
reinforced by the concluding words of the "Glory be to the Father and
the Son and the Holy Ghost," which assume a continuity between creature and creation.

The passage is not a cancellation of all views by the inclusion of many
nor a dehumanized abstract of ideas, but a typically human and individual experiencing of phenomena, including the self, from within and
without. This simultaneity of attachment and detachment is represented verbally by rhythm, the anticipation of relatedness—repetition,
similarity—heightened by its temporary absence, the absence of an expected syllable ("catalectic tetrameter") as the equivalent of momentarily closing one's eyes. Joyce represents the human "meter"—walking,
blinking, breathing—in which the continuum of nature, the sea, is experienced in segments that only the remembering and anticipating imagination can put together. In the "creation" of the sea and self, the artist's
"work" is a type of the labor to live which is common to all humanity.

I N   L A W R E N C E ' S   Australian novel *Kangaroo,* the writer-pro-
tagonist, Richard Somers, rents a cottage by the sea and often walks
alone on the shore.[8] Near the end, after a complicated emotional involvement with the leaders of a right-wing political party, he returns to
the sea for a long ambulatory meditation. Lawrence's rhythms are rarely
as compressed as Joyce's, but he, too, weaves his character's detached
thoughts with his unconscious, involuntary participation in his environment: "The thud, the pulse of the waves: that was his nearest throb of
emotion." At first, Somers, like Dedalus, "reads" the sea, finds "solace"
and "escape" in it. But the more he walks, the less interested he is in
"signatures," verbal or natural, and the more he wishes to allow himself
to drift into blank existence:

> He had it all to himself. And there, with his hands in his pockets, he
> drifted into indifference. The far-off, far-off, far-off indifference.
> The world revolved and revolved and disappeared. Like a stone
> that has fallen into the sea, his old life, the old meaning, fell, and
> rippled, and there was vacancy, with the sea and the Australian
> shore in it. Far-off, far-off, as if he had landed on another planet, as
> a man might land after death . . .
> "What have I cared about, what have I cared for? There is noth-
> ing to care about." Absolved from it all. The soft, blue, humanless
> sky . . . the pale, white unwritten atmosphere . . . *Tabula rasa.* The

world a new leaf. And on the new leaf, nothing . . . Without a mark, without a record.(365)

The abolition of thought is represented first by a simple repetition ("far-off, far-off, far-off"), which marks Somers as an observer looking out to sea and, at the same time, begins to identify him with the mindless movement of the waves. The similes of falling "like a stone" into the sea or like a dead man on "another planet" are expressions of detachment from detachment, from the self-conscious mind, from "meaning" and "caring," not from being itself, which continues to have "weight" and substance. Like Stephen Dedalus, Somers asks himself questions that are both highly specific in relation to the immediate narrative context and philosophically abstract. He is reflecting not merely on his marriage and political friendships but on the state of anxiety that has brought about the combination of involvement and critical distance that Frye describes as "distinctively human." To be "absolved" from it all seems to him momentarily to be able to become part of the "humanless" sky and sea, to be free from thought and therefore from language. Lawrence does not play with language in the same way that Joyce does, but he has his own manner of calling attention to words as words. In the last three lines of the passage, language is used to depict the absence of language; grammar falters, predication vanishes, phrases replace complete thoughts, and verbal signs are used to indicate a peculiarly verbal emptiness, an "unwritten" atmosphere, without a "mark" or a "record," except of course, the one Lawrence is in the process of making. The use of *tabula rasa* is particularly ironic since its meaning is so entirely tied to a verbal and philosophical tradition. Unlike the Australian sea, it is a "marked" phenomenon, full of linguistic associations.

Though his imaginative efforts to absolve his characters from the anxieties of human ambivalence and join them to nature go further than those of any of his contemporaries, Lawrence was no more naive than Joyce or Woolf about the obstacles. For him, as for the others, there is also a time to turn away from the sea; a time devised by self-conscious man as well as the pulse of the unconscious sea: "Home, to tea. The clicking of the clock. Tic-tac! Tic-tac! The clock. Home to tea. Just for clockwork's sake. No home, no tea. Insouciant soullessness. Eternal indifference. Perhaps it is only the great pause between carings. But it is only in this pause that one finds the meaninglessness of meanings . . . the reality of timelessness and nowhere"(367).

Somers's "pause" in eternal indifference, like Stephen's "walking into eternity" along Sandymount strand with his eyes closed, does not represent a new view of things for the artist so much as the acceptance, indeed, the inviting, of moments with no view, or at least none springing from the ego as the center of the universe. The result is the modern equivalent of the medieval *memento mori,* though the projection is not of one's own life after death but of the continued life of the world after one has ceased to live in and see it. This "absence" of view is also within the realm of the searching human imagination to anticipate and, between heartbeats and familiar verbal patterns, to experience.

T H O U G H not herself a writer or painter, Mrs. Ramsay in *To the Lighthouse* has an artist's sensitivity to order and disorder that is the informing spirit of Lily Briscoe's painting by the sea in the third section of Woolf's novel.[9] One of the key passages referring to Mrs. Ramsay and her own relation with the sea is in a very long sentence in which her mind is shown responding to the patterns of particular sounds as she leafs through a catalogue:

> The gruff murmur, irregularly broken by the taking out of pipes and the putting in of pipes which had kept on assuring her, though she could not hear what was said ... that the men were happily talking; this sound, which had lasted now half an hour and had taken its place soothingly in the scale of sounds pressing on top of her, such as the tap of balls upon bats ... of the children playing cricket, had ceased; so that the monotonous fall of the waves on the beach, which for the most part beat a measured and soothing tattoo to her thoughts and seemed consolingly to repeat over and over again as she sat with the children the words of some old cradle song, murmured by nature, "I am guarding you—I am your support," but at other times suddenly and unexpectedly, especially when her mind raised itself slightly from the task actually in hand, had no such kindly meaning, but like a ghostly roll of drums remorselessly beat the measure of life, made one think of the destruction of the island and its engulfment in the sea, and warned her whose day had slipped past in one quick doing after another that it was all ephemeral as a rainbow—this sound which had been obscured and concealed under the other sounds suddenly thundered hollow in her ears and made her look up with an impulse of terror.(27–28)

Woolf's manner is very much her own; yet she, like Joyce and Lawrence, demonstrates the peculiar importance of rhythm in this passage by placing it under great strain. The excessively long sentence seems at several points to be on the verge of wandering off into meaninglessness, but it is brought back each time by references to sounds that recur like the insistent beat the passage describes: "the gruff murmur," "this sound," "the tap of balls," "the monotonous fall." The completion of the sentence seems a triumph over inconsequential vagueness, on the one hand, and too-insistent repetitiveness, on the other. In fact, it maintains a delicate balance between human rhythms, the men's voices, the children's game, the cradle song, and the nonhuman measure of the sea. "This sound," at the beginning of the sentence refers to the voices, but the same phrase at the end has been transferred to the sea.

There is really no question of the human timing or pacing overwhelming the "ghostly roll of drums." Like the long sentence, the human rhythm is in constant need of reestablishing itself. The destructive measure is always present, but one is not always conscious of it. Mrs. Ramsay's vantage point in this scene, as in most of the novel, is peculiar. She is with neither the men nor the children, part of neither the philosophical discussion nor the games, but alone. In fact, the academic talk and cricket have very much the same function for her as the cradle song. They are all consoling conventions of harmony and human control, the specific meanings of which are unimportant to her, not because she is too stupid to grasp them but because she defines their objects in their process rather than in their ends. She sees them sharing the fate of the island, which will inevitably be engulfed.

That Mrs. Ramsay feels terror rather than relief in encountering the relentless indifference of the sea has to do with her own identity in relation to her family. If the old cradle song, "I am guarding you—I am your support," is not murmured by nature, then her own voice as a mother is not an echo but a poignantly fragile and vital improvisation. Like Rachel Vinrace, Mrs. Ramsay is drawn by the bottomless, insensible, repetitious sea not merely to a realization of the fragile brevity of life but to a terrifying sense of nothingness. But while her ability to imagine her own annihilation becomes the dominant psychological state for Rachel and leads eventually to her death, Mrs. Ramsay's extraordinary gift for penetration, like the lighthouse beam, alternates; it illuminates being, even after her death, as brilliantly as it does nonbeing.

If the forms and substances of life are temporary and, to a large extent, invented conveniences, so, in another way, are the emotional and mental constructs of death and nothingness. Life cannot be possessed, held down, thoroughly "gotten at" by the individual, least of all Mrs. Ramsay, from whom it seems continually and elusively to be slipping away. Mealtime, marriage, letter writing, philosophy, motherhood, are all activities that participate in and approximate life, but that do not in any total way contain it. But Mrs. Ramsay's encounters with death when she is alone or listening to the sea are equally and necessarily fragmented and imaginary. The insistent throbbing of the waves is no more "real" an equivalent of death than telling a story to a child is of life.

Being drawn toward death, toward a sense of one's nothingness, is finally as much an action or reaction of the mind as is being drawn toward life and identity.

Mrs. Ramsay's extraordinary gift lies in her capacity to imagine her own nothingness and then, without denying it, to turn her mind with equal concentration to the life of another; in doing so, she recovers her identity as a mother, a wife, and a friend. Her knowledge, her misgivings, and her ability to hold things together bear a marked resemblance to those of the artist who contains terror within the compass of outrageously long sentences, sensuous repetitions, and extravagant metrical games. No fixed, or comfortable, or clear view of the sea can be given. But by refusing to mix metaphors—the cradle song with the drum roll, to confuse the sign with that signified—the "sea" with the sea, or to mistake time for eternity—clockwork for the "pulse of the waves," the writer establishes an alternating perspective, a new rhythm with gaps like horizons toward which the reader is forced to look for himself.

The sea figures powerfully in crucial passages in the fiction of Joyce and Lawrence; yet it is Woolf, more than either of the others, who is most consistently preoccupied by its broken symbolic potential and its capacity, if only as a vast blank, to provide perspective on the trivial certainties of the land-locked life. Perhaps no passage in Woolf contains more sadness, anger, and disappointment than the description of the shore in the "Time Passes" section of *To the Lighthouse*, which follows the terse parenthetical announcements of the death of Mrs. Ramsay and, later, of her son Andrew in the war in France:

At that season those who had gone down to pace the beach and ask of the sea and sky what message they reported or what vision they affirmed had to consider among the usual tokens of divine bounty—the sunset on the sea, the pallor of dawn, the moon rising, fishing-boats against the moon, and children making mud pies or pelting each other with handfuls of grass, something out of harmony with this jocundity and this serenity. There was the silent apparition of an ashen-coloured ship for instance, come, gone; there was a purplish stain upon the bland surface of the sea as if something had boiled and bled, invisibly, beneath. This intrusion into a scene calculated to stir the most sublime reflections and lead to the most comfortable conclusions stayed their pacing. It was difficult blandly to overlook them; to abolish their significance in the landscape; to continue, as one walked by the sea, to marvel how beauty outside mirrored beauty within . . . That dream, of sharing, completing, of finding in solitude on the beach an answer, was then but a reflection in a mirror, and the mirror itself was but the surface glassiness which forms in quiescence when the nobler powers sleep beneath? Impatient, desparing yet loth to go (for beauty offers her lures, has her consolations), to pace the beach was impossible; contemplation was unendurable; the mirror was broken.(202)

The passage sums up better than almost anything else of the period the artist's complex and troubled relation to the natural universe. She is drawn to the real and imagined beauty of nature, to the color and movement that have inspired painters and poets for ages, but she is unable to separate that beauty and rhythmic motion from the random, destructive, and ugly shifts that are a part of it. She is perfectly capable of reading the literature of the sea, but she cannot read the sea itself and will not, though frequently tempted, pretend that she can. Her struggle for honesty, then, is first of all a struggle with artistic representations that charm and move but do not persuade her. If she cannot tame nature and present it in words of her own without falsifying it in a new way, she can at least expose the flaws in the old pictures. She may even imitate the familiar formulas—"the sunset on the sea, the pallor of the dawn"—only to intrude on them with the reminder that something is "out of harmony" and "stays the pacing" of the "most sublime reflections." Like Joyce and Lawrence, Woolf does not directly confront the sea itself, but rather confronts the falsifying harmonies and cadences that have been identified with it. As artists, they all recognized that *some* pacing, *some* harmony was necessary to them, but that by breaking the flow, creating a counterrhythm, they could show that order is earned by man, rather than given by nature.

Nature, as symbolized in the sea, still helps the onlooker to define himself. As always, it is a reminder of death and eternity, of the eventuality of a complete loss of ego. But rather than provide vague consolations or messages of moral direction, it casts the viewer back on his own kind. The sea is still a mirror, though no longer Byron's "glorious mirror where the Almighty form glasses itself." Nor is it a mirror of human nature in its totality, but rather of superficial and "quiescent" man as he is when the imagination glosses over the realities his heart knows. For the true artist, the person of complete integrity, that mirror of wishful thinking remains visible but broken. In order to discover his own depths, he must survive the hazards of the sea-view—the tow toward nothingness and the cracked literary glosses—and look for answers from those who can hear his questions.

TWO

Our Great Sweet Mother

Mother and Child

... the imagination [is] ... the mother of things, whose dream we are, who images us to herself, and to us, and images herself in us.

JAMES JOYCE, *James Clarence Mangan*

When a child leans its breast against its mother it becomes filled with a primal awareness of *her*—not of itself desiring her or partaking of her—but of her as she is in herself. This is the first great acquisition of primal objective knowledge, the objective content of the unconscious.

D. H. LAWRENCE, *Psychoanalysis and the Unconscious*

"Come, Papa, come," she said, stretching out her hand. "Mama's dying."

VIRGINIA WOOLF, *The Years*

FOR JOYCE, WOOLF, AND LAWRENCE, the
natural world, no longer taken as a mirror of God's mind or man's,
loses its structural and rational justification but not its substance. Unlike
the God of revelation and theology, it is still very much there. Though it
may not be understood in terms that make sense morally or æstheti-
cally, it can be experienced and described. These writers continued to
pose questions about nature, to explore its effects on men and women,
and to wonder whether they might be transformed into human values.

The personification of nature as a mother, and especially Wordsworth's Romantic extension of it, seemed to them an unfulfilled dream:

> blest the Babe,
> Nursed in his Mother's arms, who sinks to sleep
> Rocked on his Mother's breast; who with his soul
> Drinks in the feelings of his Mother's eye!
> For him, in one dear Presence, there exists
> A virtue which irradiates and exalts
> Objects through widest intercourse of sense;
> No outcast he, bewildered and depressed:
> Along his infant veins are interfused
> The gravitation and the filial bond
> Of nature that connect him with the world.
>   (*The Prelude*, II)

For the modern writer, Wordsworth's ascending ladder, which leads
from child to mother to nature and ultimately to God, is broken. But
even though one series of links may be damaged, that with the mother,
like that with nature, remains intact. Furthermore, certain characteristics of the mother-child relationship, though their meaning may be
questioned, remain physically constant. The new life still grows like a
seed in the dark and protective womb; it is still attached by a cord to the
mother's body; it still derives its first rhythmic stimuli from the mother's
heartbeat; and it still undergoes an abrupt separation from the maternal
environment at birth. Thus even if, after birth, the mother's relation
with the child does not conform to Wordsworth's ideal, certain conditions and events are imprinted on each new life.

Divested of its transcendent associations, the blood bond with the mother remained strong while the old contract with God seemed to weaken. Skeptical modern writers tended to think of God as an idea. Arduous as it may have seemed to challenge and eventually to uproot that idea so that man could take on the responsibility for ordering the world himself, it was a task that had been labored at for centuries and one that seemed possible. Though he puts it more arrogantly than most, Joyce was by no means alone in thinking of himself as an artist doing God's work, that is, the work of God the father, the architect, authority, and judge. The universality, power, and constancy of the mother as a creative and shaping force was more difficult to imitate and to dismiss. Even for those without Wordsworth's view of nature, the breaking of the umbilical cord seemed the rupture of a real link, not a repudiation of an idea.

T H E   D E A T H of a mother in the novels of Joyce, Lawrence, and Woolf has strong autobiographical roots. The mother of each died when the writer was still young. But what is of particular interest to the critic is how the loss of the mother is transformed from personal trauma into a key element in the artist's signature. As Stephen Dedalus argues in the Scylla and Charybdis episode in *Ulysses,* with reference to the autobiographical elements in *Hamlet,* the artist does not merely work out his own suffering in therapeutic words; he discovers and reproduces the world by coming to terms with himself. "We walk through ourselves, meeting robbers, ghosts, giants, old men, young men, wives, widows, brothers-in-love."

The nature of the frequent meetings with the mother, especially the dead mother's spirit, defines the sensibility and experience of a particular writer. But because of its deep and universal associations, it also can define a whole world. Jane Austen, who does not believe in ghosts, shows in *Northanger Abbey* that her impressionable heroine's anxieties about the dead mother of her best friends is only a result of too much exposure to Ann Radcliffe. The vacancy that death leaves is what Austen points to, and it is in keeping with her moral view that the living should usefully fill such vacancies rather than morbidly brood over them. One of the important virtues of Emma Woodhouse is that, at an early age, she assumes the role of lady of the house and looks after her widowed father. Thoughts and images of the dead mother do not come into the story. On the stage of this polite social world, death takes away the essential privilege of making an entrance. Throughout the fiction of the nineteenth century, motherless heroines assumed the nourishing and protective role of the absent parent, either for their own families, like Little Dorrit, or for other incomplete families, like Jane Eyre.

The problems of motherless sons have always differed from those of motherless daughters, but those differences were accentuated by middle-class attitudes toward the family in the nineteenth century. Sons could not, in a world that made sharp distinctions between sexual and parental roles, assume the mother's place, even in the slightly grotesque fashion of Esther Summerson in *Bleak House*. They were bereft not only of nurse and guardian but of a model of femininity that they could seek to recover, complement, or improve upon in a mistress or wife.

The son's desire to have his mother for himself, mixed with the temporal impossibility and social taboo connected with this desire, plays an important part in a number of Victorian plots. Thackeray avoided incest but still scandalized readers in having Henry Esmond marry his foster mother. David Copperfield's marriage to Dora combines, as so often in Dickens, a profound psychological truth with a stern moral. The attempt to marry the pretty, childlike image of his dead mother brings disappointment and misery to David. While Thackeray stretches legalities and years to make his hero's dream realizable, Dickens honors both the dream and the social and physical reality without pretending that they can be one. The most common way around the awkward inclinations of the motherless hero is a spiritual bond that keeps mother and son together regardless of age and situation. As Paul Dombey lies dying, he reports to his desolate sister a vision of their dead mother, her beauty encompassed by heavenly light, waiting for him on the opposite shore. In short, while the bereft daughter occupies the place left empty by the departed mother, the bereft son seeks, in his own fashion, to find her again, either on earth or in heaven.

Despite the differences in the ways in which male and female characters are shown to experience the loss of the mother, there are important common elements. The tie to the mother reflects on the character's physical, especially sexual, self: the capacity for growth, mating, and procreation, and bodily strength, beauty, and health. Complementing this link is an equally powerful spiritual bond. Not only was the Victorian mother usually the "religious" member of the family, but, after her death, she tended to represent to her children the gentler virtues of resignation, obedience, sympathy, and unselfish love. The presence of the dead mother in the character's life is invariably a highly personal, even private, matter, often symbolized in sentimental fiction by a favorite portrait and in more realistic fiction by a memory or dream peculiar to the bereaved child. The mother represents, on the one hand, the physical source of life and, on the other, that expression of vitality that, because deprived of formal authority and practical action, is vicarious, emotional, unworldly, and imaginative.

The contrast with the role of the father, living or dead, is striking. In nineteenth-century fiction, the primary function of the father is to exercise authority. When like Mr. Bennett, he fails comically, or, like Michael Henchard, fails tragically, he highlights, by contrast, the importance of the archetype from which he deviates. Most of the adventure novelists of the nineteenth century—Scott, Stevenson, Kingsley, Kipling—kill or incapacitate the hero's father so that the action can begin. The intellectual struggles of the period, though not necessarily carried to the death, can also be seen, in part, as battles to overcome the prohibitive authority of the father, as in the cases of Gosse, Butler, Rutherford, Arnold, Mill, and Darwin. The father's legacy is intellectual, moral, economic, legal, and, by virtue of the name, always social and public. Mr. Dombey seems to be speaking for a great many nineteenth century fathers when he informs his wife about the naming of their newborn son: " 'He will be christened Paul, my—Mrs. Dombey—of course . . . His father's name, Mrs. Dombey, and his grandfather's . . . There is some inconvenience in the necessity of writing Junior . . . but it is merely a private and personal complexion. It doesn't enter into the correspondence of the House. *Its* signature remains the same.' "

What distinguishes the family mythology of the early twentieth century from that of the high Victorian period is that the arbitrary character of paternal rule remains, but not the power. Different as Simon Dedalus, Walter Morel, and Mr. Ramsay may be from one another, their authority is a hollow structure, a mechanical pretense of solemn purpose propped up with boasting and bullying that imperfectly conceal a pathetic dependence. Apparently, the repeated religious, political, and social challenges of the nineteenth century had left the patriarchal figure, rather like that of Edward VII or George V, rulers without substance. They might be laughed at or pitied, but they were hardly worth a serious rebellion. Even a second-rate artist could do better than Simon Dedalus's political bluster or Mr. Ramsay's dogged efforts to get beyond Q.

The father's role as rule-maker could be assumed and improved upon—at the very least, from the point of view of entertainment and morality—by the gifted artist. Joyce's epic structures and Lawrence's moralizing are indications of their own imposition of "authoritative" order. The presence of the maternal phantom suggests another shaping power that precedes and makes possible the artist's defiance and self-knowledge and to which he must invariably submit. The artist as thinker, lawmaker, and craftsman stamping his own will and design on shapeless material—that is, the artist assuming the role of Victorian father—contrasts with the artist as matrix, a seemingly passive source of living form. As roles for the artist, the two are in sharp contradiction; each seems to deny the importance of the other and to undermine its reality. The challenge is to discover a vital equilibrium: a balance between conscious and unconscious order; design and rhythm; theory and experience; plot and moment. Haunted by the ghost of the father, the modern artist seeks to arrange, explain, extend, impose, and control. Haunted by the ghost of the mother, he seeks to contain, combine, stir, touch, and release new life.

I N *Ulysses* Joyce makes extensive use of the father-and-son relationship, not only through the Odysseus-Telemachus parallels and frequent references to Daedalus and Icarus and the first two persons of the Trinity, but through the prolonged and exaggerated debate in the library about the ghost of Hamlet's father and Shakespeare's own son, Hamnet. Mythological, literary, and theological substitutes for Stephen's weak father seem relatively easy to come by. His mother, though dead, is more difficult to replace. Her ghost repeatedly appears and speaks to him throughout the book. Unable to rid himself of her, Stephen can apply the same reasoning he does to Shakespeare and his dead son, in which the roles of parent and son, living and dead, are reversed. In the debate over *Hamlet,* he defines a ghost as "one who has faded into impalpability through death, through absence." If this is so, then, like Shakespeare, it is he, through memory and imagination, who brings his mother back, gives her a new birth.

Immediately after accusing Stephen of his mother's death, Mulligan calls him "the loveliest mummer of them all." It is one of a number of Mulligan's playful attempts to label Stephen—"Kinch," the "fearful Jesuit"—whose "absurd name" seems to have an even less firm hold on its bearer than Paul Dombey's corporate "signature" had on his newborn son. The pun plays on the identification of the artist as imitator, *mummer,* and mother, *mamma.* It incorporates a transformation from masculine to feminine with a concept of the imitative artist and suggests that Stephen wishes to be not only his own father, authority and rule-maker, but his own source of life, his own mother.[1]

But Joyce is not one to indulge his young hero's ambitions without qualification. In the discussion of Shakespeare, Stephen himself recalls the famous scene in *Coriolanus* between the hero and his mother at the gates of Rome and refers to it as Shakespeare's tribute to his own dead mother. Volumnia begs her son not to enter Rome with the Volces and destroy Rome. Coriolanus answers:

> My mother bows . . .
> Great nature cries, 'Deny not.'—Let the Volces
> Plough Rome and harrow Italy: I'll never
> Be such a gosling to obey instinct, but stand
> As if a man were author of himself,
> And knew no other kin.

Coriolanus does eventually "obey instinct" and yield to his mother's plea. That Rome was saved and Coriolanus lost is a conclusion that can hardly have escaped Joyce. The combat against instinct is a struggle to the death—for Stephen, even beyond death. The young artist's effort to rid himself of his mother's ghost is not merely a matter of repudiating her religion. What is more important is that the obsessive guilt, the flood of pity, the horror of physical decay associated with her can enter uncontrollably into his mind, mocking his aesthetic detachment and his ability to manage his own imagination.

Mulligan's mention of the dead mother reminds Stephen of her visit to him in a dream. Joyce places the reader inside of Stephen's skull, looking out with his eyes and seeing everything as though a transparency of his mother's phantom overlaid it. Despite his desire to gain "distance" on his life, his family, and himself, Stephen, whose glasses are broken, can see private dreams and memories more clearly than the distant view: "Stephen, an elbow rested on the jagged granite, leaned his palm against his brow and gazed at the fraying edge of his shiny black coat-sleeve. Pain, that was not yet the pain of love, fretted his heart. Silently, in a dream she had come to him after her death, her wasted body within its loose brown grave-clothes giving off an odour of wax and rosewood, her breath, that had bent upon him, mute, reproachful, a faint odour of wetted ashes. Across the threadbare cuffedge he saw the sea hailed as a great sweet mother by the wellfed voice beside him. The ring of bay and skyline held a dull green mass of liquid. A bowl of white china had stood beside her deathbed holding the green sluggish bile which she had torn up from her rotting liver by fits of loud groaning vomiting"(5).

Throughout the passage, Stephen is curiously still, caught in a rigid pose while the memory of his dream acts in his mind. His senses are alert and active—touch, sight, smell, sound are all evoked. Unlike conventional ghosts, the specter of Mrs. Dedalus seems to have no distinct message to deliver. Despite an impression of sensory clarity, meaning remains potential. The pain that Stephen feels is "not yet the pain of love." The vision is "reproachful," but "mute." The identification of mother and son through his black coat-sleeve and her brown grave-clothes is possible but not necessary. The circular forms, "the ring of bay" and the "bowl of white china" are juxtaposed on the page, but the logic of their connection is not shown. Stephen has obviously struck a pose, but whether it is that of an artist, thinker, or mourner is not clear. In fact, his mind is a ragbag of unassimilated images and unacknowl-edged emotions. Mulligan's glib association of the sea with a "great sweet mother" is impossible for Stephen, whose own associations, for the moment, are personal and confused.

The passage is a *tour de force* of nondetachment. Stephen is riveted by the memory of his mother. As a son, he sees and feels her so close at hand as to be unable to place her in a design. Though the narrative mode is narrated monologue rather than interior monologue, it can be taken as a reflection of Stephen's state of mind. Predicates are repeatedly separated from subjects; parallel structures are interrupted or left incomplete; con-nectives are absent from clauses; the effect is of vivid compression but not coherence. The picture is not that of a young man callous to the suf-fering of his mother, but of a mind that registers and recalls but cannot, for this instant, select, focus, or control.

When Mulligan tries to explain his reference to Mrs. Dedalus as "beastly dead" in medical terms—"I see them pop off every day . . . cerebral lobes not functioning"—Stephen finds his focus in opposition to Mulligan, whose anatomy lesson is a mock reflection of Stephen's rebel-lious image. Rejecting Mulligan's mechanistic theories and his apolo-gies, Stephen speaks of the offense of the remark to himself. When Mul-ligan sings lines from Yeats's "Who Goes With Fergus?" Stephen remembers that he used to sing them to his mother:

> And no more turn aside and brood
> Upon love's bitter mystery
> For Fergus rules the brazen cars.

The rhythm and mysterious tone of the poem help Stephen put his confused memory of his mother and his irritation with Mulligan into harmony. Yeats's words enliven his mind and enable him to create an order out of his memories and impressions. But as he wishes to escape rigid categorization, whether imposed by family or friends, he does not force order but proposes it, almost teases it, out of the situation. The three unquoted lines that complete the thought and the sentence in Yeats's poem refer to a heroic myth of male dominance over feminine nature:

And rules the shadows of the wood,
And the white breast of the dim sea,
And all dishevelled wandering stars.

Joyce's prose poem, which follows the quotation from Yeats, suggests an entirely different relationship between man and woman, artist and nature, words and things. There is no myth of dominance, but an extraordinary rendering of cooperative interaction between author and character, language and nature. Joyce is not thinking *for* Stephen but thinking *with* him in a realm in which idea, experience, and expression are in such perfect harmony as to suggest no single source: "Woodshadows floated silently by through the morning peace from the stairhead seaward where he gazed. Inshore and farther out the mirror of water whitened, spurned by lightshod hurrying feet. White breast of the dim sea. The twining stresses, two by two. A hand plucking the harpstrings merging their twining chords. Wavewhite wedded words shimmering on the dim tide"(9).

The lights and shadows, movements and sounds of nature may have no message, no moral argument in this passage, but they are allowed to be as active in their way as the viewer's consciousness is in its. The completion of thought seems so unimportant that sentences drift into unfinished phrases. Yet the order of imagery and rhythm does not conceal the lack of an explanation. Language does not pretend to rule nature, nor is it intimidated into ugliness by what it cannot control. "Twining stresses, two by two" refers as much to the movement of words as to that of the sea. The two are not equated or dissolved into one; they are presented in balance. "Wavewhite wedded words shimmering on the dim tide" is an exquisite description of language and sea at the expense of neither.

Stephen can imitate Fergus, the ruler, only up to a point. His mother's ghost is a reminder that nature can never be altogether subdued. The designing mind may do what it will with words, but just as man's conceptual longing makes nature seem impenetrable, his physical history makes words inadequate. The literary, allusive elements in the passage do not seem artificially obtrusive because their presence as words (not things) is acknowledged. By the same token, the mysterious beauty of the sea is not spoiled by classification. Words are allowed to be words, waves to be waves. That they do not solve or rule each other does not appear to mean that they cannot exist, at least occasionally, in harmony. Joyce often makes language "interfere" with nature, but he also allows language to be receptive to it, to "twine" and "shimmer" as though saturated by what it describes. For the artist-mother, words are objects and receptacles as well as indicators.

Joyce is not content with the function of the artist as one who imitates nature, improves upon it, or improvises his own replacement for it, though at various times he plays all of these roles. When he treats language not merely as a means of direct communication but as an object of contemplation, an environment, he gives it the same status as other natural phenomena open to renewal in the artist's imagination. He seems, in these instances, to be counterbalancing his imposing, paternalistic structures with a passivity akin to that admired by the Romantic poets, to be allowing new forms to emerge "naturally" from a consciousness unhampered by rules.

Joyce realized that there was an element of overingenuity, even trickery, in what he was attempting. Buck Mulligan's mock consecration on the first page of *Ulysses* introduces a major theme of the novel, the perennial human attempt to give life to inert matter. His joke about transubstantiation as galvanization ("switch off the current") is not only a mockery of a religious ritual but a reminder of one kind of company the overreaching artist keeps. The artist seen as a fake priest, magician, or mad scientist suggests the peculiarly Joycean combination of apology and bravado. Yet the eccentric sacraments, much like the overbold epic structures, confess their own artificiality quite as vehemently as they satirize the pretensions of the forms from which they are borrowed. The artist makes a fool of himself in order to escape the foolishness imposed on him by others.

To be the false mother—to presume to create new life through words—is in some ways the greatest foolishness of all. But it is an effort that may show better than anything else the counterweight of attachment and humility that balances the aloofness and arrogance of Joyce's artistic posture. To remember the mother is to remember the flesh and man's inescapable dependence on it. Stephen remembers sadly that though he refused to pray for his mother he *did* sing for her, he gave her what a poet has to give: words. The thought of this breaks the creative spell and turns him to a mental scouring of her locked drawer, where he finds random mementos, fans, dancecards, beads. As he threads together these odds and ends with fragments of song and other memories of his mother, she appears again, this time surrounded by the voices of those chanting the prayer for the dead that Stephen had refused to say: *"Liliata rutilantium te confessorum turma circumdet: iubilantium te virginum chorus excipiat"* ("May the radiant throng of confessors encompass thee; May the jubilant chorus of virgins receive thee"). Those were the words wanted at the moment of death, the words that would have helped to lay his mother to rest.

Stephen's refusal, like his rummaging through her drawer for the images of a new poem, is not only the sign of a violation of a religious duty; it is a violation but also an acknowledgment of the natural relationship between mother and son. His imagination will not let his mother rest. Whether in fear or pity, it calls her back into being, fusing her, like the sea, with the language of his new art. When the ghost cries out, "Ghoul! Chewer of corpses!" she challenges more effectively than Buck Mulligan's mock Eucharist the effort of the artist to bring life out of the dead. Stephen's pained response—"No mother. Let me be and let me live"—is the son's plea not to be haunted by guilt. It is also the artist's agonized cry to let him get on with his work of creating new forms out of dead material, without regard for his own private emotions and inhibitions. The absence of a comma between "no" and "mother" suggests a meaning not conveyed by direct address. "No mother" is a declaration straining against grammatical logic, since it eliminates the supposed object of address. It is the artist echoing Coriolanus's wish to act "as if a man were author of himself," knowing perfectly well his inability, except in fits and starts, to do so.

Though much of *Ulysses* is about the process of translating experience into words, the passages in which Stephen's mother is remembered are peculiarly alive with the contradictions implicit in that process. In the classroom at Mr. Deasy's school, Stephen is drawn to a skinny boy with weak eyes and slanted glasses who reminds him of himself as a child. After an almost Dickensian reflection on the waif, Stephen looks at his copybook: "The word *Sums* was written on the headline. Beneath were sloping figures and at the foot a crooked signature with blind loops and a blot. Cyril Sargent: his name and seal . . . Stephen touched the edges of the book. Futility"(27).

The markings on the page, crooked, sloping, and blind like the boy who made them, provide no means for getting at the mystery of their author. His signature is his "seal," his sign, but it is also what closes him off, keeps him from being known. Stephen is struck by the outward ugliness and futility of the boy, but then remembers that "someone had loved him, borne him in her arms and in her heart. But for her the race of the world would have trampled him under foot . . . She had loved his weak watery blood drained from her own. Was that then real? The only true thing in life?" His encounter with the boy is another encounter with himself and his dead mother. Again, he recalls the "odour of rosewood and wetted ashes" and feels the guilt, here associated with a fox scraping the earth, of robbing the grave for his literary subjects. Again, the filial guilt is identified with an artistic problem. The frail child with a "crooked signature" is the opposite image of the artist who, in bolder moods, associates himself with Fergus, Daedalus, Shakespeare, and a host of other heroic figures. Stephen sees the child (and, for a moment, himself) as "only a mother" could see him—weak, intense, scribbling away at hopeless sums.

It is an irony and a sign of Joyce's balance that the artist's ability to be "author of himself," to bring things together into a cohesive fusion, to do correct "sums," is brought into doubt at the very moment when it appears most to be succeeding. The pretentions of the intellect—Stephen proving by algebra "that Shakespeare's ghost is Hamlet's grandfather," trying to use mathematics to explain life—are juxtaposed with school games and the unassuming rhymes of simple poetry: "Hockeysticks rattled in the lumberroom: the hollow knock of a ball and calls from the field" (28).

The frail boy and the memory of the mother not only make Stephen feel guilty; they make him look silly. In fact, at the moment, all efforts to embroider, reorder, even comment on the essential facts of life appear futile and foolish, a matter of trickery that is really only self-deception. Even the solemn mathematical signs suddenly seem like fantastic jesters: "Across the page the symbols moved in grave morrice, in the mummery of their letters, wearing quaint caps of squares and cubes. Give hands, traverse, bow to partner: so: imps of fancy of the Moors" (28).

Algebra, like field hockey, is a way of arranging things by establishing rules. Whether they provide a clearer view of reality than the boy gets peering through his slanted glasses is by no means certain. Stephen thinks of yet another system of ordering before the scene is over. When the phrase *Amor matris* comes to mind, he identifies it as both subjective and objective genitive: mother's love and love of the mother. If, as this suggests, the two are the same, there is no escape—even through art—from the mother's claim on her son. Art, like algebra, can express the equation or, like a field sport, can imitate the conflict, but it cannot disguise the fact.

Stephen's final identification with the boy coincides with his inability to communicate with him, an acknowledgment of a link that is real but mysteriously beyond the power of language to convey except by hints and gestures:

Like him was I, these sloping shoulders, this gracelessness. My childhood bends beside me. Too far for me to lay a hand there once or lightly. Mine is far and his secret as our eyes. Secrets, silent, stony sit in the dark palaces of both our hearts: secrets weary of their tyranny: tyrants willing to be dethroned.
The sum was done.
—It is very simple, Stephen said as he stood up. (28)

Once again, poetic language provides harmony and a balance of sounds, sights, feelings, and thoughts without pretending to conceal or solve the problem of isolation. Inverted word order, alliteration, repetition, and the conceit of the "tyrant" in his "palace" mark the passage as "literary," indeed, reminiscent of a Metaphysical meditation. But unlike most Metaphysical poetry, it is undramatic. There is no exchange—not even an imagined one—between man and boy. They remain separate. The language acknowledges the gap without pretending to bridge it. Against the natural, eternal, and mysterious tie between mother and son, poetry, like field hockey and algebra, appears arbitrary and trivial, except in one essential respect. In its capacity to confess its poverty, to show what it cannot do, language acknowledges worlds outside itself and thereby lends them a dignity and assumes a dignity for itself that it had seemed to throw away. Through an extraordinary restraint within the elaborate playfulness of Joyce's language, Stephen's mind—his tendency to seek resemblances—and the boy's otherness—his unconscious resistance to that tendency—remain vividly intact.

On the beach toward evening Stephen sees a gypsy couple and imagines in the woman a combination of Eve, the Virgin Mary, Penelope, and his own mother, all containing within their forms the mysterious movement of sealike waters: "Tides, myriad-islanded, within her, blood not mine, *oinopa ponton,* a wine-dark sea. Behold the handmaid of the moon. In sleep the wet sign calls her hour, bids her rise. Bridebed, childbed, bed of death, ghostcandled" (47–48).

He pulls out a scrap of paper and scribbles the words of a poem, seeing his own shadow, like the words on the paper, as part of a fleshless birth: "I throw this ended shadow from me, manshape ineluctable, call it back." He wonders "who ever anywhere will read these written words?" He fears that his poetry, like the boy's signature, only seals him off from contact, that the "immortality" of the artist is merely a shadow, a negation, a darkness in the light. In an utterance that is part prayer and part a sensual appeal to death, he asks for deliverance from detachment: "Touch me. Soft eyes. Soft soft soft hand. I am lonely here. O, touch me soon, now. What is that word known to all men? I am quiet here alone. Sad too. Touch me, touch me" (49). There is no touch and no answer. The artist goes on thinking and spinning out words that celebrate the beauty or satirize the ugliness of what he has lost without being able to recover it. His many words are his way of questing after the one right "word," the key to life and death. The epic high adventure of *Ulysses* is largely a linguistic one in which, through repeated reorganizations of words and particular language systems, the ultimate combination may be found.

The maternal appeal is a call to quit the journey and come home, a natural anti-epic voice telling the artist that in his beginning is his end. Joyce, like Stephen, rejected that call, but in Joyce's world nothing is ever final. Everything reverberates and repeats itself. Often in Stephen's highest flights of intellect and imagination, the haunting image returns, his ingenuity falters, his artistry appears futile and false, and he sees himself—like some of the undeceived characters of *Dubliners*—vulnerable and alone.

In the library during the elaborate discussion of Shakespeare, Stephen is at his most inventive and archly jesuitical, full of hypothetical banter and recondite allusions, when, suddenly, in the midst of a reference to Ann Hathaway at Shakespeare's deathbed, the following interrupts his chain of thought: "Mother's deathbed. Candle. The sheeted mirror. Who brought me into this world lies there, bronzelidded, under few cheap flowers. *Liliata rutilantium.* I wept alone" (190). For Joyce, literary indulgence in private emotion meant the destruction of effort and of art. Stephen recovers and goes on to put into his abstract argument the reasons for breaking emotional ties with the past: "There can be no reconciliation if there has not been a sundering." The epic journey, like that of Odysseus, may lead the artist back home, but that conclusion cannot be known unless leave is taken in the first place.

In a discussion of incest a few pages later, Stephen alludes to Thomas Aquinas as having taken a view "different from that of the new Viennese school." In fact, Aquinas's view, as summarized by Stephen, though couched in moral terms, is closely analagous to Freud's. Aquinas calls incestuous desire "avarice of the emotions." According to Stephen, he means "that the love so given to one near in blood is covetously withheld from some stranger who, it may be, hungers for it" (205). This is one of the most explicit statements in Joyce's work of the psychological and ethical basis for the artist's need to break with his home in order to be free to invest sympathetic emotion elsewhere. It is also an acknowledgment not of callous indifference on the part of the young artist, but rather of feelings so deep and strong as to be either paralyzing or, if redirected, the source of his creative energy. There is no contradiction, then, when the rebellious and arrogant Stephen says, "*Amor matris,* subjective and objective genitive, may be the only true thing in life. Paternity may be a legal fiction" (207).

Stephen acknowledges the power of the mother—the attractions of earth and sea, the seasonal rhythms of natural time, the magnetism of flesh and blood, and at times, he tries to usurp it, but more often he chooses the fiction of the father, the invention of new rules of time and space. It is an act of defiance, but not one of ignorance or indifference.

Indeed, the mysterious knowledge and potency of the mother is no more weakened in the end than are the inventions and adventures of the father. When, during the Circe episode, the ghost of Mrs. Dedalus appears for the last time, Stephen begs her to tell him "the word known to all men." More blackened and withered than ever, she approaches him and for the first time reaches out to touch him, saying, " 'Beware! God's hand.' " It is at this point that Stephen cries out his famous satanic refusal, *"Non serviam!"* and, repeatedly, "No! No! No!" When the ghost identifies herself with the suffering Christ, saying "inexpressible was my anguish when expiring with love, grief and agony on Mount Calvary," Stephen cries out, "Nothung!"—the name of Siegfried's magic sword of deliverance—and smashes the chandelier with his walking stick. "Time's livid final flame leaps and, in the following darkness, ruin of all space, shattered glass and toppling masonry" (582–583).

The art of defiance seems to have triumphed. The ghost has vanished. Stephen has committed a sacrilege by imitating with his ashplant the gesture of piercing Christ's side at Calvary, but he has not been struck dead, and he has with apparent impunity violated his ghostly mother with his phallic stick. He has greeted her response to the question about the "word known to all men"—the suffering Christ or *Logos*—with *Nothung,* a sword and "nothing." He rejects incarnate order, love, the "word made flesh," passed on from mother to child throughout time, in favor of a world that is nothing except what language makes of it, the flesh made word.

This scene, indeed, this moment, is often treated as somehow final in *Ulysses,* although there are two hundred more pages in the book. There is plenty of time to be reminded that Stephen's gesture, for all of its internal significance to him, is, to say the least, quixotic. Not only does it occur during a drunken interlude in a bawdy house, but the object of his heroic violence is a cheap lamp. Long after the climactic *"Non serviam,"* intimations of Mrs. Dedalus float in and out of view. Even in his encounter with Bloom, his spiritual father, Stephen does not escape motherhood. Bloom is an androgynous figure, the "new womanly man," who confesses in the Circe episode: "Oh, I so want to be a mother." It is one of Bloom's commonplace remarks that fixes in its most concrete form the mark of Mrs. Dedalus on her son: "Face reminds me of his poor mother" (609). When Stephen leaves Bloom after being taken home by him, they both hear church bells. The echoes for Stephen are the *Liliata rutilantium* hymn for the dead.

Moreover, though Stephen may choose the way of masculine rebellion and artful assertion, Joyce himself preserves to the end the balancing rhythms of an artless, indomitable mother.[2] In a maternal phase of her monologue, Molly Bloom associates Stephen with her dead son, Rudy, and thinks how his mother would not like him wandering around the streets at night by himself. Molly's thoughts have neither the disjointedness of Stephen's when he is first seen leaning on the wall of the tower looking out to sea nor the allusive density of his poetic fusions. The source of their flow and coherence is outside of literature and, it would almost seem, outside of language: "I dont care what anybody says itd be much better for the world to be governed by the women in it you wouldnt see women going and killing one another and slaughtering when do you ever see women rolling around drunk like they do or gambling every penny they have and losing it on horses yes because a woman whatever she does she knows when to stop sure they wouldnt be in the world at all only for us they dont know what it is to be a woman and a mother how could they where would they all of them be if they hadnt all a mother to look after them" (778).

M OST discussions of the mother-and-son relationship in Lawrence's fiction center on the psychological and autobiographical.[3] Though Joyce's treatment of the theme is similarly personal in origin, it is usually assumed that Lawrence's translations into prose fiction are less distorted, less self-conscious, and somehow less artificial than Joyce's. In an essay on "Sons, Lovers, and Mothers" in Lawrence, Alfred Kazin restates a familiar critical judgment. "Unlike Henry James, James Joyce, Marcel Proust, T. S. Eliot, Lawrence always makes you feel that not art but the quality of the lived experience is his greatest concern."[4] As a comment on literary conventions and the variety of ways readers respond to and willingly allow themselves to be deceived by them, the observation makes sense. In comparison with the writers named, Lawrence, at least in certain phases, does not so often or so blatantly call attention to his own artistry.

But calling attention to artifice is not necessarily a means of calling attention away from life. One of the oldest and most persistent traditions in the history of the novel, stemming from *Don Quixote,* challenges this assumption.[5] All the quoting and posturing and conjuring in the mother-and-son passages in *Ulysses* do not obscure the recognizable human feelings associated with bereavement, nor the rebellious struggle to cast them off and proceed with life. Joyce's verbal *tours de force* are a constant reminder of the pretensions and inadequacies of language, especially because they show it at its most vivid and flexible.

Lawrence's treatment of the maternal figure is in a different mode and world from that of Joyce, but there are sufficient parallels to keep us from saying simply that Joyce gives us art while Lawrence gives us life. Lawrence, no less than Joyce, was aware that fiction demands role-playing. Looking at the famous conclusion of *Sons and Lovers,* one is struck by its rhetorical qualities, the exclamations and interrogatives, statements of paradox, metaphors and similes ("Where was he?—one tiny upright speck of flesh, less than an ear of wheat lost in the field."), the reiterations, rhythms, alliterations and near-rhymes.[6] The passage is artful and openly literary. That the rhetorical devices correspond to the protagonist's mood rather than clashing with it, as often is the case in *Ulysses,* makes them less noticeable. In fact, both authors employ a good deal of the conventional vocabulary associated with bereavement: the idea of the deceased having "gone abroad into the night"; the classical notion of her having become part of the firmament; the isolation of the son experienced as a dark void ("at the core a nothingness," in Lawrence; "Nothung" in Joyce); a desperate desire to be physically touched ("He wanted her to touch him," in Lawrence; "Touch me, touch me," in Joyce); and the ultimate denial of attachment to the dead ("But no, he would not give in," in Lawrence; and *"Non serviam,"* in Joyce.)

The most important parallel between the two books is that in each the young hero is an artist; his relationship with the mother, particularly its prolongation in the imagination after her death, is therefore bound up with the hero's conception of his art and his own most deeply felt experience of life. Paul Morel's struggle to grow up and away from the ties of home is, like that of Stephen Dedalus in *Portrait,* defined largely in terms of his efforts to attain sexual and emotional maturity in his relations with women. Though the connections are made less often and less explicitly by Lawrence than by Joyce, it is clear nonetheless that for Paul Morel, as for Stephen Dedalus, the struggle toward manhood is inextricably woven with the struggle toward self-definition as an artist.

Soon after Paul's birth, Mrs. Morel, saddened by the realization that the child was born from a union that is no longer loving, walks off into the fields with him and, in an almost religious act of consecration, promises to love him all the more. She holds him up to the sun in a gesture of offering, and the language turns formal and faintly Biblical: "Then she put him to her bosom again, ashamed almost of her impulse to give him back again whence he came. 'If he lives,' she thought to herself, 'what will become of him—what will he be?' Her heart was anxious. 'I will call him Paul,' she said suddenly; she knew not why" (37).

Lawrence does not make nearly as much of his hero's name as Joyce does of Stephen Dedalus's, but the moment and circumstances of his naming are significantly un-Dombeyesque. They call attention to an extraordinary bond with the mother as well as to foreshadowings of a divine vocation. Except for the Psalmist, no Biblical writer put more of his life's passion into words than Paul. Insofar as he was a man, he was a messenger. Quite apart from what we know of Lawrence's own sense of the sacredness of his vocation as an artist, Paul Morel's utterances about his art seem to fulfill his mother's unwitting prophecy. In response to Miriam's questions about his paintings, he claims not to be copying the outer form, the "dead crust" of nature, but the "real living." Assuming the role of another Biblical messenger, he indicates a painting of pine trees and says, "There's God's burning bush for you" (152).

Mrs. Morel has given her son life, a sense of special purpose, and she has taught him to see. When she lifts him up to the sun, her gesture and words—"Look! Look, my pretty!"—capture precisely the relationship of dependence that makes her death years later such a trauma for him, both as an artist and as a man. Having been the support and vantage point of his seeing, Mrs. Morel has provided Paul with the means to measure, assess, and order reality. Without her, he loses his will to be because he has lost—or thinks he has lost—his power to see the inner life and outer relations of things. The mother's physical absence represents an aesthetic deprivation, a loss of insight and perspective.

After the death of Mrs. Morel, we are shown the world through Paul's eyes. His feelings of disorientation and loneliness, like those of Stephen Dedalus, are universal, but his particular renderings of those sensations are those of an artist who is no longer able to organize what he sees; even more specifically, they are those of a painter who conceives of reality in spatial terms. "Nothing was distinct or distinguishable." Things happening only a few feet away appear as if at a great distance. "No, it was not that they were far away. They were in their places. But where was he himself?" The world seems literally to have lost its center and to be falling apart and away from him. "There seemed no reason why people should go along the street, and houses pile up in the daylight. There seemed no reason why these things should occupy the space, instead of leaving it empty" (410).

While Stephen Dedalus exerts every effort of will and imagination to escape the haunting memory of his mother, Paul Morel exerts his to pursue his mother beyond death. In both cases, the imagination is temporarily in opposition to the natural rhythm of death in life. In trying to force an extreme—for Stephen, a complete separation; for Paul, a perfect reunion—each son is untrue to the maternal gift of life balanced with death, containment with release, dependence with independence. Both mothers were possessive of their sons, but both foreshadowed death's breach in the physical letting go that is part of birth. In smashing the lamp, Steven tries to plunge himself into a darkness that his mother's ghost cannot penetrate. In looking for consolation in the night, Paul tries to surround himself with a darkness that only his mother can penetrate.

After his mother's death, Paul continually wanders around at night, seeking a space uncluttered by objective reality in which he can "be" alone with his mother: "The realest thing was the thick darkness at night. That seemed to him whole and comprehensible and restful. He could leave himself to it. Suddenly a piece of paper started near his feet and blew along down the pavement. He stood still, rigid with clenched fists, a flame of agony going over him. And he saw again the sick-room, his mother, her eyes. Unconsciously he had been with her, in her company. The swift hop of the paper reminded him she was gone. But he had been with her. He wanted everything to stand still, so that he could be with her again" (410).

This effort of the brooding imagination to avoid light and movement and the distractions of commonplace reality, to be rigid in itself and to wish everything to stand still, is the complete opposite of Mrs. Morel's offering to the sun and of Paul's own maternally inspired ideal of art as that which conveys the "shimmering protoplasm" with "scarcely any shadow in it." It is a signal not only of Paul's gradual self-destruction as a man but of his breakdown as an artist. Though earlier he rather arrogantly identified his artistic talent with a life-giving force, he suddenly can find no connection between art and life at all:

"You've got to carry forward her living and what she had done, go on with it."
But he did not want to. He wanted to give up.
"But you can go on with your painting," said the will in him. "Or else you can beget children. They both carry on her effort."
"Painting is not living."
"Then live."
"Marry whom?" came the sulky question. (412)

Despite Lawrence's comment on the conclusion of *Sons and Lovers* as indicative of a "drift toward death," Paul rejects darkness and paralysis, and walks "towards the faintly humming, glowing town, quickly." Whether he will marry or paint is not clear, but the dichotomy itself is a curious and significant one to pursue in Lawrence. Does the hero recover the lost mother and the perspective, the connection to earth, the fervor and energy that his bond with her represents, by replacing her with another woman, or by some effort of the imagination to defy mortality and revivify the past?

L AWRENCE'S tendency is not toward the structural and thematic density of Joyce, not toward the accumulation and superim-
position of contradictory impulses and views within a poised simultaneity. His dialectic is dramatic and extensive; it occurs between works as
well as within them. The future of the motherless hero is left unsettled in
Sons and Lovers, but with minor alterations, his situation is taken up again
in later works, and issues raised by the quandary about whether to paint
or marry are considered in the light of contrasting resolutions. Two
works that are thematic extensions of *Sons and Lovers*—"Daughters of the
Vicar" and *Aaron's Rod*—reflect a split not only in Lawrence's technique,
his way of shaping a narrative, but in his view of art and its relation to
life.

"Daughters of the Vicar" is one of Lawrence's most powerful and
well-integrated stories.[7] It bears on *Sons and Lovers* in much the same way
the second part of *Wuthering Heights* bears on the first. Louisa, one of the
vicar's two daughters, having been brought up in the unhappy and pretentious refinement of the vicarage, breaks away to marry a young miner
of whom her parents disapprove.[8] It is as though Paul Morel's parents
were being given another chance, as Katherine and Heathcliff are in the
more tempered lives of Kathy and Hareton. Yet there are differences.
The vicar's daughter is earthier than Mrs. Morel, and Alfred, the young
miner, is more sensitive and self-assured than Walter Morel. In fact,
Alfred Durant is a fascinating combination of Paul Morel and his father.
He is physically strong, an amiable, natural man who likes his work in
the mine and gets on easily with his fellows. But he is also self-taught; he
likes books, sings in the choir, and plays the piccolo. He is not an artist
but a natural man with the sensibility of an artist. Moreover, as the
youngest son, he is unusually dependent on his mother; when she is discovered to be dying, his experience of disorientation and loss is described
in language very close to that used about Paul Morel: "He could not recognize himself nor any of his surroundings. He was afraid to think of his
mother. And yet . . . he could not escape from her, she carried him with
her into an unformed, unknown chaos" (173).

As in a fairy tale, Louisa appears to replace the dying mother. The old
woman is found by the younger one in her garden, where she has
wrenched "something inside" while trying to uproot vegetables for her
son's supper. Louisa nurses her; "a natural sympathy" develops between
the two women. The old woman's pains come and go in rhythmic
spasms, but it is Louisa, in doing the mother's job of washing Alfred's
back when he returns from the mines, who feels "strange and pregnant."

In an almost perfect symmetry, Alfred's "new night" represents a sundering from the mother and a joining with another woman. But this

love, like the old woman's death, is not a matter of an individually controlled design. Alfred, too, succumbs to the "labor pains" with a dumb trust that the issue will be good: "Then his grief came on like physical pain. He held tight to the gate, biting his mouth, whispering, 'Mother!' It was a fierce, cutting, physical pain of grief, that came on in bouts, as his mother's pain came on in bouts, and was so acute he could scarcely keep erect." After the mother's death and a short awkward interval, the two young people come together or, rather, are drawn together, since they are nearly always spoken of in terms of motivations that seem not to be their own. When Louisa offers to stay, "the words were spoken from her without her intervention."

The dramatic point of the story is that it is not thought, design, imposition of will, or even common sense that brings about union or separation, but nature itself. Yet in the juxtapositions of the vicarage and the miner's cottage, the characters of the vicar's daughters, birth and death, darkness and light, mother and wife, this is one of the most carefully composed of Lawrence's works. It is not the first time that conscious art has been put to the service of unconscious nature. But, like Joyce, Lawrence seems to have been aware that sleight of hand or a contradiction might be involved in the use of artistic forms in the cause of artlessness.

Though art is not an issue in "Daughters of the Vicar," it plays a major and complicated role in *Aaron's Rod,* another working out of the destiny of Paul Morel.[9] Alfred Durant is not required to reject his mother or his dependence on her but only to transfer his sensitive energies to another woman. Aaron Sisson, also a piccolo player, has been married for a number of years when *Aaron's Rod* opens. But though it started well, his marriage and family life have become a dull and confining routine from which only his music seems capable of helping him to escape. In terms of Paul Morel's choice—to marry or to paint—Aaron has already tried marrying and is, as the book begins, about to try living by his art.

The title of the novel contains the kind of pun Joyce loved—the rod is Aaron's piccolo, his virility, and, through association with the Biblical story of Aaron, his miraculous or magical powers. But Lawrence is not satisfied that a word like "rod" might momentarily, equivocally, and humorously bring together music, magic, and sex. If there is a connection behind the apparent linguistic accident, he wants to find it. *Aaron's Rod,* which, unlike "Daughters of the Vicar," is one of Lawrence's least coherently designed narratives, pursues the pun by trying to bring each of its terms literally into the open.

In his effort to will his physical nature and his music into a perfect unity, Aaron drifts toward Florence, where he meets the Marchesa del Torre, a melancholy, aging American singer married to an Italian aristocrat who enjoys surrounding himself with artists and giving musicales. At first, the Marchesa takes a maternal interest in Aaron and his piccolo, but soon she is confiding in him her hatred of music and her reasons for refusing to sing. They find that they share a dislike—verging on disgust—for chords, harmonies, orchestrations, in fact, all music that imitates or depends on social coordination. When Aaron plays for the Marchesa, Lawrence describes his music in terms that attempt to distinguish it from what is conventionally considered art: "It was a clear, sharp, lilted run-and-fall of notes, not a tune in any sense of the word" (271).

The effect of this unmusical music on the Marchesa is extraordinary. As in a romance, she is awakened from what seems to have been a long sleep. The more the Marchesa is aroused, the more Aaron sees her not as a remote older woman but as an irresistibly seductive and mysterious enchantress. In fact, his reward for waking her from her spell is to be placed under one himself, and his playing is transformed into a sexual act: "He did as she wished . . . And the stream of sound came out with the quick wild imperiousness of the pipe . . . She seemed to go still and yielding. Her red mouth looked as if it might moan with relief" (296).

As Aaron becomes more deeply captivated, he also assumes for himself the credit for a kind of miraculous resurrection of the Marchesa's sexuality and youth through music. What is striking is the broad sarcasm with which Lawrence treats this attitude on the part of a character he had hitherto regarded with sympathy: "He had performed a little miracle, and felt himself a little wonder-worker, to whom reverence was due" (p. 301).

When Aaron takes the Marchesa to bed, he is struck by her girlishness: "Almost like a sister, a younger sister! Or like a child!" It is an unexpected observation, given the Marchesa's age and her strange power over the young man. When Paul Morel nursed his dying mother, he also had been surprised that she looked so much "like a child," "like a girl curled up in her flannel nightdress." But neither the desperate love of the son nor the passionately egocentric art of the young musician can really awaken the sleeping mother and find her a girl. The affair with the Marchesa is physically consummated, but Aaron finds it unsatisfactory, and it quickly is brought to an end.

Aaron's disastrous failure to resolve the difference between piccolo and penis, surrogate mother and young mistress, finally becomes absurd, to Lawrence as well as to the reader, despite the underlying seriousness of the story. The second half of the novel is a dream allegory of the immature artist's psyche in naturalistic guise. In some ways, its mixture of realistic detail and fantastic distortion and its continual association of artistic creativity with sexuality resemble parts of the Circe episode in *Ulysses*. What is ludicrous on the realistic plane is often painful as a projection of internal conflict. Aaron, trapped in the pride of his sex and artistry, thinks that he has the Marchesa del Torre, the lady of the tower, imprisoned under his spell, whereas, in the battle of self-gratification and willfulness, she is his master.

As a work of art (rather than as a vehicle for an argument) *Aaron's Rod* shows that coherence and harmony are not the results of transformation—the conversion of sex into music or music into words—but of a celebration of distinctions that does not confuse domination with relationship. The novel cannot reach a satisfactory conclusion because no human exchange has actually been experienced. Aaron's preoccupation with himself, his music, his piccolo, is a form of masturbation, a practice that was obnoxious to Lawrence because it seemed to him the physical expression of all that opposes creative awareness and sympathy. In seeking to charm a false mother-mistress into being the slave of his rod, Aaron has forgotten the true maternal gift: the recognition of another "as she is in herself," what Lawrence calls "primal objective knowledge."[10]

For the mature artist in possession of the mother's gift—"the treasure of the heart"—the question is no longer whether to paint or marry, whether, like Aaron, to escape into pure will or, like Alfred Durant, into pure being. As Lawrence himself developed as a writer, he argued more and more cogently that the whole person does not escape at all but embraces both poles in rhythmic alternation. He collects himself in a painting, a song, a story, a sentence; he gives himself away in friendship and love. The mother's gift is twofold: individuality and the consoling, but also humbling, reminder of the presence of life outside the self.

WHETHER to paint or to marry is one of the questions that dominate *To the Lighthouse*. The first section of the book centers on Mrs. Ramsay, wife and mother; the third and final section on Lily Briscoe, spinster and artist. Superficially, the two women appear to have nothing in common. Mrs. Ramsay is warm, pliant, gracious, and selfless to the point of seeming to give up all claims to identity. She "sacrifices" herself to her husband, children, and friends. Lily Briscoe is cool, concentrated, brittle, and self-centered. She "saves" herself for her art. The contrast, on one level, reflects the anxiety felt by Woolf and other women of her generation in trying to reconcile the demands of Victorian marriage and motherhood with those of an independent, creative spirit. The two characterizations suggest that a woman of talent either marries and thereby abandons her autonomy and identity for the sake of others or remains single, aloof, and undistracted in her pursuit of achievement.

There is no doubt that the problem has special and peculiarly painful ramifications for women, but insofar as it raises issues of dependence and independence, attachment and detachment, it concerns artists of both sexes. In some ways, Lily Briscoe is a female version of Stephen Dedalus and Paul Morel, both of whom had to break with their families, especially their mothers, before they could collect themselves sufficiently to become artists. Lily, though not Mrs. Ramsay's real daughter, is the child of her spirit. According to one familiar psychological pattern, Mrs. Ramsay's death and Lily's rejection of marriage are the liberating conditions that enable her to finish her painting.

Yet for Woolf, as for Joyce and Lawrence, the complete separation from the mother is neither possible nor desirable. Whatever the artist requires in the way of rebellion, detachment, and independence in order to perform comes to nothing without the counterbalancing experience (if only in the memory) of sympathy and dependence, a "primal objective knowledge" of another. Mrs. Ramsay and Lily need and complete one another. They also have a great deal in common. They do not simply represent two parallel ways of being artistic; rather, they represent two essential characteristics of the artist's mind: sympathy and detachment. Mrs. Ramsay's sympathetic nature obviously does not destroy her identity, since she is the single most memorable character in the book. Yet character, like beauty (which Mrs. Ramsay also possesses) must be seen to be believed. It is the artist, Lily Briscoe and, ultimately, Woolf, who sees it and, through memory and design, makes it visible to us. Similarly, the reader knows that Lily is not all cold detachment. Mrs. Ramsay, after all, loved her; through her love, Woolf makes a potentially dull caricature of a social and artistic problem into a sympathetic character.

Agonizingly aware of the "choices" forced on women of her time, Woolf saw no solution in setting a caricature—"spinster artist"—against a type—"Victorian mother." The enduring problem, is not whether to marry or to paint, but how to bring the tendencies they represent together, how to reconcile involvement with observation, sympathy with perspective. Woolf based the portrait of Mrs. Ramsay on her recollections of her own mother, and the tenderness in the result betrays a depth of feeling akin to that expressed through Stephen Dedalus's nightmares and Paul Morel's passionate grieving. Woolf herself was haunted by her mother's image and voice until she was well into her forties and had completed *To the Lighthouse*. Writing the book was obviously not only an act of homage but an attempt to resolve some of the conflicts that arose from being both artist and daughter.[11]

Perhaps the most remarkable aspect of the characterization of Mrs. Ramsay is its mixture of profound unconventionality of spirit with an ordinary and confined external life. She is shown darning stockings, reading fairy tales, gathering flowers, flattering her husband, encouraging her children, putting guests at ease, serving food, going on errands, and writing letters. She is the perfection of a type, and though it is a type about which Woolf had great misgivings, she treats her with enormous sympathy and even awe. Most important, she shows her transcending type, not only her own situation but the efforts of others to classify her. She may be the resigned victim of an unjust society, but she is also an individual, mysterious and unique. Like Mrs. Dalloway or Leopold Bloom, she tests the artist's ability to see the soul in a stereotype. It is a test that Woolf passes with genius. Somehow, in a circle of "originals"— eccentric and egotistical scholars, philosophers, poets, and painters—the self-effacing and unassertive Mrs. Ramsay is the most original of all.

Still, questions and difficulties remain. The death of Mrs. Ramsay (related in a parenthetical aside rather than a staged scene) and the attempts of Lily Briscoe, the holiday artist, to imitate and "continue" her in another medium raise doubts about the value and durability of her example. In the final section of the novel, Lily returns to the Ramsays' vacation house ten years after the visit with which the book opens. Much has changed. Mrs. Ramsay is gone; a son has been killed in the war; and a daughter has died in childbirth. Lily finds the house "full of unrelated passions." When she tries the next day to finish a painting left incomplete all those years, her mind returns again and again to Mrs. Ramsay, remembering especially her gift for "resolving everything into simplicity," bringing things together, and giving the appearance of "permanence," "shape," and "stability." Lily makes a repeated and explicit comparison between Mrs. Ramsay's maternal talent for reconciliation, for coaxing things into shape, and that of the artist searching for the right composition.

But however affectionately and gratefully Lily remembers Mrs. Ramsay, she cannot help but think of her "achievements" as spurious, her intimations of permanence and stability as illusory. After all, Mrs. Ramsay herself is no longer there, and most of her well-meant "designs" for her children and friends have not been accomplished: "But the dead, thought Lily, encountering some obstacle in her design which made her pause and ponder, stepping back a foot or so, oh, the dead! she murmured, one pitied them, one brushed them aside, one had even a little contempt for them. They are at our mercy. Mrs. Ramsay has faded and gone, she thought. We can over-ride her wishes, improve away her limited, old-fashioned ideas. She recedes further and further from us. Mockingly she seemed to see her there at the end of the corridor of years saying, of all incongruous things, 'Marry, marry!' . . . And one would have to say to her, It has all gone against your wishes" (260).

For a moment Lily takes refuge in the objective detachment of the artist, capable of regarding any representation of life as a phenomenon to be assessed in itself rather than in terms of what it is meant to illustrate. Against Mrs. Ramsay's old-fashioned, sentimental, and unsuccessful efforts at design—her wish, for example, to see Lily marry William Bankes—she sets her own rational, unemotional friendship with Bankes and their "disinterested" way of discussing the aesthetic flaws in Raphael's *Madonna and Child*. But neither the artist nor her art is invulnerable. The absence of a particular life, the memory of a vanished focal point, is almost as intrusive and compelling as the thing itself. Self-induced nostalgia and a mildly agreeable melancholy suddenly turn into a haunting and almost unbearably palpable void. "Ghost, air, nothingness, a thing you could play with easily and safely at any time of day or night, she had been that, and then suddenly she put her hand out and wrung the heart thus. Suddenly, the empty drawing room steps . . . the whole wave and whisper of the garden became like curves and arabesques flourishing round a centre of complete emptiness" (266).

The negative return of Mrs. Ramsay unsettles Lily's confidence in art as more capable of ordering, settling, and distancing things than an old-fashioned mother of arranging the lives of her children and friends. She imagines Mr. Carmichael reassuring her that even though human beings pass away, words and paint remain. But this gives her little satisfaction, since she knows that her own painting will be rolled up and put in an attic. As Lily struggles with her painting and her memories of Mrs. Ramsay, she is brought to a crisis. She has long since admitted her incapacity—or anybody else's—to control life, but her sudden inability to manage her own memory and emotion causes her command of her canvas to falter. She weeps uncontrollably and cries out for Mrs. Ramsay.

This, the highest pitch of grief expressed in the novel, comes not from one of Mrs. Ramsay's children or even from her husband, though we know he is stricken, but from a "relative" in mind and feeling only, an unmarried, childless, prim, and undemonstrative "daughter" who tries to translate into paint what she has learned from the mother of eight. But what is it that Lily has finally to inherit from Mrs. Ramsay and reformulate in her own medium? Since harmonies at dinner tables and attempts at matchmaking are tentative, fragile, and, in the long run, always unsuccessful, and since books can be forgotten on shelves and paintings in attics, what remains? The answer to this brings on Lily's keenest pang in recalling Mrs. Ramsay and gives her her clearest insight into the beauty of her dead friend and her legacy to the artist. What retains value and significance in some permanent and absolute sense is not the "actual picture," but "what it attempted."

What gives beauty and depth to Mrs. Ramsay's small designs and reconciliations, what saves them from triviality, is her steady awareness of death in every moment and crevice of life, of life itself as "terrible, hostile, and quick to pounce." Though she bravely and gaily "brandishes her sword," Mrs. Ramsay knows that there is no question of "winning." Beneath her graceful gestures and sympathetic words is a knowledge, a realism, that makes all the other characters, including her husband, appear children by contrast. The one person in the book who lives with and therefore cannot be surprised by death is Mrs. Ramsay. Lily Briscoe imagines her dying in a way that Mrs. Ramsay herself might have explained it to a child she wished to console. She sees her "raising to her forehead a wreath of white flowers . . . and going unquestioningly with her companion, a shade across the fields." This consoling vision does not disguise death or redefine it, but it does provide an imaginative gallantry in the face of it that is an alternative to thundering outrage, religious acquiescence, or, what seems more common among Mrs. Ramsay's husband and his academic friends, the pretense that it does not exist. Though the book opens with Mrs. Ramsay giving her son "false" hopes about the weather and being corrected by her husband, it is Mr. Ramsay's faith in logic and system that is shown to be the deeper and more deceptive error. Mrs. Ramsay likes to tell fairy tales, but she knows them for what they are.

For Woolf, order is not given; it is made. And once it is made, it does not endure but is forever being dissolved. Mrs. Ramsay's gift to Lily Briscoe is the resolution to repair with the imagination the continual damage life does to the mind and body. Even the consoling vision of Mrs. Ramsay gracefully crossing the fields of death has to be composed and recomposed once it has flashed upon the brain: "But always something—it might be a face, a voice, a paper boy crying *Standard, News*—thrust through, snubbed her, waked her, required and got in the end an effort of attention, so that the vision must be perpetually remade" (270).

To the Lighthouse is a strong and hopeful work, but the success it describes and achieves is precarious. Mrs. Ramsay provides a focal center for the novelist and her characters, but it is a center that is neither stable nor permanent. It cannot be grasped or defined or, except in very oblique ways, shared. Mrs. Ramsay's importance, her capacity to "bring things together," demands from the reader as well as from the other characters an act of the imagination very much akin to an act of faith. Except for the episode at the dinner table, most of the revelations of her "power" are not staged scenes witnessed by a public audience. Her beauty of character is glimpsed briefly and unexpectedly by one character or another as she hesitates at a door, pauses on a stairway, stops by a window, strolls through the garden, or sits on the beach. When she is dead, the reader, like the characters, feels that he has been touched by her without ever having seen her clearly, without ever having gotten to "know" her as one knows a character in George Eliot or Henry James. We are thrown back on the memory and vision of Lily Briscoe, as in the first section we were on the private perceptions of her guests and family.

Lily Briscoe does not invent Mrs. Ramsay. She does not give her her character or beauty. But she sees and remembers her selectively; she *pictures* her. Time provides Lily with the distance her heart fears but her eye requires; given its brutal capacity for severing bonds, self-assertion and withdrawal seem almost superfluous. The "Time Passes" section presents a catastrophic rending of tissues and opens seemingly irreparable gaps. The artist, for whom time, like the sea, is a waste across which everyone and everything eventually recedes, suddenly realizes that she needs to overcome distance, not extend it. At the very end, Lily wants to remember not only how Mrs. Ramsay looked but how she acted. She wants to render her not only in paint but in the flesh. She wants to be like her. Not that she wants to marry and bear eight children. But having felt love, she has experienced in Mrs. Ramsay's death a distancing that it was Mrs. Ramsay's gift (and curse) inherently to know all along. Lily wants Mrs. Ramsay's art, her ability to avoid the fraudulence of concealing loss with love and the despair of denying love because of loss. She wants a moment of balance that will also be a moment of truth.

The figure of Mrs. Ramsay, however different it is from that of Mrs. Dedalus and Mrs. Morel, shares with them the curiously equivocal role of the "private" parent whose relation to the artist cannot be adequately expressed in conventional public terms, the parent most intimately woven into the imagination and, at the same time, the most resistant to the excessive claims of the imagination. The mother gives birth to memory and dream, but then uses them to wake the artist back into life. Mrs. Ramsay's own beauty results from her ability to sustain a precarious balance between an awareness of life's indifference to design and the human need for it.

As Lily struggles to complete her picture, she is torn between the continually changing view of Mr. Ramsay's sailboat moving closer and closer to the lighthouse and her effort to "make things stand still" in her painting. She discovers that she does not really wish to resolve the tension in the picture but to reveal it, to "achieve that razor edge of balance between two opposite forces." The three-part structure of *To the Lighthouse*, which balances Mrs. Ramsay alive with Mrs. Ramsay dead on the fulcrum of time, parallels Lily's achievement exactly. Whether the line she draws in the center of her canvas is the lighthouse, the boat, Mrs. Ramsay, or even she herself does not matter. The "center" is Mrs. Ramsay's gift, not as a fixed, absolute point in a cosmic or family circle, but as a pivot in constant need of renewal in the unending conflict between attachment and distance.

I F , I N *To the Lighthouse,* the magnetic vitality of the mother requires the partly detached perspective of the observant daughter in order to come into focus, in *The Years* the centrality and shaping power of the mother is shown to be a false myth.[12] Characters are repeatedly arranged in a circle, around a table, a bed, a grave; they are drawn by custom, but no genuine focal point has the energy to attract their deep attention or to provide even temporary harmony to their thoughts. *The Years* is a novel of the periphery. The characters, indeed, the narrative voice as well, are all at the edge of experience—trying, as it were, to get a closer view, but repeatedly nudged aside, interrupted, distracted. It is a novel in which the shaping ability of the imagination is shown and *felt* to be as feeble as the social and literary conventions that fail to satisfy it.

The Years is Woolf's most aggressive attack on the Georgian novel, apart from her well-known essay on the subject. If the term *antinovel* can be applied to any of Woolf's works, *The Years* is the best candidate for the title. It is not Woolf's most experimental fiction nor, by any means, her most successful, but it is a fascinating example of the writer taking up one narrative and dramatic convention after another and rejecting them as unsuitable for her purposes because they are untrue to the experience she is attempting to portray. The ostensible structure of the story is that of the family chronicle, but that structure is so splintered and displaced by repeated shifts in setting, point of view, theme, chronology, and dramatic focus that it loses all but the most tenuous coherence. Though there are signs in the book of Woolf's efforts to provide another kind of coherence by means of recurrent imagery and gestures, parallel phrases, and analogous moments, this novel, unlike *Mrs. Dalloway* and *To the Lighthouse*, does not successfully present a new vision of experience. It demonstrates the failures of the new artistry as devastatingly as it does those of the old.

The Years begins with the slow death of the mother of a large, upper-middle-class family. An important and often public event in the fictional family histories of the nineteenth and early twentieth centuries, the death of the matriarch is presented here in bits and pieces, mostly as witnessed by Delia, a politically minded daughter who would rather think about Parnell and Home Rule than about her mortally ill mother. Delia sees most things pertaining to her family—including her mother's death—as part of a "scene" in which she has no part.[13] In fact, her idea of "honesty" prevents her from participating in what is happening around her except in a detached, almost trancelike fashion. She goes through the motions of family existence while observing, criticizing, and rejecting the behavior of others, including that of her dying mother. Delia wants to get on with her own life, and her mother's slow lingering on is an irritation to her. When she enters the sickroom, her mind registers visual details with as little emotion as if she were describing a stage setting. All is a matter of deceptive appearances. Even her mother "did not look as if she were dying; she looked as if she might go on existing in this borderland between life and death for ever" (21).

Despite occasional outbursts, Delia Pargiter is neither a seriously rebellious child like Stephen Dedalus nor a passionately dependent one like Paul Morel. Her problem is not an excess of emotion or ideas. She thinks and behaves erratically, is indifferent to most of her surroundings, and is hard-pressed to sustain any ordering vision for more than a moment. When she tries to be the emotionally dutiful daughter and conjure up pleasant and nostalgic memories of her mother, the effort wanes before it ever really waxes: "But the scene melted as she tried to look at it. There was the other scene of course—the man in the frock coat."

The image of Parnell in his frock coat at a political rally blots out Delia's thoughts of her mother until the mother herself stirs and interrupts with the question all of the characters throughout the novel are forever asking, "Where am I?" Delia's answer—"Here, Mamma! Here!"—is hardly much help, given where she herself has been while sitting at her mother's side. The mother's efforts at conversation, "broken" sentences, "fumbling" words, give Delia hope that the end is at last at hand. In fact, as one reads on in the book, it becomes more and more obvious that the mother's fragmented talk, like her sudden question, is not peculiar to the dying but a foretaste of the way everyone speaks in this world of unfinished sentences and unanswered questions. When Delia leaves the sickroom, she wonders, "Where am I?" and for a moment, feels that she is "in some borderland between life and death." The identification with the dying mother has not resulted from emotional sympathy or guilt, but from a shared bewilderment.

Delia's rendering of the actual death scene—a full-scale staged event with members of the family appropriately positioned in the room—is not only a parody of the social and literary conventions associated with passage from the world, but an admission that whatever it is that is really happening cannot be seen and therefore cannot be described: "There were so many of them in the room that she could get no further than the doorway ... She could not see the bed from where she stood. . . . There was complete silence in the bedroom. Is this death? Delia asked herself" (46).

In the Victorian or Georgian novel, the dying mother would be fully shown and would often be given long, grammatically complete speeches of farewell. In contrast, the central actor in Woolf's scene is silent and invisible, the event all but unknowable except through the stock and slightly ludicrous behavior of "witnesses" who are acting presumably not out of direct relation to what they feel, but out of their knowledge of what one does on such occasions. At least, that is the way Delia judges it and it is what the reader sees her and the others doing. "Then there was a stir, a shuffle of feet in the bedroom and out came her father, stumbling. 'Rose!' he cried. 'Rose! Rose!' He held his arms with the fists clenched out in front of him. You did that very well, Delia told him as he passed her. It was like a scene in a play" (46–47).

The effect of Woolf's presentation of this scene is curious. For all Delia's critical detachment, there is none of the biting mockery or satire of which Joyce is capable, largely because the characters, including the parents, are too little developed to take on the weight of real anger. Delia's discomfort is a form of awkwardness. She does not know how to behave since her feelings are no guide, and she is irritated with others for seeming to follow an established pattern hypocritically. Even her outburst at her father—who we know has a mistress—is inconsequential. Either he does not hear it or she does not really say it but only thinks it. In any case, the scene almost immediately shifts to Oxford and another set of characters. Hence, too little sustained connection exists between any of the characters for satire or drama to develop. There is no more opportunity for interchange, good or bad, with the living father than there had been with the dying mother.

For a moment, at the funeral, Delia is able to break through the enforced symmetries of the event, to look into the grave and experience something other than what has been channeled, approved, and modeled by others. But, as invariably in *The Years,* there is an interruption. The minister begins a prayer of thanksgiving that infuriates Delia and breaks the spell. If her feeling is worthwhile, why does Delia not fight her way back to it in spite of the obstacles of conventional language and behavior? That is one way of describing the efforts of Lily Briscoe, Stephen Dedalus, and Paul Morel, but it is clearly not the story Woolf wishes to tell in *The Years*. Delia does not transcend her wavering ego. She is not an artist; her function in the book is nearly over after the funeral, and she hardly appears again until the end.

The narrative is not about the struggle and possible triumph of an individual imagination over traditional restraint, however deceptively it may seem to be that at the outset. That Delia's genuine feeling is interrupted, her vision incomplete, is finally seen to be not so much the fault of a particular custom, phrase, or set of beliefs as in the very nature of things unmediated by art. If she has learned anything from watching her mother die, it is that the process of dying—separation, decomposition—is constantly eating into life, emotional and mental as well as physical. Once she has faced this, Delia (and to some extent the reader) modifies her attitude toward any integrating structures, however inadequate. Trivial order and even some posing do not win her faith but they do eventually elicit tolerance and cooperation. Delia's compromise between egocentricity and conventionality is the compromise of the uncreative mind. As Mrs. Pargiter is to Mrs. Ramsay, Delia is to Lily Briscoe, an unresourceful opposite.

When the burial service ends and the mourners begin to disperse, Delia observes that "the attempt at concentration was over." The phrase applies as much to Mrs. Pargiter's dying and to Delia's state of mind as it does to the concluding of the ceremony. The "attempt," the need to bring things together, is itself what unites people despite the awkward, imperfect, and often foolish forms that result. Without a ritual to react to, Delia is no longer angry but merely bewildered and lost. That people are taking polite leave as if going home from a party is remarked on without irritation or humor, but only a mild and melancholy irony: "People shook hands rather furtively, among the graves, and even smiled. 'How good of you to come!' . . . It was becoming a shrouded and subdued morning party among the graves. She hesitated—she did not know what she ought to do next" (88).

The long middle section of the book shifts back and forth from one member of the family to another with little more than an occasional passing reference to Delia and almost none to the departed mother. When Delia does reappear at the book's conclusion, it is as an old woman, married and matriarchal, presiding at a family reunion that in its preservation of tattered forms is not so terribly different from the "shrouded and subdued morning party among the graves" with which her adult life began. The pun on "morning"/"mourning" is not a mystical paradox, a parenthetical "Little Gidding," but a melancholy comment on time.

In what appears to be a pointlessly rapid passage of years, Delia has, like her mother, become the vague center of a family ceremony to which all come and none seems to belong. As she judged her mother, she, in turn, is judged by her nieces and nephews for having married, instead of a wild rebel, "the most King-respecting, Empire-admiring of country gentlemen." The book ends with Delia bidding goodbye to her guests and playing with ease the role she had hesitated about at the funeral: " 'It's been so good of you to come!' Delia exclaimed, turning towards them with her hand outstretched" (434).

When her sister Eleanor pauses to thank her, Delia tries to call her attention to an arrangement of flowers, as if, for one last moment, to hold her within the compass of the ceremony she has created. But Eleanor has already begun to drift off into her own world and is watching a taxi stopping in front of a house down the road: " 'Aren't they lovely?' said Delia, holding out the flowers. Eleanor started. 'The roses? Yes . . .' she said. But she was watching the cab. A young man had got out; he paid the driver. Then a girl in a tweed travelling suit followed him. He fitted his latch-key to the door. 'There,' Eleanor murmured, as he opened the door and they stood for a moment on the threshold" (434).

Within a few lines the book is finished, and the young couple, never seen before, will not be seen again. The reader is not told what particularly attracts Eleanor to them, whether she sees a purpose and clarity in their movements that she cannot find in her own family, whether, never having married, she envies their imagined happiness, or whether she has momentarily invented a life across the threshold for them that is more coherent and real than her own has been. The main point is that Eleanor's connection to her sister, the party, and, indeed, to the reader is a fragile one capable of being changed or broken in an instant. This inconclusive ending is one more repudiation on Woolf's part of the kind of novel that ties together loose ends and settles all the characters. As long as life goes on, there is no settling. Even death is final only for the one to whom it happens. For everyone else it is a threshold, a leave-taking, and a beginning, earth falling on a coffin and sparrows chirping, guests leaving a party and a young couple entering their new home.

In the end, *The Years* fails to provide a strong alternative to the kind of family chronicle it opposes. Although Woolf regarded this novel as "one book" with *Three Guineas,* the death of the ineffectual mother—a prisoner of her family's and society's prejudices—leaves the narrative as well as the surviving characters strangely unfocused. Mrs. Pargiter is not presented as warped or wounded by the world because she is not presented at all. She is a cipher who appears to have orphaned her children from the outset. But her nullity damages her children more than if she were overbearing and possessive. She has neither dominated nor nourished them but, deprived of her own identity, leaves them without a pattern to be authors of themselves. Unlike Mrs. Ramsay, Mrs. Dedalus, and Mrs. Morel, she provides no object of imitation or rebellion for the child or would-be artist.

No book seems to have given Woolf more trouble in conception and execution than *The Years*. Among her frequent complaints about the difficulties she endured in writing it, she confessed in her diary, "It's like a long childbirth."[14] Since none of Mrs. Pargiter's daughters is employed by Woolf as surrogate artist-heroine, an unusually heavy burden falls on the "absent" narrator as the one who must try, without reference to personal viewpoint, to create focus and vitality. This effort and the seemingly insurmountable problems it causes come to dominate the book and to overshadow the feminist themes that link it to *Three Guineas*. Despite a good deal of concrete detail and Woolf's intention to make it more realistic than *The Waves*, *The Years* turns in on itself. It is a novel in which the old image of the father as a creator has gone under and the author, like an orphaned child, is left trying to piece together bit by bit something that is not an imitation of the paternal longing for linearity, explanation, and completeness.

Even more important, however, this is the book in which Woolf tried to kill both the mother *and* her ghost, to eliminate a conventional literary transformation of maternal "heart" as well as paternal "head." She seemed to wish to discover what the offspring (and the artist) could do on their own. The result is painful and at the end nearly chaotic, for the novel shows at great length that no effort, moral or aesthetic, can hold things together except in the transitory, faltering, and artificial ways exposed but ultimately tolerated and used by the characters and narrator. A book that seems to begin, like Delia, full of confidence about what it opposes, in the way of domestic and literary convention, turns into an apologetic mourner at the funeral of its adversary.

At the party a game is played that is a satire of the family and a grotesque parody of the book, echoing the section on decorum in Horace's *Ars Poetica*. A niece "stretched out her hand and Renny gave her the paper. It was folded; they had been playing a game. Each of them had drawn a different part of a picture. On top there was a woman's head like Queen Alexandra, with a fuzz of little curls; then a bird's neck; the body of a tiger; and stout elephant's legs dressed in child's drawers completed the picture" (389).

The hitherto solemn niece's reaction to the absurd composite "family portrait" is hysterical laughter, which relaxes her. "She felt, or rather she saw, not a place, but a state of being, in which there was real laughter, real happiness, and this fractured world was whole; whole, vast and free. But how could she say it?" (390). She tries, but of course she cannot say it. Neither, in this novel, can Woolf. The admission is hardly full of glee or triumph. The novel that began with the charade of a mother's death, as an exposure of family life and a critique of the fictional chronicle, points in the end, with a grotesque stillbirth, toward a repudiation of itself. What mother—or author—would choose to inhabit a "fractured world" or willingly bear a monstrous child?

To the Lighthouse (1927) and *The Years* (1937) are narrative experiments of very different kinds. One chronicles the life of a family during two brief periods separated by ten years; the other follows the members of a family during eleven intervals over fifty years. One focuses on the powerful figure of a beautiful and loving mother; the other begins with the death of a faded, ineffectual mother and splinters among her children and grandchildren. Mrs. Ramsay and Mrs. Pargiter seem complete opposites: one is unforgettable even in death; the other, difficult to see and remember while still alive. *The Years* dashes the myth of the mother as a figure of creative energy and reconciliation, while *To the Lighthouse*, through the agency of Lily Briscoe, keeps it alive.

Significantly, it is as much the absence of a Lily Briscoe in *The Years* as it is the death of Mrs. Pargiter that leaves the narrative, like the family, in such a fractured state. Woolf withdraws the artist with the mother. Poor Mrs. Pargiter has no one to remember her, but, like all mothers, she cannot be ignored with impunity. She has her revenge on her children and their story. Having lost touch with their vital source and center, her descendants cannot create new centers of coherence of their own. Male and female alike, they are as unfocused and forgettable to one another (and the reader) as she was.

The novels of Woolf, Joyce, and Lawrence teach us that the ghostly mother will not be denied by daughters or sons. She haunts her artist-offspring by a too palpable presence or a disabling absence. Either way, she keeps the artist honest. She abhors egotists and aesthetes. She will not be banished, buried without reverence, shattered like a lamp, turned into a girl or an enchantress or even into an exquisite ideal of beauty without finding a way to chide the dreaming child and call him back to earth.

To the modern writer, the absent mother represents a lost focus and link to concrete reality, a memory of rupture and abandonment. In dying, she appears to have completed her detachment from the child, which began at birth. Yet the very gap created by her death is a reminder of an old and necessary liaison, a "primal objective knowledge" prior to separation. What is perceived as "fractured" must once have been whole. To repair the break, the artist, like the maturing child, is forced to look for new links with life outside the self.

THREE

A Long Event of Perpetual Change
Marriage

Leopold Bloom: As God made them He matched them ...
Twice nought makes one.

Molly Bloom: youre looking blooming Josie used to say after I
married him.

JAMES JOYCE, Ulysses

It is this establishing of pure relationships which makes
heaven.

D. H. LAWRENCE, Collected Letters

Arnold Bennett says that the horror of marriage lies in its
"dailiness." All acuteness of relationship is rubbed away by
this. The truth is more like this: life—say 4 days out of 7—becomes automatic; but on the 5th day a bead of sensation (between husband and wife) forms which is all the fuller and more
sensitive because of the automatic customary days on either
side. That is to say the year is marked by moments of great intensity ... How can a relationship endure for any length of
time except under these conditions?

VIRGINIA WOOLF, A Writer's Diary

L AWRENCE'S DEFINITION of marriage as "a long event of perpetual change" describes the literary as well as the social history of institutionalized mating. When, during the eighteenth century, the novel began to emerge as a genre with tendencies different from those of epic and romance, one of its most distinctive characteristics was its preoccupation with marriage. Though particular marriages were often shown to be foolish or unhappy, the institution itself was almost invariably held to be the natural and virtuous goal for reasonable men and women in a secular age. Above all, marriage was a sign of order, a structure by means of which sexual, financial, and social instability could be alleviated if not entirely eliminated.

However different the contents of the story or the particulars of the courtship or apparent flight from courtship, marriage tended to function structurally in the same way in most fiction written between the mid-eighteenth and the late nineteenth centuries. It was a sign of harmony and resolution, of predictability and conclusiveness, toward which all but the most extravagant or unlucky of youthful adventures led. In a sense, it served as a retroactive license for unruly behavior since the eventual submission to its rule was understood by author and reader to be inevitable. Indeed, the elements of its rule affected the simplest and most fundamental mechanics of narrative form as a supposed imitation of life. It was assumed, for example, that human relations and the verbal relationships that described them had a purpose, an achievable goal that could be defined and earned. It was also assumed that beneath the apparently infinite diversity of life and language lay meaningful similarities. The mating of people, like the coupling of words, was a sign that the world made sense.

As in earlier narrative forms, the young hero or heroine of the novels of this period encountered a variety of good and bad examples of the goal being sought, as well as distractions and obstacles en route. Plot turned on delayed gratification, the postponement of a clearly defined and anticipated harmony. The language of these narratives took a great measure of its significance from matrimony as a symbol of human completion, which governs the meaning of all the actions and words that come before. The ultimacy of marriage often made plot seem a mere matter of preliminaries. But, in fictional terms as well, marriage contained a peculiar contradiction. On one hand, it was the source of ideal happiness, a goal to be sought by all right-thinking characters. On the other hand, it was the end of every good story, a nonadventure, a long silence, a victory almost indistinguishable from defeat, since "they lived happily ever after" was just as unimaginable a dismissal as "they roasted eternally in hell."

The conception of marriage as a resting place, as conclusive in literary terms as the "final resting place," suggests not only that plot is preparation but that it is preparation for a time in which the old, more interesting self ceases to exist. Precisely the qualities that were taken to make the ideal husband or wife—stability, equanimity, patience, resignation—meant the annihilation of heroic effort, however modestly defined. A *Tom Jones,* part II, in which the hero is happily settled into family life would have been as dull and disappointing as the second half of *Pamela.*

The fiction of Jane Austen provides the clearest, most polished example of the extent to which marriage—abstractly conceived as a harmonious union—governs the shape and symmetry of the narrative structure as well as its contents. A bad marriage, like bad grammar, is always to be regretted, sometimes to be corrected, but never to be blamed on the institution itself. A good marriage, like a well-constructed sentence, is the consequence of foresight, discipline, and understanding. It reveals its direction from the start and leaves nothing unfinished or unclear in the end. Austen's happy marriages, like her felicitous sentences, are perfect in the sense that they never exceed their own limits. They create only expectations that they are able to fulfill.

Although the happy marriage continued throughout the nineteenth century to be synonymous with last chapters, it is striking how many of these occasions are tinged with melancholy. The marriages of Edward Waverley and Rose Bradwardine, Jane Eyre and Rochester, Katherine Linton and Hareton Earnshaw, Amelia Sedley and William Dobbin, Little Dorritt and Arthur Clenham, Adam Bede and Dinah Morris, Gabriel Oak and Bathsheba Everdene are some of the most obvious examples of unions that are inevitable but hardly jubilant. In virtually every case, some false or forbidden passion remains in the past, and the wedding ceremony doubles as its burial service. The moral significance of this mixed blessing is clear: one or both of the characters is presumed to have been purged of a false love and is seen as sufficiently mature to accept a quiet but "better" alternative.

Unfortunate, even disastrous marriages are the subject of major nineteenth-century novels like *Middlemarch* and *Portrait of a Lady;* yet it was Hardy in *Jude the Obscure* who did most damage to the literary structures and social myths that had been so long kept alive, however ambivalently, by the novel. Unlike Eliot, Hardy does not produce a "good" marriage as a sign of partial healing at the end of his book; nor, like James, does he allow his characters sufficient moral imagination to transcend a bad marriage. Jude and Sue are victims of an institution for which neither is suited. As Phillotson carries Sue to his bedroom near the end of the novel, the old housekeeper mutters, "Weddings be funerals." The phrase is like a charm uttered to break a magic spell. It articulates what was implied indirectly by generations of novelists and, by doing so, cracks the myth of perfect union, empties it of automatic, unexamined signification, and returns it to the realm of free inquiry.

A T T H E beginning of *Women in Love,* Ursula and Gudrun Brangwen discuss marriage.[1] When Ursula seems skeptical, Gudrun argues that at the very least it is "bound to be an experience of some sort." " 'Not really,' said Ursula. 'More likely to be the end of experience.' " This exchange marks the novel as unmistakably modern not simply because Mr. and Mrs. Bennett have been replaced by two smart and relatively liberated young women discussing marriage in a tone that combines curiosity with sarcasm, but because the phenomenon of marriage itself is open to definition. The question is not simply whether the girls will marry—though that obviously concerns them—but what marriage means. The phrase "the end of experience" perfectly captures the double significance of the nineteenth-century social myth and novelistic formula that proclaimed marriage to be the object of life as well as the conclusion of the restlessness and misadventure that make for good reading but bad lives if unchecked. Ursula's tone suggests a third meaning, which shifts the moral weight of the question and implies a reexamination of sequence as well as value. Is marriage to be the end of feeling and growth as well as of instability and anxiety? If so, is it so much to be sought after? If not, what does it do? Is it, in fact, an ending in any way that makes sense in life as it is supposed to do in novels?

Joyce, Lawrence, and Woolf suggested radical answers to these questions in a number of works, including three of their finest short stories. "The Dead," "The Shadow in the Rose Garden," and "The Legacy" are remarkably alike in their treatment of marriage and especially in their endings.[2] Each story, as the titles indicate, deals with a form of death— death not as an absolute finality but as a condition that intermingles with and affects life. In each case an apparently happy and ordinary marriage undergoes a sudden and violent rupture. Each husband is complacent, self-absorbed, and certain of his wife's total devotion until, by chance, he discovers that she has loved someone else with an intense passion that cannot be forgotten or duplicated in marriage. It is as though some of the "happy" melancholy marriages with which so many Victorian novels were concluded have been pursued and found to be neither so safe nor so tranquil as literary convention pretended.

In none of the stories is adultery the issue; in fact, only in Woolf's "The Legacy" is it likely that adultery has actually occurred. The crux of each tale is the husband's realization that his wife—the one person he supposedly knows through and through, a woman he thinks belongs to him—is capable of a life, if only in her memories, that he cannot share. Nor can he influence or know it except in fragments that inform him of little more than his distance from her. Moral outrage, which only the husband in Lawrence's story goes to the trouble of expressing, gives way to shock and despair at the extent to which human beings, including married couples, are isolated from one another.

The marriages in the three short stories are not "good" or "bad." The wives are not beautiful, noble heroines, nor the husbands grizzly Phillotsons or decrepit Casaubons. In none of the stories is marriage a beginning or an end; the sustained relationship of husband and wife is a condition of their being that predates the events of the plot and, except in Woolf's story, continues after the narrative concludes. Neither Joyce nor Lawrence suggests that the couples will separate. Indeed, without conclusive evidence or sentimental emphasis, each tale provides some sign that the shock of discovery has made a hitherto insensitive husband slightly more aware of himself and his wife. Joyce's Gabriel Conroy sheds "generous tears" in a moment of sympathy that, for once, is as much for his wife as for himself. And in Lawrence's story, there is a definite sense of gain in the seemingly ironic authorial observation at the end that the couple "no longer hated each other." In two cases, the lover is dead, and in one he is mad. There is no one for the husband to confront and nothing to be stopped. Like marriage itself, the other love is a condition of the couple's existence, which produces a crisis in understanding that corresponds to a crisis in event only in Woolf's story.

The myth of marriage as an end to change and therefore as an appropriate end in fiction ceases to operate in these stories. Tying the knot no longer seems an accurate image of marriage or a good pattern for composing fiction—not so much because the institution itself has altered radically, but because it is presented as both husband and wife experience it, rather than as either does alone or as the "public" is supposed to do. Jane Austen expects us to accept the fact that it is a good thing for Emma Woodhouse to marry Knightley, but we are never allowed to ask at any length how good, in the long run, it will be for Knightley to marry Emma. Similarly, characters like Shirley, Pendennis, and Nicholas Nickleby are shown to be fortunate in their marriages, but it is almost invariably for a particular heroine or hero that we are primarily satisfied. The main interest of the plot has been hers or his, and the "tying of the knot" is the end of that individual's adventures.

The story of marriage becomes an entirely different matter for the modern writer when he begins to treat it as a plot with two authors. Even when the narrative voice is that of a third person or when the point of view seems to be primarily that of one character, the scheme of the story, as well as its moral and psychological tone, is equivocal. Plot defined as the anticipated design of a single imagination seems no more appropriate than marriage defined in a similarly rigid and single-minded fashion. The husbands in the three stories are "obtuse" narrators of marriage plots over which they ultimately discover they have only limited control. The story has been lived simultaneously by wives with chapters in mind that the husbands have not even begun to imagine. The crisis occurs when the "texts" of the two marriage plots are brought together. There is no *corpus delicti,* no naked intruder under the marriage bed to be thrashed or chased trouserless out the window. The confrontation is a verbal one, a clash not of events but of languages that have derived from differing situations and failed to merge.

By the time the Conroys in "The Dead" arrive at their hotel room, we have already witnessed Gabriel's verbal pretentiousness and Gretta's relative silence at a family party. Feeling desire for his wife, but unable, as usual, to express himself simply or directly, Gabriel begins a little story to illustrate his own generosity. Gretta's apparent indifference irritates him; when she kisses him and tells him that he is a "very generous person," however, he imagines that "her thoughts had been running with his." In fact, her thoughts are not with or against him, but entirely elsewhere. When, for a moment, she not only tells him the story of her youthful lover, but creates the present scene with her words, it comes as an illumination to the reader as well as to Gabriel. There are no recriminations or outbursts. Gretta simply falls asleep and so does Gabriel, realizing with the reader how irrevocably the one text has become two.

The confrontation of Lawrence's couple in "The Shadow in the Rose Garden" is more melodramatic than that of Gabriel and Gretta, and in places it is comic. But it, too, is presented largely in terms of verbal disparity. At times it is as if two writers are trying to find the correct words for the same situation and nearly coming to blows over terminology. After visiting her old lover in an asylum, the wife tries to explain her feelings to her husband. Despite her obvious agitation, her language is that of a polite romance. She speaks of her lover's rank in the army, their ages, and the fact that "he was awfully fond of me, and I was of him—awfully." When her husband translates this into "carrying on," she replies:

> "I don't know what you mean, by carrying on. I loved him from the first days I met him . . ."
> "And how far did it go between you?" he asked . . .
> "I hate your not-straightforward questions," she cried . . .
> "We loved each other, and we *were* lovers . . ."
> "Lovers—lovers," he said white with fury. "You mean you had your fling with an army man . . .
> "Do you mean to say you used to go the whole hogger?"(232)

Between being "awfully fond" and going "the whole hogger" there is at once no difference and a world of difference. What is at issue in the marriage, as in the plot, is not the fact but the meaning, which quite obviously cannot be the same for the two character-narrators. Even if the husband's language and attitude were less gross, he could hardly tell, interpret, or respond to the story as his wife has done. The sharp differences in language reveal the chasm the episode has placed between them, while the very existence of the exchange shows it as an undeniable element in their relationship.[3]

In Woolf's "The Legacy," the wife is not alive to dispute terminology with her husband, but she has literally left her own written account of her married life in "fifteen little volumes bound in green leather." In the early volumes, the wife's text seems largely to follow the husband's in style and subject matter. Gilbert Clandon's tale of his marriage is summed up in his grateful remembrance that Angela "had been the greatest help to him in his career"(134). For years and years (and pages and pages) Angela's narrative shows that she, like Gilbert, was proud of him, regarded his career as the central fact of their life, and saw her role as that of a supporting character in a plot that he created and in which he figured as the undoubted hero. One of her recorded experiences is the feeling of pride she took in him when at a political rally the audience sang, "For he's a jolly good fellow."

After a while, Angela begins to do volunteer work; she meets other people, and as "his own name occurred less frequently . . . [Gilbert's] interest slackened." But, like the husbands in the other two stories, Gilbert is not merely bored by his wife's version of things; he very soon becomes puzzled by it. He finds that he is a poor reader of her text, that initials and references make no sense to him, in short, that her plot has so diverged from his that he cannot understand it or recognize in it the wife of his own plot. Both wife and lover have killed themselves by the time

Gilbert realizes that in return for the secondary role he has given her in his life story, she has written him out of hers altogether.

In each of these stories several narrative conventions are placed in new perspectives in ways that correspond exactly to those of the conventions of marriage. The outlines of an old-fashioned story with a beginning, middle, and end are still to be seen. Each story had an apparent protagonist, an apparent direction, and an apparent balance of opposites or equilibrium. The complication comes not from a subplot, or even a counterplot, but from a revised version of the same story told reluctantly by a "minor" character who turns out to be a coauthor. The familiar structures remain, but the binding materials of sequence, prediction, correspondence, emphasis, and meaning are curiously broken and transformed.

The unsettling of the reader's expectations about fictional marriage coincides with his liberation from certain formal constraints associated with narrative prose. A story that, told in one way, is that of complacent egotism becomes, in the words of a different author, a tale of passion. The reader may choose one version or another and place blame on one of the character-narrators; he may make no choice and simply see the equivocal story as a case for moral relativity. But the best of such fictions call neither for narrow judgments nor for absolute neutrality, rather they require a moral perspective cleared of visions of "perfect union" and a literary sensibility enlivened by a suspicion of all-wise narrators settled comfortably in their stories like husbands in armchairs with slippers (and wives) at their feet.

THE MARRIAGE of Leopold and Molly Bloom, like the rest of *Ulysses,* elaborately and eccentrically organized as literary pattern, appears on the "unadorned" level of everyday life to be a pathetic shambles. The heroic, Biblical, Shakespearian allusions seem only to draw attention to the bare unattractive facts: that Molly is a lazy, uneducated, self-indulgent slut and that Leopold is a sensual, half-impotent, good-natured cuckold. The question posed is not only why such a couple remains together at all but what their marriage has to do with the outpouring of verbiage that surrounds it in the novel.

The answer to the first question remains to be seen, but to the second, we have Joyce's (and Lawrence's and Woolf's) earlier fiction as a clue. Though by contrast with *Ulysses* "The Dead" is the essence of simplicity, it nevertheless makes the point that there is no such thing as an "unadorned" fact or situation, especially where marriage is concerned. Humanity's most universal and ancient means of seeking completeness—

union with the opposite sex—exposes both the variety and persistence of the need and the incompleteness out of which the need grows in the first place. The perfect marriage, like the beatific union, is silent. It is the end of all stories. All the rest need explaining, by interested bystanders as well as by those involved.

Since marriage is a state of mind as well as a state of body and being, stories about it do, in fact, enter into the total reality. *Ulysses* is well known as a book of parodies, exaggerated literary imitations, but it is also a book of nonliterary responses to literature. The most modest thoughts and feelings about marriage are verbalized in terms of existing texts or in deliberate contrast to them. Bloom's purchase of *Sweets of Sin* for Molly becomes a curious act of generosity toward an unfaithful wife, a kind of collusion, a vicarious participation in his own cuckolding. Bloom reads excerpts in the shop and experiences pleasure:

> —*All the dollarbills her husband gave her were spent in the stores on won-drous gowns and costliest frillies. For him! For Raoul!*
> Yes. This. Here. Try.
> —*Her mouth glued on his in a luscious voluptuous kiss while his hands felt for the opulent curves inside her deshabillé.*
> Yes. Take this.(236)

The pretentious, provocative language of the cheap novel helps Bloom translate his anxiety into a momentary feeling of luxurious warmth. In one sense, Bloom is a man of vulgar taste who is easily deceived by big words with an aura of wealth and of the exotic into romanticizing his wife's infidelity with the crude Blazes Boylan. But this very quality puts Bloom into a position of sympathy and union with Molly that Boylan cannot share or remove. The passage is an early indication that Bloom's marriage to Molly, his identification with and understanding of her, goes well beyond his ability to penetrate her physically, a talent in which Boylan is his obvious superior. The need for sensual gratification, euphemistically labeled, is shared by Leopold and Molly. That each can provide it only indirectly for the other may be a sign either that the marriage has deteriorated or that it flourishes in subtle and unexpected ways.

Gerty MacDowell, the lame girl Bloom sees on the beach, whose reading habits differ from Molly Bloom's, imagines marriage in the words of the innocent domestic romances permitted to Catholic girls of her generation in Ireland. In sharp contrast with the foreignness and extravagance of *l'affaire Raoul*, Gerty's scene is one of economical domestic bliss. She dreams of a "snug and cosy little homely house" in which she would give her husband his morning "brekky" and he would call her his "dear little wifey." As Gerty thinks about decorating her dream house, her description includes a model husband who would fit in with the furniture and, in several important respects, resemble it: "They would have a beautifully appointed drawingroom with pictures and engravings and the photograph of Grandpa Giltrap's lovely dog Garryowen that almost talked, it was so human, and chintz covers for the chairs and that silver toastrack in Clery's summer jumble sales like they have in rich houses. He would be tall with broad shoulders (she had always admired tall men for a husband) with glistening white teeth under his carefully trimmed sweeping moustache"(352).

Bloom cannot read Gerty's mind or her text on married life, but we can; and we can therefore compare it with the Bloom household in which brekky is cooked not by wifey but by Poldy and the furniture, which has been moved about by the time Bloom returns home, bears telltale stains and indentations that speak almost as clearly as Grandpa Giltrap's dog. At first, the contrast seems to be the most cynical repudiation of marriage as a happy idyll and an exposure of it as an untidy nest of deception and disappointment. Yet to conclude this is to ignore entirely the tones of the texts in question. Gerty's is not merely naive, but lifeless and static. She has imagined a dollhouse in which the husband is manicured and arranged like the furnishings. It has everything but vitality. The scenes of Bloom cooking breakfast, serving Molly tea, or creeping into bed next to her at the novel's end have, by contrast, a poverty of signs of domestic efficiency and bliss, but an unmistakable sensuousness and warmth. Molly's clothes are strewn about the room, crumbs are in the bed—the house, like the marriage, seems in a state of disorder. Still, with so much against it—the death of their only son, Bloom's impotence, Molly's adultery—the marriage survives with a mixture of affection, humor, comfort, and tension that defies ordinary assumptions. The bond between Leopold and Molly is not conventionally sexual nor domestic, yet that it endures is one of the least disputed facts in this complicated book.

A third literary text that serves as a commentary on marriage in general and on that of Molly and Leopold in particular is the Dickens parody that celebrates marital bliss in the lying-in ward where Mina Purefoy has just given birth to her eighth child. The point of view adopted in this parody is that of "those who have passed on" and "gaze down and smile upon the touching scene." Aside from the obvious fun at the expense of Dickensian sentimentality, the passage introduces the notion of marriage as a divine union ordained by God in imitation of his own relationship with mankind for the purpose of the multiplication of the species. The mother breathes

> a silent prayer of thanksgiving to One above, the Universal Husband. And as her loving eyes behold her babe she wishes only . . . to have her dear Doady there with her to share her joy, to lay in his arms that mite of God's clay, the fruit of their lawful embraces . . . O Doady, loved one of old, faithful lifemate now, it may never be again, that faroff time of the roses! . . . But their children are grouped in her imagination about the bedside . . . and now this last pledge of their union . . . And Doady, knock the ashes from your pipe, the seasoned briar you still fancy when the curfew rings for you (may it be the distant day!) and dout the light whereby you read in the Sacred Book for the oil too has run low and so with a tranquil heart to bed, to rest.(420–421)

The cloying tones do not conceal an important sacramental view of marriage as a union of man and woman under contract to God. To be loyal to the contract is to remain faithful to the union and to produce children, which is seen as "fighting the good fight," "playing one's part," performing one's service to the Lord. In return, God provides happy memories, a gentle old age, and a peaceful death. The Dickensian combination of metaphysics and sentiment seems no more appropriate to Leopold and Molly than does the Edwardian vocabulary of pseudo-pornography in *Sweets of Sin* or the prim domesticity of Gerty MacDowell's fantasy. Yet, like the other two, it does provide a means to form a part of the composite picture of the Blooms.

The reader is obviously not expected to take language as a transparent window through which the characters can be clearly seen and understood. But neither is language, even the language of literary parody, simply an opaque absurdity from which the reader is expected to reverse images in order to see the positive and true picture. When it comes to "the fruit of their lawful embraces," Molly and Leopold, with only one daughter to show for their efforts, cannot hold a candle to the Purefoys. In terms of "fighting the good fight," they both seem to have failed miserably and therefore to have little or no place in God's grand and benevolent design. Yet, as the book eventually reveals, Molly, too, has her memories of a "faroff time of the roses," and Leopold, at the end of a full if not fruitful day, goes "with a tranquil heart to bed."

The parodies serve as examples of a sort, but they also serve as warnings about language. We can neither trust it too far nor suspect it too much. They remind us to test our own misgivings and smart solutions as well as formulas of literary bias. They remind us of our own narrowness of mind and sensibility, as we are quick to recognize the same character-istics in the verbal mannerisms of popular and classic literature. They remind us that verbal structures are related to but not the same as the phenomena to which they point. Above all, they remind us to approach fiction with a constant ear, not for the perfect combination, but for the variety of imperfect combinations through which the genuine human voice is heard.

Leopold and Molly have their own narrated versions of marriage that, in juxtaposition with the texts prepared by others, describe and imitate in their deepest structure the phenomena of sexual coupling, social con-tract, and sacramental union. Leopold Bloom is said to have a "touch of the artist" in him, and it is of course true that Bloom, like all human beings, constructs his life while living it. Most of the time he appears to have little more success as an artist then he does as a husband. His head is full of half-remembered rhymes, fragments of song lyrics, jumbled proverbs, incomplete phrases from the Bible and Shakespeare, advertis-ing jingles, old wives' sayings, and trite expressions. He does somehow manage to put things together with words, though the result often re-sembles a random patchwork rather than a deliberate design.

In fact, Bloom's attempts at verbal coherence are not at all random. His use of words, including his borrowing of familiar lines for his own purposes, is always rooted in experience. One of his longest meditations on marriage at first appears to be a ragbag of commonplace observa-tions. But when related to Bloom's immediate situation (he has just masturbated while watching Gerty MacDowell on the beach) and his own marital history, the words connect into an outline of a particular, recognizable man:

Still it was a kind of language between us. It couldnt be? No, Gerty they called her. Might be false name however like my and the ad-dress Dolphin's barn a blind.
Her maiden name was Jemima Brown
And she lived with her mother in Irishtown.
Place made me think of that I suppose. All tarred with the same brush. Wiping pens in their stockings. But the ball rolled down to her as if it understood. Every bullet has its billet. Course I never could throw anything straight at school. Crooked as a ram's horn.
(372-373)

Bloom is feeling a vague mixture of satisfaction, discomfort, and shame, none of which would seem appropriate to a happily married man. His imaginary coupling with Gerty, like his correspondence with Martha and his marriage to Molly are examples of bullets not finding their billets, of crooked throws and forced rhymes like "Irishtown" and

"Jemima Brown." His preoccupation with his sexual failure as a husband and his Jewishness dominates his thoughts and gives meaning to his apparently random words. The child's ball rolling to Gerty's feet, the cliché about bullets and billets, and the ritual ram's horn come together as emblems of a game that he, by nature, is not good at playing. Still, his art has not been entirely inward and futile. Gerty has not been unaware of his interest. There has, in fact, been "a kind of language between" them. Even if metaphorically she would only wipe his pen on her stockings, she is not unaware of him as an author, a creator of a text to which she in her own silent fashion replies. The unseen correspondent Martha does write back and, most important, the absent, unpossessed Molly is a major contributor to his mood and language.

Earlier, while reading a story by Mr. Philip Beaufoy, he imagines himself and Molly as coauthors of a "sketch by Mr. and Mrs. L. M. Bloom." Like so many of Bloom's dreams, this one is realized in its own fashion. Even while watching girlies on the beach, Bloom is the thoroughly married man whose wife informs his mind and helps shape his words. Molly is never far from Bloom's thoughts, even when it is the sight of Gerty that is supposedly bringing him to a climax. When his excitement has subsided, he mulls over marriage, thinks of how pretty young girls turn into ugly wives, and dwells on Molly with pride:

> That's where Molly can knock spots off them. It is the blood of the south. Moorish. Also the form, the figure. Hands felt for the opulent. Just compare for instance those others. Wife locked up at home, skeleton in the cupboard. Allow me to introduce my. Then they trot you out some kind of nondescript, wouldn't know what to call her. Always see a fellow's weak point in his wife. Still, there's destiny in it, falling in love ... As God made them He matched them. Sometimes children turn out well enough. Twice nought makes one. Or old rich chap of seventy and blushing bride. Marry in May and repent in December. This wet is very unpleasant. Stuck. Well the foreskin is not back. Better detach.
> Ow!
> Other hand a sixfooter with a wifey up to his watchpocket. Long and the short of it. Big he and little she. (373)

In figure and form, Molly is central to this passage. Not only does she dominate the scene even though not physically in it, but her way of thinking and talking affects the way Bloom forms his thoughts. The proud "blood of the south" and the cattiness about other men's wives are Mollyisms. And "hands felt for the opulent" is a phrase from *Sweets of Sin,* which Molly has not yet read but which we know is just her taste in literary style. Furthermore, as always, Bloom is preoccupied with

God's matchmaking and particularly with the coupling of opposites, which appear to be ludicrous mistakes rather than destiny. His own far from perfect match with Molly does not seem, by comparison, so absurd. He is still capable of being aroused by her, if only at a distance. Though he is uneasy about being an uncircumcised Jew, still in possession of his foreskin—what the citizen calls a "half-and-half"—Molly with her "Moorish" (Jewish) blood is a half-and-half, too. And though, contrary to the saying, twice nought makes nought, two halves do, when given the chance, make one.

Bloom is no more a polished rhymster than he is a model husband. His couplings, verbal and physical, are filled with flaws. But in the Aeolus section, an entry entitled "Rhymes and Reasons" suggests that rhyme is not really very reasonable, that the seemingly perfect match of sounds and appearances may be an arbitrary and meaningless conjunction: "Mouth, south. Is the mouth south someway? Or the south a mouth? Must be some. South, pout, out, shout, drouth. Rhymes: two men dressed the same, looking the same, two by two" (138).

Though he goes earnestly along trying to make reason out of rhyme and, correspondingly, to imagine some ideal relationship between himself and Molly-Martha-Gerty, Bloom's genuine artistry, that is, his ability to fashion verbal equivalents of actual relationships, is not expressed in superficial resemblances. His fondness for jingles, his curiosity about religious rituals, and his taste for sumptuous pseudo-literature are all signs of a ludicrously unachieved idealism. His real strength is in his ability to root himself deeply in concrete experience and, on occasion, to make every word reverberate with dramatic vitality.

In a comic scene of almost Shakespearian quality, Bloom meets M'Coy outside the post office where he has just picked up a letter from Martha. During his conversation with M'Coy, Bloom watches an attractively dressed woman across the road and then glances at an advertisement in the morning paper:

What is home without
Plumtree's Potted Meat?
Incomplete.
With it an abode of bliss.

—My missus has just got an engagement. At least it's not settled yet . . .

Mr. Bloom turned his largelidded eyes with unhasty friendliness.

—My wife too, he said. She's going to sing at a swagger affair in the Ulster Hall, Belfast, on the twentyfifth.

—That so? M'Coy said. Glad to hear that, old man. Who's getting it up?

Mrs. Marion Bloom. Not up yet. Queen was in her bedroom eating bread and. No book. Blackened court cards laid along her thigh by sevens. Dark lady and fair man. Cat furry black ball. Torn strip of envelope.

> *Love's*
> *Old*
> *Sweet*
> *Song*
> *Comes lo-ve's old . . .*

—It's a kind of a tour, don't you see? Mr Bloom said thoughtfully. *Sweet song.* There's a committee formed. Part shares and part profits. (75)

Bloom's recollection of Molly in bed with her Tarot cards and the envelope addressed to Mrs. Marion Bloom by Blazes Boylan gives the conversation a significance for him and for the reader that it does not have for M'Coy. Since Boylan is organizing Molly's tour and, as Bloom suspects, arranging a lover's meeting with her that very day, the words and phrases associated with the recital form in Bloom's mind a separate code with a significance of its own. Terms like "engagement," "swagger affair," and "getting it up" accumulate a meaning at first farcical and then pathetic and painful, as Bloom imagines Molly, the dark lady, and Boylan, the fair man, lying together like cards, and spells out LOSS with the words of "Love's Old Sweet Song." The final phrase, "part shares and part profits" is Bloom's artful and humane resolution of the discord, a description of the business arrangement made for the concert tour, which also serves as a knowing, resigned, but not ungenerous definition of marriage. In a world of material complexity and mutability, the pun seems inevitable, but Bloom, the everyday artist and incorrigible husband, reveals a surprising capacity for control through insight and love.

As Bloom continues his journey through Dublin, his mind returns again and again to Molly and Boylan. Crossing O'Connell Bridge, he looks down at the gulls hovering over the Liffey and remembers a rhyme and then two lines from Shakespeare recalling Hamlet's father, who was dishonored by his wife and brother. The reader's expectation is that the "gulled" Bloom will identify himself with the forlorn and hungry birds:

They wheeled, flapping.

> *The hungry famished gull*
> *Flaps o'er the waters dull.*

That is how poets write, the similar sounds. But then Shakespeare has no rhymes: blank verse. The flow of the language it is. The thoughts. Solemn.

> *Hamlet, I am thy father's spirit*
> *Doomed for a certain time to walk the earth.*

—Two apples a penny! Two for a penny!

His gaze passed over the glazed apples serried on her stand . . .
Wait. Those poor birds.

He halted again and bought from the old applewoman two Banbury cakes for a penny and broke the brittle paste and threw its fragments down into the Liffey. See that? The gulls swooped silently two, then all, from their heights, pouncing on prey. Gone. Every morsel. (152–153)

This is the kind of scene in which Joyce, with only a few strokes of the brush, fashions a picture of Bloom that is unsentimental but unforgettably sympathetic. Ready to indulge in self-pity, to savor his role as "dull gull," to make easy poetry of his misery, to comfort himself with shiny apples, "gaze-glazed," Bloom throws off literary allusions and self-absorption and acts with perfect simplicity and charity. For a moment, in this labyrinthine text, he is shown merely as a man feeding birds. Out of this passage emerge a narrative voice in which Bloom the character and Joyce the author are indistinguishable and a rhythmic alliterative poetry of ancient freshness without rhyme or reason. In this book of intricate connections and elaborate parallels, it is a stroke of artistry of a rare but important kind that presents Bloom unencumbered. This is a glimpse of Bloom-not-gull whom Blazes Boylan can never reach.

For a moment it seems that language and event, author and character, are one in a breathtakingly simple equation. Such instances are usually so brief as to seem even more illusory than the complex meanderings that lead toward and away from them. Within a moment, a phrase, Bloom's equilibrium is unsettled. "Aware of their greed and cunning he shook the powdery crumb from his hands. They never expected that. Manna" (153).

"Aware" has much the same function as "forlorn" in Keats's "Ode to a Nightingale." It brings author, reader, and character back to a "reality" that is self-conscious, analytical, thoughtful. As Bloom begins to assign human attributes of "greed" and "cunning" to the birds, he calls a new kind of attention to himself and to his words and away from the gulls. The link is by no means broken, but it is complicated. When the image of "manna" occurs to him, a whole new structure is superimposed on the act of scattering bread that has the paradoxical function of enriching the idea of the act while seeming to impoverish it as a unique gesture. In order to "keep" the moment, Bloom has first to experience its loss and then to translate it into associative terms that bind it to other timeless events, like the Exodus, with which it fits imperfectly. The more outrageous and labored Bloom's associative mythmaking is, the more likely it is to result from felt, though fleeting, correspondences. Language, like Bloom's crooked throwing arm, tends to miss the mark. But the reader is left with the distinct impression that there *is* a mark that neither foolish combinations of words nor people can always conceal.

Later that night, when Bloom returns home with Stephen Dedalus and eventually lies down in bed next to the sleeping Molly, the words that represent the movement of his mind are no longer mimetically his. In this most intimate moment, as he drifts off to sleep touching his wife's body and literally feeling the contours of Boylan's form on the mattress, Joyce chooses to convey Bloom's thoughts in words that are so excessively pedantic as to bear almost no clear relation to the mood the reader expects under the circumstances. In fact, the words do tell with extraordinary precision what Bloom is feeling (envy, jealousy, abnegation, and equanimity) while, at the same time, demonstrating once again that telling is not the same as showing. At best, it is showing of a decidedly indirect and crude sort. The more pretentious the language becomes in its implicit claim of exactitude for itself, the more it is exposed as a blunt and blundering instrument. As S. L. Goldberg has observed in his superb analysis of *Ulysses,* "It points to what it cannot reduce to its terms."[4]

Ulysses provides a number of texts by means of which the reader reads, among other things, Bloom and his marital condition. In addition to the literary parodies, Joyce seems in some instances to let Bloom ramble on by himself; in other moments, author and protagonist are indistinguishable narrators; in still others, like the *Ithaca* section, the author assumes an exaggerated superiority over his creation and speaks superlogically and superpoetically on his behalf: "Equanimity? As natural as any and every natural act of a nature expressed or understood executed in natured nature by natural creatures in accordance with his, her and their natured natures, of dissimilar similarity. As not as calamitous as a cataclysmic annihilation of the planet in consequence of collision with a dark sun" (733).

What the words say is that Bloom is to some extent able to calm his emotions by telling himself that there are worse crimes than adultery, which, after all, consists of a natural act between a man and a woman. The effect of the repetitious, alliterative, legalistic, and ingenious language is curious. It goes to great and unnecessary lengths to say something very simple while omitting all evocative reference to Bloom. These words convey thoughts about adultery and thoughts about feelings, but not the feelings themselves. By this time in the novel, the reader knows Bloom well enough to supply his own version of how he feels and perhaps even to experience irritation with Joyce for remaining aloof from his hero, for playing amusing but slightly cruel games with poor Bloom when he most needs sympathy. Yet, of course, if the reader "knows" and sympathizes with "poor" Bloom it is because Joyce has provided him with the means to do so. The author remains infuriatingly blameless precisely because his overall success depends on the reader's recognition of his particular failures. Every text, every section, almost every passage along the way, simultaneously makes a claim and flaunts an inadequacy. It is in the recognition of both that the reader cooperates in shaping the imperfectly worded and wedded but completely believable Bloom.

The relationship between marriage and language is made most explicit when Molly half wakes up and questions Bloom about his day. Bloom is referred to as a "narrator" who tells a modified story and Molly as a "listener" well aware of the limits of "this intermittent and increasingly more laconic narration." As far as they may be from the ideal author and reader or husband and wife, their interdependence is unmistakable. Bloom's narration exists only insofar as Molly listens to it, figures in it, and repeats it in her own fashion. Her own text, which follows immediately on the punctuation mark at the end of his, begins and ends with Bloom. Although Molly's monologue is notorious for its expansive, not to say imaginatively promiscuous, attitude toward men in general, its focal point, its cohesive center, is Bloom. In her nostalgic romantic reveries earlier suitors come to mind, but they tend to blur into the young Bloom "trying to look like Lord Byron," "very handsome at that time," "too beautiful for a man." Even her most immediate and erotic memory of Boylan and his "tremendous big red brute of a thing" leads her to a comparison with Bloom—"Poldy has more spunk in him"—in which a slang reference to a physiological detail implies a moral preference.

In one of her reveries on marriage, she recalls a friend whose husband went to bed with his boots on: "well its not the one way everyone goes mad Poldy anyway whatever he does always wipes his feet on the mat when he comes in wet or shine and always blacks his own boots too and he always takes off his hat when he comes up in the street . . . O Sweetheart May wouldnt a thing like that simply bore you stiff to extinction actually too stupid to take his boots off now what could you make of a man like that Id rather die 20 times over than marry another of their sex of course hed never find another woman like me to put up with him the way I do know me come sleep with me yes and he knows that too at the bottom of his heart" (744).

A trivial and amusing comparison with someone else's mad husband leads Molly to acknowledge her satisfaction with Bloom, their mutual need for forbearance. Most important of all, at bottom, they understand one another and share, like their marriage bed, an inviolable field of experience that extends through their daughter Milly into new life, through Rudy into death, and through their consciousness and memory into the continual narration, revision, and interpretation of their own story. Molly's mind and desires wander, but, like the voyaging Bloom, she returns to her mate in memory ("yes I said yes"), in fact ("mute immutable mature animality"), and in word: "well hes beyond everything I declare somebody ought to put him in the budget if I only could remember the one half of the things and write a book out of it the works of Master Poldy" (754).

In some ways Molly and Leopold seem the exact opposite of Gretta and Gabriel Conroy (or the couples in Lawrence's and Woolf's stories), who appear well-matched while, in fact, they are totally out of touch with one another. The Blooms' marriage seems to have nearly everything wrong with it, except that both appear to take comfort from it and will it into surviving through their intense awareness of and involvement in one another's being and modes of expression. They are unlikely, outlandish collaborators in the preparation of their intermingled texts, but they are collaborators nonetheless. Molly's "know me come sleep with me" could as well be spoken by Bloom, which is one reason why the jealousy of both is tempered with comprehension and resignation. Even Bloom's effort to explain metempsychosis, though jumbled by Molly into "met him pike hoses" and "met something with hoses in it," is not a simple misunderstanding but the token of an exchange between them, a word that has fulfilled its meaning by losing it and having it replaced for Bloom by Molly and for Molly by Bloom.

In the Circe episode, while supposedly peeking through a keyhole at Molly and Blazes Boylan, Bloom is shown a mirror—"the mirror up to nature." In it he sees Shakespeare—according to Stephen, another cuckold—who says to Bloom, "Thou thoughtest as how thou wastest invisible. Gaze." Bloom sees himself. The keyhole through which he imagines himself watching his wife's adultery is a reflection of himself, of his anxieties and desires. In a way, he participates in his own cuckolding, since in his imagination he enjoys Boylan's pleasure and, in his sexual passivity, he encourages and duplicates Molly's receptivity. As he had observed earlier, you "always see a fellow's weak point in his wife."

The implication is that a true marriage is a mirror, like the one in the Bloom's parlor that reflects Bloom regarding the various "matrimonial gifts"—a stopped clock, a dwarf tree under glass, and an embalmed owl—that decorate the mantelpiece. The first images are, like the endings of Victorian novels, emblems of marriage as static, an end of time, a kind of death. Beyond these reflections is Bloom himself, "solitary" and "mutable," a man alone but capable of change, momentarily single but open to otherness. Finally, beyond Bloom, is the reflection of "several inverted volumes improperly arranged and not in the order of their common letters." These books bring Bloom once again back to Molly—to her sloppy housekeeping, "the deficient appreciation of literature possessed by females," to various incongruities in the room that may be clues to Boylan's visit, and, finally, to "the insecurity of hiding any secret document behind, beneath or between the pages of a book."

Bloom's and Molly's ideas of order are not the same, but they intersect and overlap often enough to remain mutually recognizable. Neither can hide any secrets in the pages of the "books" they are writing. Their lives, like their words and names, are inextricably intertwined. Molly takes on Bloom's name with a relish that goes beyond legal formality: "I never thought that would be my name Bloom when I used to write it in print to how it looked on a visiting card or practising for the butcher and oblige M Bloom Youre looking blooming Josie used to say after I married him well its better than Breen or Briggs does brig or those awful names with bottom in them Mrs. Ramsbottom or some kind of a bottom" (761).

Bloom, the artist, recalls a poem in which he worked an acrostic of his nickname into sentiments about Miss Marion Tweedy:

> *Poets oft have sung in rhyme*
> *Of music sweet their praise divine.*
> *Let them hymn it nine times nine.*
> *Dearer far than song or wine,*
> *You are mine. The world is mine. (678)*

The amateur rhymster, inadequate husband, is married to an un-grammatical dreamer, an adulterous wife—but for all that, they are more a mockery of the "perfect" matchings of embalmed owls than of themselves. Each travels away from the other only to return in dream and memory, flesh and word. To call them Mr. and Mrs. L. M. Bloom, coauthors, is too pretentious. While playing one of his childish word and letter games, Leopold comes up with "Molldopeloob," a more appropriate name for their almost comic, almost incomprehensible union.

L A W R E N C E is not one for anagrams, acrostics, limericks, parodies, or other games with language, but his treatment of marriage in *The Rainbow* is, among other things, an elaborate interweaving of ways of talking about as well as seeing and experiencing the married state.[5] Casting the story as a family chronicle of three generations gives the novel a conventional movement forward. Yet the recurrence of the basic situation—a man and woman attempting to live together—the relative scarcity of historical information, the stability of symbolic language, and the repetition of peculiar linguistic structures counteract the forward motion. In a sense, Lydia, Anna, and Ursula are all contemporaries, as are Tom, Will, and Anton. There is no more finality in the novel than there is in *Ulysses*. Obviously, marriage is not an "end," since, despite the marital achievements of two generations, the book concludes with Ursula Brangwen unmarried, as restless and dissatisfied as her widowed grandmother and foster grandfather were at the novel's beginning.

Lawrence does show the effects of education and the gradual breakdown of rural village life on marriage. Anna's religious skepticism and Ursula's going away from her family to teach and, even more, her taking a lover, are signs of "modern" development. But these external considerations appear, in this novel at least, to interest Lawrence less than the emotional and physical intimacies that change relatively little from generation to generation. In fact, *The Rainbow* can be seen as a family history that, in an odd way, refuses to go forward but repeatedly turns back on itself, as if trying to determine whether there is a logic in human mating that is stronger than historical circumstance and personality.

Joyce presents the marriage of Leopold and Molly in multiple layers of complex textual variation; Lawrence provides three primary texts on marriage that overlap, resemble, and differ from one another in subtle ways. The first text is essentially that of Tom Brangwen, who does not so much narrate as see and feel what the author records. The second is shared by Anna Lensky and her husband, Will Brangwen, sometimes in dialogue, sometimes by means of a narration with a rapidly alternating viewpoint. The third text is almost exclusively Ursula Brangwen's, with the major exception of a crucial and devastating episode in which the reader is taken into the mind of her lover, Anton Skrebensky. Interspersed among these are commentaries and digressions by minor characters.

Throughout all three marriage narratives, the dominant structural as well as thematic and metaphorical concern is spatial. Marriage is not treated primarily in temporal terms, as a significant moment or an end of significant moments. Rather, it is seen first and last as a matter of place, of a man and a woman coming together to "share a bed," "live under the same roof," and in doing so to create, if possible, a new space. The verbal equivalent of this process is not the exchange of vows—

which Lawrence never shows—nor the woman's taking the man's name, but the creation of a new language through which husband and wife not only understand one another but communicate with the world, whether or not the other is present.

Lawrence wastes few words in marrying Tom Brangwen, the young, inarticulate English farmer, to Lydia Lensky, the Polish widow and mother of Anna. On the face of it, there seems to be little to say about them except that they appear to have almost nothing in common, and therefore little to say to one another. When Tom first sees Lydia, he simply thinks to himself, "That's her." When, in fact, he does learn something of her history, he is not really very interested in it: "He had learned a little of her. She was poor, quite alone, and had had a hard time in London, both before and after her husband died. But in Poland she was a lady well-born, a landowner's daughter. All these things were only words to him, the fact of her superior birth, the fact that her husband had been a brilliant doctor, the fact that he himself was her inferior in almost every way of distinction. There was an inner reality, a logic of the soul, which connected her with him" (41).

The facts of this highly concentrated narrative summary are enough for whole chapters in another kind of novel, but Lawrence, through the mind of Tom Brangwen, introduces them only to dismiss them as unimportant to the relationship the two are in the process of forming. It is a curious reversal of the theme and narrative structure of the three short stories discussed earlier, in which the husband's discovery of the wife's narrated text, complete with facts about another life, comes as an overwhelming revelation. Tom finds out about Lydia's other life, her other man, her foreignness and distinctness from himself, at the very beginning. Yet he is conscious of an "inner reality," a "logic of the soul," that does not cancel out these facts but makes room for them. Lydia's difference from himself is not a surprise or a threat. Each feels the awareness of the mystery of the other as a condition of their mutual attraction.

Tom's formal proposal to Lydia is an awkward, impersonal event in which he finds himself nearly speechless and collapses into a chair to recover from faintness. As usual, very little is said. But after Lydia accepts, he leaves the house where she is working and goes into the night, where the activity of his mind—translated into words by Lawrence—becomes indistinguishable from the nonverbal chaos of a turbulent sky. "He could not bear to be near her, and know the utter foreignness between them, know how entirely they were strangers to each other. He went out into the wind. Big holes were blown into the sky, the moonlight blew about. Sometimes a high moon, liquid-brilliant, scudded across a hollow space and took cover under electric, brown-irridescent cloud-edges.

Then there was a blot of cloud, and shadow. Then somewhere in the night a radiance again, like a vapour. And all the sky was teeming and tearing along, a vast disorder of flying shapes and darkness and ragged fumes of light and a great brown circling halo, then the terror of a moon running liquid-brilliant into the open for a moment, hurting the eyes before she plunged under cover of cloud again" (49).

The most obvious thing to notice about such a passage in terms of narrative space is its relative length in contrast with the perfunctory summary of Lydia's life in Poland. Even when further details are added to that story in the following chapter, they, like the external details of Lydia's and Tom's day-to-day life together, pale beside the nonfactual, nonlinear, seemingly incoherent efforts to express an inner state of being. In this passage, Tom is responding to the unique and intense experience of the coincidence of "intimacy" and "foreignness," of a union made pleasing to the point of pain by a knowledge of the difference that makes it possible.

The language Lawrence chooses to approximate Tom's state of mind does not refer directly to him or to Lydia, but to the spaciousness of the sky in turmoil. There are intense moments without single direction; great flashes of light without steady illumination; vivid images without apparent pattern or meaning. It is, in other words, the kind of passage in which Lawrence appears to be indulging in Romantic excess and losing control along with his character. In fact, however, the passage has a structure within the "vast disorder of flying shapes and darkness." Words are linked to one another as if in self-defense against the frantic pace of the phrasing. Through hyphenation, internal rhyme, and alliteration, unexpected resemblance and cohesion are revealed within the confusion. Perhaps most important of all is the iteration of the feminine personal pronoun. Early in the paragraph, "he could not bear to be near her" refers to Lydia. In the final clause, the reference is to the moon, fused by grammatical as well as emotional association with the woman whose "radiance" will guide Tom to a new but by no means static sense of place.

Just before the wedding, it worries Tom that "they were such strangers," that "they could not talk to each other." Their conversations after marriage show that, in this regard, there is little change.

"I'm betimes," he said.
"Yes," she answered. (59–60)

"They blow up with a rattle," he said.
"What?" she asked.
"The leaves." (65)

Despite its failure to inspire conversation, their union changes both profoundly. Tom does not become more articulate, but his silences result not from a frustrated groping after understanding but from a peaceful rapport with things that resolves the apparent contradiction between detachment and continuity: "It made a great difference to him, marriage. Things became so remote and of so little significance, as he knew the powerful source of his life, his eyes opened on a new universe, and he wondered in thinking of his triviality before. A new, calm relationship showed to him in the things he saw, in the cattle he used, the young wheat as it eddied in a wind" (59).

The elements of external nature are unchanged, but marriage has provided Tom with a key by means of which he reinterprets them, sees them for the first time in a relation to one another and to himself that he had not known existed. Once the key is provided, the muddle becomes a language that "shows" itself to him—not an arbitrary invention of his own, but a universal system that was always there, though illegible to him. The remoteness and diminished "significance" refer partly to his past confused view of things but also to the false idea that meaning and importance reside in or behind things in themselves, rather than in relationships. His detachment from this idea and from himself as a "significant" but dead weight is part of his transformation into the wedded state. It, in turn, reveals his unpossessive, living bond with his animals and crops. The symmetrical phrasing, the unhurried pacing, the uncomplicated syntax provide a linguistic contrast to the cluttered and frenzied passage in which Tom watches the moon after proposing to Lydia. They also provide a rhetorical, if not a logical, coherence between two apparently contradictory conceptions, remoteness and binding. At the same time that Tom recognizes that things have become remote after his marriage, he senses a new and calm relationship with nature.

Whatever bond Lawrence is trying to portray through Tom and Lydia, it is not associated with the kind of domestic confinement or coziness so often connected with country marriages. In fact, though Lydia moves into the Marsh, Tom's family house, and they remain there throughout their married life, the inner experience is more like a release from the particularity of place than a restriction to it. The early scenes of Tom at home on the farm are reminiscent of George Eliot's verbal imitation of the Dutch school of painting, all glowing, warm, and comfortable. On one of her first visits to the Marsh before their marriage, Lydia sees the house not at all with the eyes of a Gerty MacDowell eager to move into a dollhouse, but rather with anxious misgivings: "She looked around the room he lived in. It had a close intimacy that fascinated and almost frightened her. The furniture was old and familiar as old people, the whole place seemed so kin to him, as if it partook of his being, that she was uneasy" (37).

The Marsh is for Lydia what Poland and her previous marriage are for Tom, particularly as personified in her child, Anna Lensky. The house, like the child, each with a name that marriage does not change, is an outward sign of an untranslatable past, of an aspect of self that unalterably is. The fact that each partner's difference from the other is so palpable and vivid helps the marriage to avoid the complacency and blindness to distinctiveness that so often comes in unions between people with superficial likenesses of background, class, and nationality—like Gabriel and Gretta Conroy or Gilbert and Angela Clandon.

For Lydia and Tom, the instances of union are extraordinarily moving moments of sharing and transformation throughout their marriage. On the first morning after the wedding, when Anna goes to the bedroom and tries to send Brangwen out of her mother's bed, his answer is a touching expression of his union with Lydia. " 'There's room for you as well,' he said. 'It's a big bed enough.' " Later in the year, when Lydia is in labor with their first child, Tom takes Anna to the barn to watch the cattle feeding and, by comforting and cradling her in her distress, makes her his child.

Tom's assumption of the role of father to Anna, like Lydia's moving into the Marsh, are shown, contrary to expectation, as liberating rather than confining actions. Because performed in love and trust—not according to duty or presumption—they become the visible signs of an expanded life in marriage. When, after two years, Tom shows signs of feeling confined, Lydia is able to reveal even further possibilities in their relationship. Though the external contours of this new encounter are emotional and physical, the language used to describe it is again spatial, though with a stronger religious tone than hitherto. "They had passed through the doorway in to the further space, where movement was so big, that it contained bonds and constraints and labours, and still was complete liberty. She was the doorway to him, he to her. . . . He went his way, as before, she went her way, to the rest of the world there seemed no change. But to the two of them, there was the perpetual wonder of the transfiguration . . . Anna's soul was put at peace between them . . . Her father and mother now met to the span of the heavens, and she, the child, was free to play in the space, between" (96–97).

It is important to see that memory, history, and language, like "bonds, constraints and labours," are not so much rejected by this conception of marriage as contained within the vast new space that it creates. The symbol of the arch, which pervades the novel in natural and artificial form, suggests the balance between union and detachment that

Lawrence sees as necessary in a true marriage. The bases of the arch remain forever apart while the tops tend inward and join. Marriage is not denied as a social convenience, a meshing of fortunes or families, an orderly means of procreation, a stay against solitude and insecurity, but it is also explored, perhaps for the first time in such depth, as it is experienced by the inarticulate, unhistoric self.

Lawrence, like Joyce, was deeply skeptical of philosophical idealism, yet, also like Joyce, he was drawn to the elements in human character that are universal and unchanging. Lacking Joyce's self-conscious humor, he borrows vocabularies, especially Scriptural, that do not remove his characters altogether from chronology or linear plot, from "bonds, constraints and labours," but reveal them to the reader in a new and unexpected perspective. By the time the passage above occurs in the book, the reader has encountered sufficient instances of the trivial, day-to-day life of the Brangwens to be jolted and refreshed by the language of "tranfiguration" and heavenly space. It is as though Lawrence is asking the reader to share vicariously in the rare relationship of Tom and Lydia by following the exhilarating movement of language from the finite to the infinite, to believe in the actual link by traveling the distance he creates between words.

Like Joyce, Lawrence was a novelist's novelist. He loved stories and facts. But, also like Joyce, he was a philosophical novelist who loved ideas and wanted to incorporate them into his fiction. Though it was Joyce who lectured on Defoe and Blake, Lawrence would have appreciated the polarity. Certainly, he shared Joyce's impulse to join the mundane and the mystical in a new narrative form. Their impulses may have been similar, but, little reflects their different backgrounds more than their efforts to wed metaphysics to fiction.

With his "metaphysics in Mecklenberg Street," Joyce is in the great Catholic tradition of Dante, Aquinas, and Chaucer. His interweaving of languages and systems is part of a vast comedy in which learning is elaborately and often beautifully employed to show its own futility and in which form is imposed not because it is a perfect reflection of truth but because, with all its obvious imperfections, it is all that is available to humanity to express what is beyond itself.

Lawrence is closer to the Puritan tradition of Calvin, Milton, and Bunyan, in which learning is used as a weapon to challenge the ambiguities of language and to create ever more perfect forms. If Joyce were to use the word "tranfiguration" for an experience within marriage, he would be likely to anticipate the reader's response to linguistic incongruity ironically; his treatment would not necessarily discredit ecstasy but would expose the poverty of language (at least, in the twentieth century) that tries to express it directly. Lawrence, equally aware of the linguistic problem, usually refuses to accept or play with incongruities of this kind. If religious language seems out of place with the sexual character of marriage, the fault is not with language but with conventional attitudes. Perfectly aware when they are "out of place," he flaunts words like "transfiguration," not as sophisitcated exposés of verbal inadequacy but as challenges to conscience.

Still, though he does not capitalize on it to the extent that Joyce does, Lawrence is aware of the potential for humor in juxtaposing languages of very different sorts. A mismating of words, as of people, may be a joke as disconcerting and far-reaching in its way as the comic happy matings in the novels of Jane Austen are comforting and significant. When Anna grows up and marries Tom's nephew, Will Brangwen, Tom decides to make a speech at their wedding reception. "For the first time in his life, he must spread himself wordily." Most of the party is drunk while Tom rambles on about marriage, trying to explain and define it: "A married couple makes one Angel." One of his brothers says, "It's the brandy." Another makes a joke about addition. The women begin trading stories about angels appearing in mirrors or getting stuck in noses. Finally, the talk deteriorates into sexual advice to the groom in the form of crude metaphorical banter: "When the fat's in th'fire, let it frizzle"; "This road can't be lost by a blind man."

Having followed Tom's text this far, the reader may be amused by the colorful language of the wedding guests, but he is more likely to be touched by Tom's awkward attempt to summarize in a speech what marriage means. The image of the angel is neither so foolish as the guests think nor so clear as Tom obviously wishes. The episode adds to our understanding of marriage and the androgynous character of the marital experience, but it adds even more to our comprehension of the writer's difficulty in trying, like his hero, to find the right words to define an experience that is at once public and private, common and unique, physical and spiritual, endlessly discussable and silent.

The discrepancy between Tom's sentimental speech and the crude talk of the guests is laughable, a minor incongruity. But the discrepancy between Tom's earnest analogy and the experience he is trying to describe is of major importance. Tom's "angel," like Lawrence's "rainbow" or "arch," does not "capture" the phenomenon, but one's sense of its failure to do so is a measure of the extent to which the book has convinced us that there is a reality that can only be communicated indirectly. In an imaginative imitation of Tom's rapport with Lydia, the reader can know the author's "meaning" without "understanding" what he says. Between Tom and Lydia and the Angel, between "transfiguration" and "the fat in the fire," are connections that are not altogether frivolous or illogical and still spaces in which to move, interpret, and create for ourselves meanings that Lawrence suggests but does not complete.

The laughter of the wedding guests at Tom's analogy of the angel is an ominous echo of his stepdaughter Anna's laughter at Will Brangwen in church during their first outing together. What initially appears to be the giggling fit of a young girl turns out to be a response as intuitive, inarticulate, and significant as the wordless attraction between Tom and Lydia at their first meeting. Will and Anna share a strong physical attraction, but not long after their wedding it becomes clear that there is an absence of sympathy between them, a discrepancy much wider than mere laughter seems to indicate. The problem is expressed in terms of Will's love of the Church—its music, architecture, and symbolism—which Anna cannot share and, more important, will not let him have as a mysterious portion of himself. Though Anna proves to be the stronger of the two, Will also begins by assuming too much about his wife: "He did not attach any vital importance to his life in the drafting office, or his life among men. That was just merely the margin to the text. The verity was his connexion with Anna and his connexion with the Church, his real being lay in his dark emotional experience of the Infinite, of the Absolute. And the great mysterious, illuminated capitals to the text, were his feelings with the Church"(159).

Will muddles his text by mixing his union with Anna with his attachment to the Church. Unlike Tom Brangwen's deepened experience of marriage as a "transfiguration"—Lawrence's narrated equivalent of Tom's speech about the angel—Will's religious terminology has not been earned through his wedded life. Words like "infinite" and "absolute," so often used by Lawrence in evoking the power of human passion, are almost ludicrously inappropriate to the relationship of Will and Anna because Lawrence will not let the reader forget that they are meaningless to Anna, who "could not get out of the Church the satisfaction he got" but sees everything in concrete, literal, and self-centered terms.

Unlike Tom and Lydia, Will and Anna talk and argue a good deal. They repeatedly disagree not only about the meaning of particular words and images, but about the meaning of meaning itself. Will loves to pore over old books of illuminations and religious paintings. But when Anna looks with him, she cannot share his feelings or let him have them in peace. She becomes furious at the sight of a Pietà:

"I do think they're loathsome," she cried.
"What?" he said, surprised, abstracted.

"Those bodies with slits in them . . ."

"You see, it means the Sacraments, the Bread," he said . . .

". . . It's horrible, you wallowing in your own dead body, and thinking of eating it in the Sacrament."

"You've to take it for what it means."

"It means your human body put up to be slit and killed and then worshipped—what else?"

They lapsed into silence. His soul grew angry and aloof.

"And I think that Lamb in Church," she said, "is the biggest joke in the parish—"

. . . "It might be, to those that see nothing in it," he said. "You know it's the symbol of Christ, of His innocence and sacrifice."

"Whatever it means, it's a *lamb!*" she said. "And I like lambs too much to treat them as if they had to mean something . . ."

. . . "It's because you don't know anything," he said violently, harshly. "Laugh at what you know, not at what you don't know."

"What don't I know?"

"What things mean."(161)

This could almost be a dialogue between a caricature T. S. Eliot, prim and traditional, and a caricature Lawrence, the impetuous and ignorant heretic. In fact, the dramatic context of the dialogue and the complexity with which both characters are presented shows how wrong Eliot was in depicting Lawrence as wild and untutored in comparison with the sophisticated and "orthodox" Joyce. Lawrence's detachment in presenting the argument between Will and Anna is as great as Joyce's is in the famous Christmas dinner debate in *Portrait*. The reader is not invited to side with either Will or Anna, but to perceive, through a verbal confrontation, how the distance between two people can remain barren and unbridged rather than become a fertile space arched over by trust and love.

The chapter is entitled "Anna Victrix," not simply because Anna's will is stronger than her husband's, but because both seem to see the object of marriage, rather like the settlement of an argument, or the editing of a definitive text, as fixed and final. In the debate about symbols and things, one hears Lawrence in both voices, a mind rooted in the concrete, impatient with abstraction, yet continually attracted by the mysterious and infinite potential of things. In certain moods, Lawrence would say with Anna that a lamb is only a lamb; yet in others he knows, with Will, that potent associations carry the creature and the word beyond themselves. As in a marriage, both apparently opposite acts of comprehension need each other. The true visionary must be able, again and again, to humble himself and see the demystified insignificant lamb.

Meaning, if it is to exist at all, is what fills the distance between object and subject; it is relationship, and, insofar as it occurs between living creatures, it is, by definition, ever-changing.

Lawrence's most extensive exposition of this theme appears in his discussion of law and love in an essay on Thomas Hardy, in which the phrase "artistic form" might well be replaced by "marriage." "Artistic form is a revelation of the two principles of Love and the Law in a state of conflict and yet reconciled: pure motion struggling against and yet reconciled with the Spirit: active force meeting and overcoming and yet not overcoming inertia. It is the conjunction of the two which makes form. And since the two must always meet under fresh conditions, form must always be different."[6] In Lawrence's dialectic, no one can win the argument about the lamb.

The climactic scene between Will and Anna takes place during their visit to Lincoln Cathedral. Will becomes ecstatic over the scope, the symmetry, the depth and darkness of the cathedral, but his idea of space, like his interpretation of the lamb, is utterly different from Anna's. Lawrence's language mocks neither experience. Will's satisfaction with the church is described in terms of sexual consummation: "Then again he gathered himself together, in transit, every jet of him strained and leaped, leaped clear into the darkness above, to the fecundity and the unique mystery, to the touch, the clasp, the consummation, the climax of eternity, the apex of the arch"(202). The cathedral seems to carry Will away from Anna and she is jealous. What for him is the ultimate is to her, "the ultimate confine," which gives her the "sense of being roofed in." The disagreement here is not over words but, more important for a married couple, over the sense of place. Anna "remembered that the open sky was no blue vault, no dark dome hung with many twinkling lamps, but a space where stars were wheeling in freedom"(203).

The language of Anna's reverie of freedom is as intense and lyrical in its own way as that of Will's communion with the building. Once again, it is not their distinctiveness that ultimately separates them but their inability to love one another enough to accept it. Anna maliciously breaks Will's mood by calling his attention to little carved faces in the stone and insisting that they are of a woman.

> "He knew her, the man who carved her," said Anna.
> "I'm sure she was his wife" . . .
> "It's a man's face, no woman's at all—a monk's—clean shaven," he said . . .
> "You hate to think he put his wife in your cathedral, don't you?" she mocked, with a tinkle of profane laughter.
> And she laughed with malicious triumph.(204–205)

What began as girlish giggling at her young man in church turns into a wife's mockery. Anna's laughter and Will's petulance are gestures of repudiation and refusal, not of ignorance or incomprehension. It is because she knows what he is experiencing in the cathedral without wanting to share or allow it that her interruption is so well calculated to destroy his pleasure. From the beginning, Will and Anna know much more about one another than Tom and Lydia, and they talk a great deal more. But their knowledge and words have no power whatever to soften their wills or bring them together. What Tom calls "the logic of the soul" is missing. Their conversations are no improvement on the silences of Tom and Lydia; even their arguments are not exchanges of ideas so much as statements of fixed positions. The debate over whether the carved head is a man or a woman is their perverse and articulate variation on Tom's halting description at their wedding feast of an angel as "the soul of a man and woman in one."

Will and Anna stay together; their physical passion even increases, but their souls remain separate and their discourse hollow. In a summary of Will's defeat, Lawrence observes that "he had failed to become really articulate, failed to find real expression." Thus the collapse of his marriage is seen to result in a failure of language, understood in the broadest sense as the means by which a person establishes relationship between the self and the world. Unlike Tom, Will sees no "calm relationship" in things. His carvings remain incomplete, his drafting becomes mechanical, his talk with his wife is reduced to faltering quarrels, even his bond with Ursula, the daughter who most loves him, is blighted.

Ursula Brangwen is damaged by the incompleteness of her parents' marriage. Her lack of confidence in herself and her ambivalent feelings about love, though "modern" in expression, are treated by Lawrence as a curse visited on the child because of the sins of the parents. In one episode Ursula and her lover are strolling by a river and talking. Their talk is even more argumentative than Will's and Anna's. It is also more repetitious, almost ritualistic in its rigid stylization. It is talk so filled with irony that definitions are disputed as a matter of course. A word uttered by one partner is repeated by the other in an utterly different tone and tossed back. The effect of the repetitions is the reverse of that of the euphonic word linkings in the night passage following Tom's proposal to Lydia, in which subtle, unexpected harmonies are discovered to exist in the midst of apparent chaos. With Ursula and Skrebensky, the surface order of two lovers walking arm in arm, engaged in seemingly calm and rational discourse, is in fact a chaos of noncommunication, the prevention of meaning.

An extraordinary parody of a human exchange ends in the repetition of the word "nothing," which sums up its meaning: " 'It seems to me,' she answered, 'as if you weren't anybody . . . You seem like nothing to me' "(311). Each speaker negates the other by using language as a hard surface. For Skrebensky it is a protective shield; for Ursula, a mirror of ridicule with which she tries to expose her lover's folly and conceal herself. The tone of the dialogue makes it seem part of a dead ceremony, and, in fact, it follows the celebration of a family wedding. Ursula is dressed in white, and bits of confetti are still in her hair. As the two walk away from the family party to stroll along the river, they appear to be rehearsing for their own wedding, but the rehearsal, like the exchange of words, is the sharp antithesis of communion.

The only genuine exchange occurs when Ursula boards a dirty river barge and offers her name to the infant daughter of the bargeman and his wife. The couple have been quarreling and are delighted with the beautiful lady's exotic name. They accept the offer, and Ursula gives the child her necklace as a token of the occasion. The bargeman watches Ursula, who is radiant and "white as a moth," "as if she were a strange being, as if she lit up his face." Once again, the image of an angel suggests itself. Ursula has appeared like a guardian angel to these poor and grimy people, given their daughter a mysterious name with a precious token, and disappeared with a smile.

The scene has a kind of charm, largely because of the spontaneous warmth and gratitude of the couple, especially the husband. But on Ursula's side, it rings false. Her "angelic" gesture is a whim to spite Skrebensky as much as to indulge her own sentimentality. Ursula appears to be acting out an unconscious wish for marriage without a husband and childbirth without a father. Giving away her name and necklace to the infant simply adds a spurious baptism to a false marriage. To call the strangers' child Ursula is another form of repetition, an extension of the conversation with Skrebensky, in which the self is asserted and reasserted with reference to no one with whom a relationship can be formed. There is no doubt that for Ursula the key to the infant's appeal is the fact that she will never see her again.

Given the scenes in the Marsh between Tom and Lydia and in Lincoln Cathedral between Anna and Will, the treatment of space in the section that focuses on Ursula and Skrebensky is telling. One of Ursula's pronouncements while walking with Skrebensky is, "I hate houses that never go away, and people just living in the houses." It seems an idle and passing remark until later, when it becomes clear that Lawrence is going to carry the logic of this kind of talk, as well as the complementary structures of his narrative, to an extreme conclusion. At first the reader takes it as a sign of Ursula's "advanced" ideas as well as a "sign of the times" that she and Skrebensky make love before discussing marriage. But soon it becomes clear that Ursula's preference for love in the woods is not a wholesome sign of liberation, but a hysterical attempt to dissociate love from society so completely that it is not merely marriage, home, and family she is fleeing but the presence of any company at all, including that of a lover.

Acts of individual rebellion can appear as remote from life as automatic collective rituals. If law without love is rigid and sterile, love without law is the chaotic lurching of will running wild. A reader who, with Joyce, thinks of Lawrence as continually defending "nudity in the woods" may be surprised by his ability to show it as a laughable, almost insane form of a childish and willful autoeroticism. While they are guests in the country, Ursula is forever leading Skrebensky on long night excursions on the downs. "Skrebensky wandered dazed, not knowing where he was or what he was doing with her . . . She would not love him in a house any more. She said she hated houses, and particularly she hated beds"(464).

Lawrence goes on to describe a midsummer evening that for other pairs of his lovers might be a perfect and glamorous setting. But for Ursula and Skrebensky the mood is strange, forlorn, obsessive. "She took off her clothes, and made him take off all his, and they ran over the smooth, moonless turf . . . And then suddenly she started back, running swiftly. He was there, beside her, but only on sufferance. He was a screen for her fears. He served her. She took him, she clasped him, clenched him close, but her eyes were open looking at the stars, it was as if the stars were lying with her and entering the unfathomable darkness of her womb . . . It was not him"(465).

Ursula's space, far from being shared with Skrebensky as Tom's and Lydia's was shared, is gained at his expense. The more she expands, the more he contracts, until he is "clasped" and "clenched" into something that occupies no space. He becomes what she has called him from the start, nothing, "not him." He is, for her, a soulless accomplice in her "intercourse" with the stars, which is really to say that he is an accomplice to her illusion, since the unspoken but right word for her act is masturbation. She is not entering the night, but rather imagining that it is entering her through his body. The sexual drama could hardly be more different from the comparatively innocent outdoor love scenes in *Lady Chatterley's Lover* or *Women in Love*. Indeed, it might be more accurate to say that there is no sexual drama at all, but merely an erotic monologue.

The final love-making scene between Ursula and Skrebensky takes place on a beach. It is one of the few episodes in which the narration takes Skrebensky's feelings into account. Through much of Ursula's text, he is depicted as a forerunner of Gerald Crich, attractive and virile, but a kind of hollow machine that behaves and speaks automatically. Ursula's frustrated petulance and even her narcissicism seem understandable, given this view of Skrebensky. But when she refuses to marry him and he breaks down and weeps, the reader, if not Ursula, begins to see him as something other than a tin soldier. The coming together on the beach is a test he is destined to fail. It is described primarily as he experiences it; Ursula's hunger for freedom and space are translated into confinement, suffocation, and death for him. "She seized hold of his arm, held him fast, as if captive, and walked him a little way by the edge of the dazzling, dazing water . . . she clinched hold of him . . . she fastened her arms around him and tightened him in her grip . . . He knew what she wanted . . . He felt as if the ordeal of proof was upon him . . . He came direct to her, without preliminaries. She held him pinned down at the chest . . . it was agony to his soul . . . he only wanted to be buried . . . He felt as if the knife were being pushed into his already dead body"(480)

Ursula, too, seems dead, her "rigid face like metal in the moonlight," her eyes "fixed" and "unseeing." Skrebensky wanders away from her along the beach and finally curls "in the deepest darkness he could find, under the sea-grass, and lay there without consciousness." The confinements of bed, house, and marriage have been avoided, leaving two experienced bodies with virgin souls dead on the strand.

As in the short stories about marriage in which the wife's narration is ignored until a moment of crisis, this is a case of catastrophically uninterpolated texts. The reader is presented primarily with Ursula's version of things and, only when it is too late, is forced to see that Skrebensky might have told the story differently. But it does not really matter. Each wished to impose will and words on the other. It is as though an author, through a trick of rhetorical coercion, tried to be his own reader in order to ensure that his writing would be interpreted only *his* way. Lawrence, despite his own overactive will, saw the calamitous futility of such an ambition. He saw that it was the surest way to kill a book as well as a marriage. The "resemblance is not fortuitous," as Frank Kermode has observed. "A novel might resemble a Lawrentian marriage . . . since they are both types of the living universe."[7]

Anna wanted to turn everything into nature, to demythologize the lamb. Her daughter wants only spirit. But after much suffering and disappointment, the sky-entranced Ursula realizes that "the rainbow stood on the earth." For Lawrence, the angel, the lamb, and the Gothic arch lose vitality and mystery if bound too rigidly to the earth, but they become impotent and lifeless if allowed to float detached in the ether. Space is a given in creation, yet the recognition and filling of it, the mediation between poles, is an essential act of human comprehension, a reverential engagement in life that imitates what Saint Paul refers to as Christ's saving act of "reconciling in himself the heights and the depths." The mating of man and woman has a potentially sacramental, even divine, meaning for Lawrence, since for him, as for Tom Brangwen, it is not within the power of man or woman to enact the reconciliation alone.

Like the silences and gaps between words, space can either separate or unite people. After their final embrace on the beach, Skrebensky literally drags himself away from Ursula and wanders down to the water's edge. At the novel's end, he is in India and she in England. His telegram, "I am married," uses words to express the social as well as the spiritual and geographical distance between them. In the most important sense, they have never really touched one another. Their physical separation at the end is simply the dramatic embodiment of the emptiness that has always existed. In the end, they are "finished" with one another because all along they have both been fixed and finished characters with no capacity to bend or grow.

Their situation provides a striking contrast with that of Ursula's grandparents. As Tom Brangwen tries to prepare himself for Anna's wedding, he is startled to realize how "unsure," "unfixed," "unfinished," "unformed," he feels as a married man of forty-five. But as Lawrence has him realize, that is precisely the clue to his success as a man and husband. "He might be getting married over again—he and his wife. He felt himself tiny, a little, upright figure on a plain circled round with the immense, roaring sky: he and his wife, two little, upright figures walking across this plain, whilst the heavens shimmered and roared about them. When did one come to an end? In which direction was it finished? There was no end, no finish, only this roaring vast space. Did one never get old, never die? That was the clue. He exulted strangely, with torture. He would go on with his wife, he and she like two children camping on the plains"(135).

Not only does Tom continually relive his own uncertain betrothal, but his words call the reader back to the legendary beginnings of the human race. The echo of the last lines of *Paradise Lost* is unmistakable:

> In either hand the hastening angel caught
> Our lingering parents, and to th' eastern gate
> Led them direct, and down the cliff as fast

To the subjected plain; then disappeared.
They, looking back, all th' eastern side beheld
Of Paradise, so late their happy seat,
Waved over by that flaming brand; the gate
With dreadful faces thronged and fiery arms.
Some natural tears they dropped, but wiped them soon;
The world was all before them, where to choose
Their place of rest, and Providence their guide.
They, hand in hand, with wandering steps and slow,
Through Eden took their solitary way.

The Miltonic picture of man and woman, abandoned together on a vast plain, as Matthew Arnold recalled, is one of danger and desolation. But it is one of enormous scope and promise as well, the end of one story but the beginning of innumerable others. The archetypal husband and wife are vulnerable, interdependent, more like children than gods. Their union is hardly a sign of the triumph of the individual will, a finished life, or a conclusive plot. Rather, it is the opposite: a reminder of limitation, of the insufficiency of self, the uncertainty of the future and of the earth waiting like a great blank page to be written on by "wandering steps and slow."

V IRGINIA WOOLF may not have had Richardson's heroine in mind when she named the protagonist of *Mrs. Dalloway* Clarissa, but the coincidence underlines the contrasting significance of the two titles. It is not merely that one novel deals with the life of an unmarried woman and the other with that of one who is married. Both titles are responses to a literary convention as well as indications of the marital status of their heroines. Richardson, seeming to follow the tradition of popular romance in using his heroine's first name for his title, produced a work that overturned some of the most hallowed premises of that tradition. The narrative does not lead to a happy marriage or any kind of marriage; the conventionally poetic name does not belong to a simple, agreeable character blandly indistinguishable from others of her social class; finally, the first name standing alone goes beyond prettiness to symbolize the character's break with her family, her separation from society, and the impossibility of a respectable marriage. A modern reader can still take *Clarissa* seriously partly because the heroine's struggle to preserve her chastity becomes a matter less and less of saving family honor (the family name) than of saving her own integrity and identity. In the long course of the novel, she is reduced to being just Clarissa, but then proves to the astonishment of almost everyone that, deprived of all the usual ties and associations, it is a name with an indestructible content of its own.

Whether or not she was thinking of *Clarissa,* Woolf was certainly aware of the conventions governing the titles of novels of English domestic life. While novels with male protagonists ordinarily included both first and family names—*Joseph Andrews, Roderick Random, Tristram Shandy, Guy Mannering, David Copperfield, Henry Esmond, Phineas Finn*—titles of novels with female protagonists—*Amelia, Pamela, Evelina, Emma, Shirley, Romola*—often stopped with first names because one of the primary assumptions of the form was that the last name would change. The symbolism suggests that the unmarried male character, however imperfect morally, represents the stability and completeness of society, while the unmarried female character, however perfect morally, is somehow unstable and incomplete and must find her fulfillment in union with a husband. Unlike a son, the daughter seems only to have borrowed her father's name until the time comes to exchange it for that of another man. By calling her novel *Mrs. Dalloway,* Woolf breaks an old tradition and advertizes the fact that the exchange has already taken place. Like Joyce and Lawrence, she has little interest in presenting marriage as a final solution to life or as a convenient stopping point for narrative fiction.[8]

Far from having given Clarissa Dalloway a settled identity, marriage seems, over the years, to have contributed to her sense of nonbeing. "But often now this body she wore ... this body, with all its capacities, seemed nothing—nothing at all. She had the oddest sense of being herself invisible; unseen; unknown; there being no more marrying, no more having of children now, but only this astonishing and rather solemn progress with the rest of them, up Bond Street, this being Mrs. Dalloway; not even Clarissa any more; this being Mrs. Richard Dalloway"(14).

At the novel's beginning, Clarissa Dalloway has obviously already given up something of the separate integrity that Clarissa Harlowe fights to retain. Yet the Dalloways' marriage, while not ecstatic, is not depicted as oppressive or unhappy. Richard Dalloway is not shown to be a particularly interesting husband, but he is not possessive enough to keep Clarissa from doing largely as she pleases and leading an interior life separate from his own. As in the case of Bloom and Molly, the Dalloways are seen more often apart than together; this permits the reader to trace in their interior monologues their movements back and forth between separation and mutual involvement. What the modern Clarissa faces is not a choice between marriage and an honorable death but the task of discovering life between the poles of individual separateness and relationship with others.

Woolf's protagonist alternates between concentrating so intensely on herself that she loses sight of her surroundings and emptying herself so completely in the lives of others that she loses sight of herself. While looking at her face in her bedroom mirror, she compares herself with a diamond, sharp, concentrated, and hard. But at other moments, she thinks of herself as a mist mingling in the branches of other lives. In her ordinary day, she experiences countless minor births and deaths, marriages and divorces. Though she may feel herself to be a part of the general and "rather solemn progress" up Bond Street, the plot of her own life and day is not one of progression but of movement back and forth between isolation and relationship, the diamond and the mist, Clarissa and Mrs. Dalloway.

The "solemn progress" describes not Clarissa's actions or thoughts but the background or context within which they occur. Just as images of space—the vast plains, the "roaring" skies, the Gothic arches, the rainbow—dominate Lawrence's novel of marriage, images of time dominate Woolf's. Recollections of the past—missed opportunities, momentary joys, unbearable losses—are juxtaposed with Clarissa's plans for her party and the anxiety of Septimus and Rezia for their future. Throughout it all, Big Ben tolls the hours in a constant reminder that time is running out with equal speed and inevitability for them all.

Lawrence's imagery suggests that marriage is a sign of man's essential connection with the earth and his best means of affirming and sustaining that connection. A good marriage is a sacrament, an embodiment of a power greater than the individual, because it imitates the active resolution of natural discord and the creation of new life. Marriage has no such significance for Woolf because for her human life seems to have no sustainable relationship with earth. All connections, good and bad, are continually diminished and destroyed by the passage of time. Marriage, like all other forms of human ordering, is an expression of a fond wish with little firm basis in reality. Insofar as it has its source in the human will and imagination, it is genuine; but insofar as it presumes a field of stability and permanence outside itself, it is an illusion. Yet since absolute isolation, like absolute intermingling, is a form of death, marriage, like much else in life, is a willed compromise, a constructed form in constant need of alteration and reshaping—not so different from Peter Walsh's adventures, Richard's committees, Rezia's hats, and Clarissa's parties.

These are all forms of communication, languages through which the self is recreated by a process of objective simplification and projection.

Whatever effectiveness such languages have, whatever meaning is shaped, flows between poles of no meaning. On one side, there is a conventionality so extreme that it goes beyond its function as conveyer of meaning and becomes its own content; on the other is an unconventionality so extreme that it loses all contact with recognizable networks of communication. One is a language so excessively "for others" as to be incapable of referring intelligibly to the particularity of the speaker; the other is one so excessively "for the self" as to be incapable of referring intelligibly to others.

As a novel about marriage and other forms of communication, *Mrs. Dalloway* explores the movements of life and partial meaning snatched from the shifting field between these two dead poles. The altogether "conventional" Mrs. Dalloway and the mad Septimus Smith feel the attractions of these opposite poles so keenly that they meet (without having seen one another or spoken) in the common experience of death in life. Like Bloom and Dedalus on another level, they are, by all the usual standards of society and realistic fiction, a hopelessly incongruous, unrelated pair. Yet without the intervention of Dickensian coincidence or secret blood ties, a kinship deeper than words and stronger than social classification is shown to exist between them. Though Clarissa survives it and Septimus does not, both are harrowed by a private, incomprehensible, and incommunicable mixture of pain and joy that is derived from human contact but, at the same time, makes further human contact seem impossible.

The primary difference between them is not sex or class, but time. Septimus's incommunicable experience is the love and sudden loss of a friend in the war, a quick and violent collision of attachment and detachment that he cannot understand, put in order for himself, or arrange into words and actions presentable to others. His madness takes the form of trying over and over to convey a message: "the supreme secret must be told," "I must tell the whole world," "the message hidden in the beauty of words," "the secret signal." In fact, except for a series of disconnected declarations, Septimus can tell nothing. When his wife, Rezia, asks him the time, he promises to tell her but cannot because his own time has been stopped by the death of his friend, whose uniformed ghost summons him to a world without time. " 'I will tell you the time,' said Septimus, very slowly, very drowsily, smiling mysteriously. As he sat smiling at the dead man in the grey suit the quarter struck—the quarter to twelve"(106).

In sharp contrast with Septimus, Clarissa has led a life without catastrophe, need, or passion. Her feelings for her husband are, from the very first, affectionate rather than intense. There is a reticence, a coolness that she regrets but cannot seem to help. Even her adolescent infatuation with Sally Seton was marked by restraint and timidity on her part. The return of Peter Walsh, a former suitor, fills her with nostalgia and wistful memories of the past, but she is not sorry she refused to marry him. Yet, like Septimus, Clarissa tastes and smells and feels death, the end of time, not in a split second at the bursting of a shell, but gradually narrowing her existence, reducing her possibilities, and shaping her interior life so that she, too, begins reading and interpreting signs in ways that cannot easily be explained to others.

Soon after Septimus is seen trying to decipher sky-writing, Clarissa returns home, reads a simple message to her husband on the telephone pad (an invitation to lunch with Lady Bruton), and translates the words into a confusion of emotions and thoughts that are consistent enough with her inner life but would appear nearly as insane as the ravings of Septimus if spoken: ". . . as a plant on the river-bed feels the shock of a passing oar and shivers: so she rocked: so she shivered . . . No vulgar jealousy could separate her from Richard. But she feared time itself, and read on Lady Bruton's face, as if it had been a dial cut in impassive stone, the dwindling of life; how year by year her share was sliced; how little the margin that remained was capable any longer of stretching"(44).

Woolf's technique of third-person narrated monologue suits the situation perfectly. Since communication is one of the major subjects of the book, as well as one of the difficulties for the characters, it is appropriate that Clarissa's inner reactions be approximated by the author rather than imitated literally in what Woolf called the "ventriloquist" style. It is not necessary that the images of the "river-bed" or the "impassive stone" be articulated by Clarissa to herself, as happens in many of the interior monologues in *Ulysses*. The narration is a rendering not of what the character might just as well say for herself, but precisely of what the character experiences but cannot say. Woolf obviously would not agree with Wittgenstein that one can only experience what can be said. If Clarissa has, like Septimus and Bloom, a touch of the poet, it is not revealed in her choice of words, which is as conventional as her choice of husband, furniture, and friends, but in the depth and honesty of an inner life that qualifies and refines those commonplace choices.

Throughout the day, as Clarissa shops, receives Peter Walsh, speaks with her husband and daughter, and prepares for her party—all ordinary outgoing activities—she returns again and again to a private self that seems to have almost nothing to do with these routine gestures. In her life, there is a spare moral reality (reminiscent of *Everyman* without the Christian theology) of a journey that must be taken unaccompanied, a passage through which husbands, friends, servants, silver, and fine pictures cannot come. This experience does not occur for Clarissa at the end of life, but episodically throughout life in rhythmic alternation with ordinary daily activity. Again, there is no doubt that the awareness is Clarissa's, even though the highly imagistic verbalization of it is Woolf's. "Like a nun withdrawing, or a child exploring a tower, she went upstairs . . . There was an emptiness about the heart of life; an attic room . . . The sheets were clean, tight stretched . . . Narrower and narrower would her bed be. The candle was half burnt down and she had read deep in Baron Marbot's *Memoirs*" (45–46).

When Clarissa's awareness of the continuous juxtaposition of life and death, attachment and detachment, is expressed in thoughts and words of her own, a certain meaning is abstractly conveyed, but it is so barren of nuance and particularity that the reader experiences a linguistic frigidity that nearly kills what it captures. For example, when Richard brings her roses after lunch, she explains his awkward formality to herself in words consistent with her reputation for prim aloofness: "And there is a dignity in people; a solitude; even between husband and wife a gulf; and that one must respect, thought Clarissa, watching him open the door; for one would not part with it oneself, or take it, against his will, from one's husband, without losing one's independence, one's self-respect—something, after all, is priceless"(181).

Put in this way, the subject nearly goes dead; suddenly it seems dry and tedious, a dull justification for an upper-middle-class marriage of convenience. That is certainly the way Peter Walsh sees it, and there are indications that Clarissa herself entertains similar suspicions. But a particular grouping of words or thoughts does not settle matters any more firmly than marriage itself does. The effort to communicate is identical with the effort to live. Both are subject to prolonged spells of incoherence and vacuity; both are capable of sudden unexpected successes.

The reader is able to believe that Clarissa and Richard's marriage is more than empty formality not so much because of what Clarissa says to Richard (they talk about the party, their daughter's friend, Miss Kilman, and his committees), or what they are shown doing together (he gives her flowers and holds her hand), but because of her genius for sympathetic identification. She is like a mute poet, capable of sending herself into another body and then returning to her own, filled with understanding, sorrow, and a kind of love beyond words and action.

The process may produce a descriptive lyricism of sorts, but the poetic text is Woolf's, not Clarissa's. Her attempts to generalize about the old woman at the window of the opposite house are as barren as her thoughts about the dignity of marriage. Clarissa's remarkable gift is not her ability to reflect on the old lady or speak of her (which she never does) but in her being able to *see* her and imaginatively *be* with her. "How extraordinary it was, strange, yes, touching, to see the old lady . . . move away from the window . . . Clarissa tried to follow her as she turned and disappeared and could still just see her white cap . . . that old lady, she meant, whom she could see going from chest of drawers to dressing-table. She could still see her. And the supreme mystery . . . was simply this: here was one room; there was another"(193).

Clarissa, who is hostile to and ignorant of religion, politics, and philosophy, cuts across these categories to be momentarily with the old woman in her solitude. It is an imaginative leap without apparent meaning or practical issue. "Here was one room; there was another" is so baldly concrete and unanalytical a statement as to defy coherent systems—like Miss Kilman's religion or Sir William Bradshaw's psychology—that presume causation and comprehensive meanings. It reflects a view of life in which there is much to be experienced and little to be said or done. To imagine that Clarissa would rush out of her room and embrace the old woman, offer her money, reform her life, cure her lumbago, discover her to be a long-lost grandmother, or hire her as a laundress is not merely to conjure up Victorian plots but to be reminded of the fictions of a lost world, in which networks of meaning had validity only insofar as they could be translated into action.

In most nineteenth-century novels, despite varieties of viewpoint, there was a fundamental text, provided by the author and apparent to the reader, which it was the task of the good characters to discover and harmonize with their own text. Through the tolling of Big Ben, the selection of characters, and the preparation for the party, Woolf provides the outlines of a single text, but she does not offer a ground against which all else is to be judged and understood. The realization that there is no "ground," no given or permanent sense or structure, is Clarissa's peculiar weakness and gift. Of all the characters, she and Septimus are the only ones who have not found a single coherent and recognizable language through which to express themselves. Throughout the day, she comes in and out of focus (for herself as well as the reader), dissolves and materializes, lapses into dull conventionality, and bursts into exquisite originality. She needs a narrator as she needs a husband, friends, a household, to provide her with semblances of structure, but she does not mistake those structures for her soul. In her virginal aloofness, she is not simply a woman with a sexual problem, but a person, like all others, who is not capable of being totally possessed by words, ideas, or people. Her great gift is her recognition of this fact about herself and about Richard, the old woman, and Septimus. The secret and paradox of her attractiveness is that she can share, with an intimacy beyond touch and sound, her acquaintance with the solitude of human nature.

Contact with Clarissa can bring about a momentary release from the carefully composed languages and systems of thought and behavior that most of the other characters use to protect themselves from solitude. Peter Walsh bursts into tears in the midst of his excited talk about himself and his plans, not because of anything Clarissa has said or done but because he is mysteriously moved by her presence. When he leaves Clarissa and follows a pretty girl on the street, he has a momentary revelation as the girl disappears and Clarissa's voice comes back to him. "Well, I've had my fun . . . And it was smashed to atoms—his fun, for it was half made up, as he knew very well; invented, this escapade with the girl; made up, as one makes up the better part of life, he thought—making oneself up"(81). But when Walsh wanders toward Regents Park, he resumes his old habit of "making up" his life as he narrates to himself the story of Clarissa's refusal of his proposal of marriage and her courtship with Richard. By letting Walsh tell this part of the story in a comic-melodramatic mode reminiscent of Wilde or Shaw, Woolf gives the reader another illustration of the gulf between things ("here was one room; there was another"). The more conventionally "dramatic" the language, the less convinced we are of the sequence, emphasis, and causation it imposes on events: "For of course it was that afternoon, that very afternoon, that Dalloway had come over . . . that was the beginning of it all"(92).

Walsh's recollection of his proposal to Clarissa is like the reconstruction of the setting for a play. He recalls his urgent note to Clarissa asking her to meet him by a fountain "far from the house, with shrubs and trees all around it." He thinks of the moment as "the final scene, the terrible scene which he believed had mattered more than anything in the whole of his life." Even Walsh realizes that this is all an "exaggeration," but it is his habitual way of giving form to his experience. Moreover, it is the only sustained account Woolf gives of the events leading up to Clarissa's marriage to Dalloway. Though we may resist Walsh's theatricality, we have no firmer textual ground on which to base our understanding. "Terrible scenes" and "marriages of convenience" are unsatisfactory labels for rejected proposals and imperfect relationships; if we can see beyond them, however, it is not to a perfect language or a perfect love, but to the desolation that makes even foolish talk tolerable.

Richard Dalloway, member of Parliament and of a number of committees, has also developed a language through which his thoughts and actions are predictably and safely channeled. If anything, it is a language even more limited than Walsh's, the language of the public man, composed of sporting phrases ("Really it was a miracle thinking of the war, and thousands of poor chaps, with all their lives before them, shov-elled together"), vague judgments ("our detestable social system and so forth"), good-natured clichés ("you can't deny it a certain dignity"), and sentimental generalizations ("it was a great age in which to have lived"). As he walks home to present Clarissa with a bunch of roses, Richard thinks about how he would like to tell her "in so many words" how he loves her, but when the time arrives the words refuse to come: "(But he could not bring himself to say he loved her; not in so many words.)"

The communication, nonetheless, is achieved. Clarissa understands his meaning, and though they speak of commonplace things, it is as if silent vows have been repeated and the marriage made again. In fact, what happens between them is analagous to what happens between au-thor and reader. It is a collaboration and completion that requires a text but does not end with it. Since the book itself holds together only insofar as the reader is able to "read between the lines" of the various speeches and interior texts, one is prepared to believe that Clarissa has inter-preted Richard's meaning correctly even if he has not articulated it "in so many words." The bouquet, the polite words and gestures are the oc-casions of their coming together without constraint. Neither forces the other to say or do anything in particular. Richard proffers the flowers as a sign Clarissa is free to interpret. That she reads the sign so quickly and correctly gives Richard enormous satisfaction and shows the reader the extent to which she accepts him. The episode reflects an attitude analo-gous to Sartre's view of the art of writing as an act of trust in human freedom, since it involves offering words that provide guides to meaning but cannot force a particular interpretation or guarantee interest or at-tention. The author is in the continual state of proposing, while the reader is free to accept, reject, or ignore the proposal altogether.

The marriage that parallels that of the Dalloways throughout the novel is that of Septimus Smith and Rezia, his Italian wife. In fact, al-most as soon as the reader sees them together, it becomes clear that there is no marriage, that sharing and communication are absent. Since the death of his friend Evans, time has stopped for Septimus. When his wife speaks to him, he is not there. He is like a reader who has closed the book, leaving her words unread and inert. " 'For you should see the Milan gardens,' she said aloud. But to whom? There was nobody. Her words faded. So a rocket fades. Its sparks, having grazed their way into the night, surrender to it, dark descends"(34).

Rezia tries to tell herself that she is a married woman, that she must stand by her husband and not admit to herself or to anyone else that he is mad. But their scenes together reveal moments of unbridgeable isolation. Their attempts at communication are not filled with the comic irony of Joyce or marked by violent ruptures, as in Lawrence; instead, they are desolate monologues, signs not of mismatching or impending divorce but of nonmarriage. When Septimus notices that Rezia is not wearing her wedding ring, he thinks to himself "with agony, with relief," that "their marriage was over." But as Rezia gradually admits to herself, there never was a marriage. Nothing has been broken because nothing was created between them. "It was not marriage; it was not being one's husband to look strange like that, always to be starting, laughing, sitting hour after hour silent, or clutching her and telling her to write. The table drawer was full of those writings; about war; about Shakespeare; about great discoveries; how there is no death"(212). The picture of Septimus dictating to Rezia provides an important contrast with the shared moment between Richard and Clarissa, in which so little is said and so much meant. Richard's reticence and Clarissa's (felt by both as faults in their own characters) are momentarily seen by the reader as positive qualities. Neither wishes, by uttering "so many words," to force or dictate a response from the other.

Septimus's dictation to Rezia is of course a kind of madness, but, insofar as marriage and communication are concerned, it is madness of a particularly revealing kind. Though the subjects—death, Shakespeare, and war—are much grander than those discussed by the Dalloways, they are not tokens of rapport between two people but rather the funneling of one person's random thoughts through the uninterpreting, nonparticipating vehicle of another. It is one of the many examples in the novel of words that have lost the power to communicate meaning, of a coincidental misuse of persons and language.

It is perfectly consistent with the parallelism between the relationships of words and people that, after hearing of the death of Septimus Smith, Clarissa should enter an empty room in her own house while her party is in progress and there, alone, receive a "message" from the dead man in total silence. Without dictation or prompting, Clarissa "reads" Septimus's suicide as no one else can. "A thing there was that mattered; a thing, wreathed about with chatter, defaced, obscured in her own life, let drop every day in corruption, lies, chatter. This he had preserved. Death was defiance. Death was an attempt to communicate . . . closeness drew apart; rapture faded, one was alone"(280–281).

Clarissa sees the opposite of life not in death, since it is so much a part of living, but in the denials of death in life, solitude in relationship, detachment within attachment, that are represented by Sir William Bradshaw's and Miss Kilman's denials of reality. "Forcing your soul, that was it." Having encountered a core of absolute solitude within herself,

Clarissa employs sentences and social graces as gestures of reverence and consolation toward others rather than as ends in themselves or efforts to conceal the truth by an imposition of will. Returning, as she does over and over throughout the day, to the simple, absolute fact, that "one was alone," is not for Clarissa a melancholy obsession, but the starting point for what she most vitally is, the nuances of meaning in her commonplace talk, the extraordinary revelations of beauty in her ordinary day, the moments of unexpected joy in her unremarkable marriage.

As the party and the novel draw to a close, Peter Walsh is overheard weaving together an exciting narrative once again, trying desperately to make connections between his old life and his new, to bring about coherence in the way storytellers and novelists do. "There was someone in India. He would like to tell Sally about her. He would like Sally to know her. She was married, he said. She had two small children. They must all come to Manchester, said Sally—he must promise before they left"(295).

But it is Clarissa, not at all articulate, in fact rather bad at putting things together in words, who brings about a moment of true communication. She presents herself not as part of a plot or a scene or even a sentence. She imposes no connection whatsoever. The wonder of her appearance, rather like that of the old woman at the window, does not reside so much in where she has been or where she is going, upstairs, downstairs, to India or Manchester, but that she is mysteriously, completely there. "It is Clarissa, he said. For there she was"(296). Mrs. Dalloway is still Clarissa. She is attached but not imprisoned by marriage. The relationship permits her to give (or lend) herself to others, including Peter Walsh, precisely because it does not make the claims on her freedom that Miss Kilman's un-Christian religion and Dr. Bradshaw's pragmatic psychology do.

One does not see Clarissa's intense empathy for Septimus or her magnetic appeal to Peter Walsh as "infidelities" to Richard, partly because such heavy stress is laid on her sexual primness throughout the book and partly because the moments of sharing are not described in sensual or judgmental terms. In both cases, Clarissa cannot help herself. She is what she is. But that is the point. She has a self, apart from Richard, that responds powerfully to others and is capable of calling up responses unknown to him. Molly Bloom's Chaucerian earthiness and Leopold's wandering eye are also more than merely promiscuous; they are signs of separate vitalities, which may be psychologically and morally problematic, but for which we are nonetheless grateful. Tom and Lydia Brangwen are faithful to one another, but as their marriage becomes better, Lawrence tells us, "he went his way, as before, she went her way." Each marriage derives its character and strength not only from what is shared but from its capacity to tolerate whatever in each partner cannot be taken or given.

For Woolf, as for Joyce and Lawrence, the precondition of true espousal is the same as that for a fruitful wedding of author and reader: the acknowledgment of an ultimate core of inviolability. Far from making communication impossible, this awareness defines its limits without restricting the particularity and dignity of the individual. Whether attributed to sex, existential solitude, class, or cultural distinction, the aspects of self that are incommunicable can lead to marital and artistic despair, to a battle of the wills trying to dominate and convert, or, more happily (though not necessarily more simply), to a tentative and respectful proposal of a bond that requires constant renewal and withers without freedom.

FOUR

Between Us Is This Line

Friendship

—Alone, quite alone. You have no fear of that. And you know what that word means? Not only to be separate from all others but to have not even one friend.

—I will take the risk, said Stephen.

JAMES JOYCE, *A Portrait of the Artist as a Young Man*

Friendship should be a rare, choice, immortal thing, sacred and inviolable as marriage. Marriage and deathless friendship. . . . : two great creative passions, separate, apart, but complementary: the one pivotal, the other adventurous: the one, marriage, the center of human life; and the other, the leap ahead.

D. H. LAWRENCE, *Education of the People*

How curiously one is changed by the addition, even at a distance, of a friend.

VIRGINIA WOOLF, *The Waves*

WITHOUT THE BACKING of a strong social hierarchy or the institutional ramifications of marriage or other family ties, friendship has come to be treated in literature as the most nearly free and ambiguous of human relationships. Friendship has no doctrine or policy, no sacramental seal. It has not only been the most private and unregulated of relationships within the total social structure, but it has also been the least well defined in itself. The powerful Judeo-Christian taboo against homosexuality combined with the equally powerful Platonic idea of the mating of the "souls" of those of the same sex has tended to make friendship either an idea without substance or a content with no acceptable form.

In English, perhaps more than in any other language, friendship has no tone proper to itself. Far more than a declaration of love or a proposal of marriage, a confession of friendship is peculiarly open to misinterpretation, precisely because it has no obvious connection with anything, not even sex or money—though neither is necessarily ruled out, which is part of the problem. Nothing is ruled out except a clear and concrete demonstration of meaning, and nothing is ruled in at all.

During the Romantic period, in particular, the poet's friend often appears in the poem as a silent partner, a good listener, the eternally agreeable and cooperative companion. Indeed, despite the conversational tone of many poems by Wordsworth and Coleridge, conversation rarely occurs because the friend is absent or dissolved into the poet's ego. Coleridge's "This Lime-Tree Bower My Prison" epitomizes the literary treatment of the friend as a reassuringly impalpable presence, a blurred double, an indistinct echo. A group of the author's friends has gone on a country walk while he sits at home in his garden nursing an injured leg. One of them, the absent Lamb, to whom the poem is addressed, becomes the author's eyes, the agent through which he "sees" the view he has been prevented from seeing for himself: "and I am glad / As I myself were there!"

The poem is not simply about Lamb or even to him since his role is not stable. He undergoes a grammatical transformation from being included in third person plural ("Well, they are gone") to second person singular ("thou hast pined and hunger'd after Nature") to first, which

[133]

blends with the voice of the author ("Henceforth I shall know"). The friend has neither the immediacy of a lover nor the distant grandeur of God. He poses no threat, demands nothing, is conveniently protean. Yet he—or some idea of him—is apparently necessary to the poet and the poem. He provides focus, though not too sharply. He justifies the easy and amiable tone of much of the piece but does not prohibit the poet from wandering off into his own private thoughts. He gives the poem its shape—that of an implied conversation—but it is a shape that is neither obtrusive nor rigid.

Just as human love and religious faith are intimated more than declared, the drama of the poem is hinted at but dissolved before it is realized. The distance between the poet and his friend is eliminated. And the friend is obviously not permitted the independence to fall off a cliff or say that he finds the scenery dull. What begins as a story becomes a meditation; what appears as one side of a conversation is in fact a monologue; what almost looked like a poem about more than one person is resolved into a single lyrical note.

Friendship thus conceived and poetically employed enables a writer to appear to be coming to terms with another human being without actually doing so at all. Although the novel has always been a vehicle for dialogue and character differentiation, in much nineteenth-century fiction the relations among close friends are rarely in clearer focus than in the poetry of the period. The unassertive, patient, indistinct Dobbinses, Pockets, and Ada Clares outnumber and outlive the bold Steerforths and dangerous Miss Wades. It is not altogether surprisng, therefore, that one variation on the Modernist reaction to Romantic egotism and emotional vagueness is to let the friend come in out of the fog and speak forcefully, sometimes bluntly, for himself.

"A LITTLE CLOUD" is the story in Joyce's *Dubliners* in which the word "friend" occurs most frequently.[1] Though it is in part about disillusionment, it is also, in its very composition, a dismantling of many of the literary conventions of Romantic friendship. The protagonist, Little Chandler, a would-be poet, a sensitive, slightly dreamy man, is about to meet his old friend, Gallaher, whom he has not seen for eight years. The potential for irony is present from the beginning, but the author does not at first dissociate himself and the reader from Chandler's nostalgia for the good old days or from his eager anticipation of a reunion with a friend he once idolized. Even the title of the story, taken from 1 Kings 18:44, echoes the titles of Romantic poems about freedom, nature, and companionship. By the end, the cloud is seen as something that can cast shadows as well as wander blissfully across the sky or promise the end of drought. Still, it is important to notice that, as in conversation poems, the point of view is at first a unified one. Little Chandler's rejoicing that his friend has "become a brilliant figure on the London Press" is metaphorically mingled with the view from his office window of "the glow of a late autumn sunset" and "a shower of kindly golden dust on the untidy nurses and decrepit old men who drowsed on the benches."

When Little Chandler hurries through the streets of Dublin to meet Ignatius Gallaher, the Romantic convention of the friend who is "useful" only insofar as he is an extension of the subjective imagination begins to break down. The thought that there will be an actual encounter with the glorified Gallaher begins to disturb the reader almost as much as it does the protagonist. Whatever identification there was at the beginning between author and Chandler weakens as Chandler ceases thinking metaphorically about his friend and his city and begins to calculate rather than imagine. "He wondered whether he could write a poem to express his idea. Perhaps Gallaher might be able to get it into some London paper for him. Could he write something original?"(73).

Even as Chandler thinks these thoughts, the streets of Dublin slip away from his sentimentalizing imagination and become strange and threatening, making him "tremble like a leaf." The city and, very soon, the friend are given identities and contours of their own, which the "poetic" protagonist cannot control. The unity of author, actor, and audience, which characterizes so many Romantic friendship poems, and stories, is shown in the process of disintegrating. Indeed, when the friend whose heroic names conjure up visions of Loyola and Galahad is seen and heard, the result seems more an explosion than a disintegration. "There, sure enough, was Ignatius Gallaher leaning with his back against the counter and his feet planted far apart. 'Hallo, Tommy, old hero, here you are! What is it to be? What will you have? . . . Well, and how have you been pulling along since I saw you last? Dear God, how old we're getting! Do you see any signs of aging in me—eh, what? A little grey and thin on the top—what?' "(74–75).

Gallaher's talk gets worse and worse—that is, less and less like Chandler's pleasantly vague image, part memory, part invention. He patronizes Chandler, gossips about mutual acquaintances, and brags about his success. Thus, without explicit comment from the author, the word "friend" becomes more painfully ironic every time it is used. As the protagonist splits off from reader and author, friend splits off from friend and "friend." " 'Well, Tommy,' he said, 'I wish you and yours every joy in life, old chap, and tons of money, and may you never die till I shoot you. And that's the wish of a sincere friend, an old friend. You know that?' "(79). This vacuous speech precedes Gallaher's unfeeling refusal of Chandler's invitation to spend an evening with him and his wife. Gallaher unconsciously parodies the Arthurian Galahad by giving his *parole d'honneur* to pay them a visit the following year. Though no explicit definition of friendship is offered in the story, it is clear that the term changes—or, more precisely, loses—meaning in the course of the narrative.

Little Chandler is not supported, guided, consoled, or encouraged; he is disappointed by his friend's coarseness and humiliated by his ostentatious success. He feels lonelier than ever, and when he goes home to his drab flat and crying baby, he turns to a volume of Byron for comfort. But the screams of the child and his own irritation make reading the poetry impossible. Just as well, since the poem he had turned to was "On the Death of a Young Lady," one of Byron's earliest and crudest effusions, written at the age of fourteen in memory of his first cousin. The inflated language and forced rhymes, which do little but betray the poet's confused emotional state—somewhere between puppy love and affectation—provide the last ironic blow to Little Chandler's conception of himself as poet and sentimentalist.

Little Chandler's hero is not merely a bad friend; his obvious grossness is also a sign to the reader of the radical inadequacy of Little Chandler's taste, memory, and imagination. A double pathos comes in seeing simultaneously Little Chandler's disappointment in his friend and his own hopeless unsuitability as a poet, that is, his inability to use his mind as a transforming vehicle of experience rather than as a storehouse of sentimental clichés. The story is as much about a failure of imagination as it is about a failure in friendship. The true artist, the controlling, observant, creative mind, unlike that represented in Coleridge's poem, remains outside the story.

I N *A Portrait of the Artist as a Young Man,* Stephen Dedalus prepares to leave not only his family and church, but his friends. Since the claims and therefore the faults of the first two are more familiar and extreme than those of friendship, they are easier to outline and theoretically easier to repudiate. Stephen's university friends are a mixed group, rowdy, reserved, radical, reactionary, pious, and irreverent. His relationship with most of them is affectionate and bantering, despite his self-image as one who is more formal than most young men of his age. The long section near the end of the novel in which he is seen among his classmates deals on the surface narrative level with his refusal to sign a peace petition and his subsequent rambling conversations about religion, politics, and art. But below the surface is a complex drama of friendship. Stephen's speeches are typically arrogant and didactic, but his relationship with each of his friends is different. Unlike the silent companions of the Romantic conversation poems, Stephen's friends do speak and are physically particularized. They are not blurred extensions of himself, but sharply realized characters against which his own character is shaped and expressed.

Though stubborn, independent, antisocial, Stephen feels bandied about by his friends, not because they are his intellectual superiors or even because any of them has a particularly strong personality, but simply because of their otherness. In a sense, Stephen is remade every time he encounters another schoolmate, since his effort to distinguish himself from them is limited by the particular tone, color, and shape of their natures. He appears to be locked into an inescapable bond: either he yields to the temptation of relaxing and becoming like whomever he happens to be talking to, or he sets himself in opposition. In either case, his freedom is curtailed and his identity becomes a predictable, almost mechanical, consequence of circumstances outside his control. His problem—the need to establish integrity and originality while among his contemporaries—parallels exactly a technical as well as psychological problem encountered by the artist.

The temptation of friendship, the tendency to become one with the companion, is experienced by Stephen in sensuous, even to some extent sexual, terms. There is little to suggest that he undergoes a specifically homosexual struggle; rather, his sensibility, rich and imaginative, is potentially androgynous, capable of a sympathetic understanding almost physical in character. The other side of Dedalus the fierce opponent and debator is Dedalus the passive and congenial completer of half-formed ideas and unfulfilled wishes, the artist who has no identity of his own but takes on the shape of whatever he contemplates. Stephen's defense against this tendency in himself is his conceptualizing intellect. When he feels himself sinking into the pores of another person, he rears up and attacks with an abstraction.

Davin, Lynch, and Cranly, the three friends who figure most importantly in the university section, are all, in different ways, seductive physical and emotional presences, capable of drawing Stephen out of himself and into the imagined circumference of their being. But in conversation, Stephen shows that he tries to distinguish and distance himself from his friends by typing or classifying them. He talks politics to Davin, aesthetics to Lynch, and religion to Cranly, making them emblems of abstract theories and generalized practices he wishes to oppose. By doing so, he makes them much more and much less than friends. They are not really intellectual opponents since none seems capable of carrying on a debate with Stephen's zest. Yet they are more than mere straw men. As Joyce presents them, both in dialogue with Stephen and as they appear in his imagination, they move back and forth between the insufficiently defined and the too neatly defined, the seductive uncertainty of unclassified reality and the repellant clarity of rigid allegory.

Of all Stephen's friends, the one who seems easiest to classify and establish distance from is Davin, a sturdy country boy, loyal to Irish ways, hostile to all things English, and ignorant of everything else foreign except "the foreign legion of France in which he spoke of serving." Stephen has a number of pet names for Davin, names that express a combination of affection and condescension: "Firbolg," "the young peasant," "my little tame goose." Stephen is reminded of Davin when he walks past a statue of the national poet of Ireland, Thomas Moore, whom he thinks of as a Firbolg dressed in a borrowed cloak of a Milesian. Stephen attempts to create an emblem of rural Ireland out of the features of his friend, but Joyce shows the process to be difficult, perhaps impossible.

Though Davin is no match for Stephen in political debate, he is capable of touching his friend directly in a way that upsets Stephen's schematic intentions because it has nothing to do with logic or patriotism. "—Go on, Stevie, I have a hard head, you tell me. Call me what you will ... The homely version of his christian name on the lips of his friend had touched Stephen pleasantly"(180). Stephen's nicknames may or may not have an effect on Davin's hard head, but Davin's unpremeditated "Stevie" goes directly to Stephen's heart, as does his country courtliness and quaint speech. Stephen is too attracted by Davin to be able to make a statue of him with perfect success, and he is too repelled by him to get away with the old Romantic trick of using him as a silent partner to whom he can recite self-indulgent verse without interruption.

Davin may not argue very well, but he does talk back to Stephen. In fact, he tells him a long, strange story of a walk at night through the Ballyhoura Hills, stopping by a lonely cottage for a glass of water, and being invited to spend the night by a half-dressed young woman whom he refuses and leaves standing by the door. Davin draws no moral from his story; he tells it without interpretation. Stephen is quick to generalize from it, to see the woman "as a type of her race and his own, a batlike soul waking to the consciousness of itself." His response is at once an act of imaginative collaboration with Davin, similar to that which exists between author and reader, and an act of differentiation between the two friends, in which Stephen, dissatisfied with the mysterious simplicity of a folk narrative, imposes his own abstract order on it. The pretentious intellectuality of Stephen's interpretation contrasts so sharply with the erotic, magical possibilities of the tale that it highlights the extraordinary ambition and the extreme limitations of a mind too ready to put everything in its place.

Joyce provides us with the uninterpreted story and the interpreted one much as he provides us with the strongly felt but unclearly perceived Davin of Stephen's imagination and the emblematic Irish peasant of his will. Davin submits to but also escapes Stephen's efforts to classify him; and Joyce, by letting the reader see Stephen's obvious failures as well as his partial successes, allows Stephen as a character to escape from a rigid identification with the author that would impose constraints on both.

It is appropriate—more than that, necessary—for Stephen to "get away" from Joyce, not merely to be seen making mistakes but speaking and behaving in ways that remain unexplained or at least "inconvenient" within the typical patterns of explanation of his character. A peculiar episode, in which Davin appears in an unexpected light for Stephen and Stephen for the reader, follows on a brief exchange with Dixon in the library. Dixon's genteel accent, love of Scott, and shrunken frame make Stephen wonder whether he was born of an incestuous love. Characteristically, Stephen imagines a scene, a brother and sister embracing in a park on a rainy day. But the misty vague Swinburnian reverie is curiously interrupted: "He had loose redbrown hair and tender shapely strong freckled hands. Face. There was no face seen. The brother's face was bent upon her fair rainfragrant hair. The hand freckled and strong and shapely and caressing was Davin's hand. He frowned angrily upon his thought and on the shrivelled mannikin who had called it forth . . . Why were they not Cranly's hands? Had Davin's simplicity and innocence stung him more secretly?"(228).

Stephen's question remains unanswered. Though quick to interpret Davin's strange vision, he turns from his own and approaches another group of friends. Yet Stephen's earlier thoughts about Davin and Ireland and the "batlike" woman give the reader plenty to play with. On the verge of flight, Stephen is preoccupied by Ireland's ingrown provinciality, its fear and ignorance of the outside world. Thus the picture of Davin embracing his sister in the park can be taken as one more sign of Ireland's perverse turning in on itself. Yet to insist on this as the primary meaning of the episode is to fall into precisely the kind of abstract and overly simplified conceptualization that is Stephen's most characteristic and least convincing defense against the complexity of his friends.

The image of the "strong and shapely and caressing" hand of Davin is disturbing and surprising to Stephen. It suggests that the vision itself, unlike a "reading" of it, is not entirely under his control; that he is some-how in and of the scene as well as outside of it contemplating it and won-dering what it means. Though he likes to represent himself as cool and aloof, Stephen is too susceptible a friend with much too sympathetic an imagination to detach himself without an enormous struggle. In some ways, Joyce's *Portrait* resembles Keats's first fragmentary *Hyperion:* young Dedalus is too gifted with the "old" Romantic sensitivities to become a new (modern) artist without undergoing agonizing birth pains.

The friend with whom Stephen discusses his aesthetic theory is Lynch, heavy-set, dull, and inarticulate, the most barbarous of his young associ-ates. In trying to distance himself from Davin, Stephen attempts to deny the side of himself that he sees as emotional, staunch, and tame. He is attracted as a fond brother (or sister) would be to Davin's quaint inno-cence, but he sees succumbing to it as an act of betrayal, a perversion of his "true" self, which seeks to balance dark affections with luminous judgments. Lynch is quite as unconscious as Davin, but his effect on Stephen is even more basely tempting. He does not evoke mysterious and erotic visions of Ireland; he is merely a commonplace, ordinary young man who speaks in trite phrases, whose idea of humor is adoles-cent and scatological, for whom art and theories of art can be reduced, like all else, to "flaming yellow excrement."

Stephen's efforts at turning Lynch into a respectable adversary or even a partially responsive audience for his remarks on aesthetic theory are even less successful and more ludicrous than his attempts to remake Davin into an emblem of Ireland. From the beginning, the reader sees Lynch not in opposition to Stephen's ideas but simply without interest in them. Stephen tries insulting Lynch, but fails to get out of him more than a friendly "curse" delivered in undergraduate jargon: "Damn your yellow insolence." Again, Stephen tries prodding with an insult: "It was a great day for European culture, he said, when you made up your mind to swear in yellow." But nothing penetrates Lynch, and nothing can save him from his sheer prosaic lack of interest and originality: "—Stop! I won't listen! I am sick. I was out last night on a yellow drunk with Horan and Goggins"(204).

Stephen nonetheless goes right ahead with his theories as if addressing an attentive, intelligent class of sharply critical students. In fact, what-ever criticism of his ideas there is, emerges from his own monologue, not from Lynch, who merely punctuates the "lecture" with inane remarks about writing his name in pencil on the backside of the Venus of Praxit-eles, eating cowdung as a schoolboy, and a story about "them flaming fat devils of pigs." Lynch himself is described as diabolical; "his face re-sembled a devil's mask," and "the long slender flattened skull beneath the long pointed cap brought before Stephen's mind the image of a hooded reptile." But Lynch is tempting and satanic not because he is arch, clever, or capable of challenging Stephen's ideas with notions of his own. He is the artist's despair, the inattentive audience whose mind keeps returning to pigs and excrement and mechanically repeated words one remove from a grunt. He does not oppose Stephen's ordering of things with another narrower or more mysterious order (as Davin does). Rather, he reduces words and theories to waste: "I have an excrementious intelligence."

Lynch's very presence and being ridicule and parody Stephen's attempt at philosophical seriousness. He makes dialogue impossible not because he has submissively allowed himself to be absorbed by the artist-speaker or because he tries to dominate the conversation. His cut is the lowest of all, because it is not aimed at particular words or ideas but at all words and ideas. Whatever Stephen may say or do, Lynch is living proof that he is wasting his time. Even Stephen's efforts to address him as a barbarian, to label him as an animal, can give no satisfaction since if the labels are accurate they can have no effect.

Stephen can turn away from Lynch, of course, and he eventually does. But the escape is not so simple, since Lynch obviously represents a part of him just as Davin does. That the struggle is a deeply internal one is borne out by the one really genuine exchange between the two friends: "—What do you mean, Lynch asked surlily, by prating about beauty and the imagination in this miserable God-forsaken island? No wonder the artist retired within or behind his handiwork after having perpetrated this country ... Lynch was right. [Stephen's] mind, emptied of theory and courage, lapsed back into a listless peace"(216).

Like Davin, whose rude Firbolg mind "had drawn his [Stephen's] mind towards it and flung it back again," Lynch has an almost physical effect on Stephen, first spurring him on to flights of intellectual superiority by means of his cloddishness and then using his own words mockingly against him and thereby "emptying" him of theory and courage and causing him to fall (like a suddenly lapsed Catholic) from his own doctrine.

When Stephen first thinks of Cranly, the third friend, myriad images come to his mind, a severed head like that of John the Baptist, "a priest-like face," and "dark womanish eyes." His friend's eyes remind him of a "strange dark cavern" from which he turns away because "it was not yet the hour to enter it." These images of Cranly, his "darkness" and "list-lessness," momentarily disorient Stephen so that the words written on signs and buildings around him seem "emptied" of sense and he feels that he is walking in a lane "among heaps of dead language." Apparently, without intending it, Stephen has, for a moment, entered the "dark cavern" of his friend's being; he has found himself in a mysterious world where signifiers have been detached from signification, his identity tied to no recognizable form, his name presumably swept along with the others as "his own consciousness of language was ebbing from his brain."

When Stephen is actually with Cranly, he does not allow himself to get lost in the labyrinth. His distance from his friend and his control of the situation and of himself are expressed through his peculiar awareness and manipulation of language. He refuses to speak dog Latin until his friend is out of temper, and then he uses it to taunt him. Rather than allow himself to be lulled by the warmth of good fellowship and playful language, he tries to use words not so much to express as to protect himself. His mind generalizes about "dead friendships" and the varieties of Irish dialects, and thus he temporarily escapes the emotional specificity of the encounter and the intriguing ambiguity of his friend's jealous outburst.

The last time Stephen and Cranly are shown in sustained conversation, Stephen chooses to confide to his friend the details of his religious doubts and the quarrel with his mother about his refusal to make his Easter duty. Of the many images and ideas of Cranly that drifted through his imagination earlier, Stephen chooses that of the priest-confessor, the representative of the Church, to address. He defines himself by forcing Cranly into a conventional role he can use and reject without the distraction of imprecise emotions and uncompleted thoughts. In contrast with Stephen's impulse toward clarity, Cranly speaks and behaves in an unsure and ambiguous manner, trying in a variety of ways to turn Stephen from his single-minded pursuit of the argument to recollections of familial and romantic love and the platonic love that can exist between friends. After Stephen dramatically declares that he "will not serve," Cranly tries to alter the tone if not the course of the conversation:

Cranly pressed Stephen's arm, saying:
—Go easy, my dear man. You're an excitable bloody man, do you know . . . Do you know that you are an excitable man?
—I daresay I am, said Stephen, laughing also.
Their minds, lately estranged, seemed suddenly to have been drawn closer, one to the other. (239)

As the discussion turns to the validity of the Eucharist, Cranly takes a fig from his pocket and begins to eat it. The gesture is innocent, but Stephen is offended by it and refuses to continue talking until Cranly throws away the fig. As a reader of Dante and the Elizabethans, Stephen is conscious, as Cranly evidently is not, that the fig is a crude emblem of the penis. Cranly thus unintentionally mocks the sacrament he is trying to defend, detracts from the seriousness of Stephen's mood, and calls attention to his own physical presence. The reader is once again put into a line of communication with Stephen that Cranly does not share. He can decipher the emblem and interpret Stephen's annoyance as Cranly cannot and thus can share in Stephen's growing detachment from his friend by perceiving the variety of minute ways in which their worlds do not meet.

Joyce allows Cranly enough individuality and substance for us to experience the failure of communication from his viewpoint, too. He tries to question Stephen about happiness and love, first the love of a son for his mother and then other kinds of love:

—Have you never loved anyone? Cranly asked.
—Do you mean women?
—I am not speaking of that, Cranly said in a colder tone. I ask you if you ever felt love towards anyone or anything.
Stephen walked on beside his friend, staring gloomily at the footpath.

Eventually Stephen begins lamely to talk about his youthful efforts to love God, but Cranly cuts him short and returns the conversation to Stephen's family.

The generality of Cranly's question and the quick shift in his mood, which leads him twice within the same exchange to a surprising abruptness, suggests that his question and Stephen's response (or his failure to respond) have a personal significance for him beyond the ostensible meaning of the words. Since that significance is not articulated, it may seem extreme to claim that Cranly is hoping for some declaration from Stephen about the importance of their friendship. Yet that hope, especially its suspension between probability and absurdity, gives dramatic edge to Stephen's theoretical rejection of religious doctrine. The reader is carried through more than a sequence of abstract logic; he is made to experience, first through Stephen and then through Cranly, the strain of discourse as a struggle for identity. Cranly's response to Stephen's unorthodoxy is an inarticulate appeal to love, a word that, from a friend, evokes not so much duty as a vague, "listless," dreamy condition in which definitions, principles, distinctions, and theories have no place.

The blurring of love with religious sentiment is seen not merely as a peculiarity of Cranly's but as a real temptation for Stephen. When the two friends hear a girl singing, Cranly murmurs, *"Mulier cantat,"* and immediately sends Stephen into a reverie in which the "figure of woman" and the "liturgy of the church" blend in an "enchanting" and obscure harmony of memory and the senses. But this kind of harmony, dependent for its effect on muted notes and hazy images, is not, for Stephen Dedalus, a good model for poetry or religion or friendship. When Cranly asks if Stephen considers the words of the song *Rosie O'Grady* to be poetry, Stephen deliberately rouses himself from his trance and breaks the mood: "I want to see Rosie first, said Stephen."

This blunt return to unsentimental realism signals the end of the friendship between Stephen and Cranly. Stephen looks at his friend with a detachment that balances admiration for his "large dark eyes," "handsome" face, and "strong and hard" body with criticism of his sympathy for the weakness and sufferings of women, which causes him to "bow his mind to them." That this "womanish" side of Cranly has been a real temptation for Stephen is suggested by his echoing of the opening line of the fourth stanza of Keats's "Ode to a Nightingale": "Away then: it is time to go. A voice spoke softly to Stephen's heart, bidding him go and telling him that his friendship was coming to an end. Yes; he would go. He could not strive against another. He knew his part"(245).

As in the ode, "away" can be taken both as a command to the seductive object of external address (the friend) and as an internal decision to remove himself from the painful limitations of mortality on the "viewless wings of poesy." Like Keats, Joyce saw poetry as a "solution" to the fragmentation and constraints of experience only insofar as it returns again and again to the concrete reality it seeks to reorder and transcend. The flight—its necessity and achievement—can be realized only in terms of a departure point and return. Each one of Stephen's soaring moments has its "forlorn" conclusion, which gradually becomes the starting place for the next imagined journey.

Until he has physically removed himself from Ireland, Stephen will be susceptible to the familiar attractions of his friends and nation. Even after he has told Cranly of his decision to go into exile, his friend literally retains a "hold" on him:

> Cranly seized his arm and steered him round . . .
> —Cunning indeed! he said. Is it you? You poor poet, you!
> —And you made me confess to you, Stephen said, thrilled by his touch.

The forlorn word that quickly follows is "alone," repeated by Cranly in awe of Stephen's determination and in recognition of his own loss:

—Alone, quite alone. You have no fear of that. And you know what that word means? Not only to be separate from all others but to have not even one friend.

—I will take the risk, said Stephen.

—And not to have any one person, Cranly said, who would be more than a friend, more even than the noblest the truest friend a man ever had.

His words seemed to have struck some deep chord in his own nature. Had he spoken of himself, of himself as he was or wished to be? Stephen watched his face for some moments in silence. A cold sadness was there. He had spoken of himself, of his own loneliness which he feared.

—Of whom are you speaking? Stephen asked at length. Cranly did not answer.

At last Cranly has come as close as he ever will to declaring his love for Stephen and his willingness to be "more than a friend," a perfect soulmate. But the declaration is curiously empty, not because Cranly does not "mean" it sincerely but because "meaning," as has been demonstrated throughout the exchange, is not exclusively within the control of either speaker. Cranly's final words are sad and hollow because the ideal they attempt to portray has been shown throughout the encouter to be false. Yet when Stephen's diary entries begin, immediately afterwards, the reader is struck by the even more shallow and empty effort of Stephen to "put away" his friend: "20 March: Long talk with Cranly on the subject of my revolt. He had his grand manner on. I supple and suave."

As an indication of Stephen's character, this entry can be taken either as an extraordinary sign of callousness or as a pathetic attempt to wish away a painful leave-taking. But more important than the psychology of Stephen Dedalus is Joyce's persistent and powerful ability to revive interest (even parenthetically) in an idea after having seemed to demolish it. The effect of Stephen's diary entry is to raise the question in an entirely new way. Friendship may be an impossible ideal, but how possible is Stephen Dedalus's determination to live without it?

IN JOYCE'S world every solution creates a new problem, every answer a new question, every finality the need for another beginning. Neither the artist nor the fictitious artist-hero is exempt from this condition. Stephen Dedalus's celebrated arrogance, wit, and intellectual independence do not by any means put him automatically above and beyond the world out of which he wishes to forge new shapes and meanings. As A. Walton Litz has remarked, "We see Stephen as a sterile egoist, cut off from humanity by his lonely pride; yet we also appreciate his imaginative powers, and sympathize with his plight."[2] We watch Stephen struggling for control over himself and his friends, trying vigorously to establish principles of thought and behavior, attempting to place his friends in categories that will render them consistent, predictable, and benign. He does not ultimately succeed or fail; he repeatedly succeeds and fails. He alternately loses himself in the seductive shapelessness of his friends and saves himself by imposing a pattern or shape on them and on himself that steadies and strengthens him until the next plunge.

The Daedelian artist may best imitate life not by what he says about it but in his ability to represent its recurrent movement (or the recurrent movement of the minds that perceive it) back and forth between sense and nonsense, order and confusion, control and chaos. Rhythm, for Joyce, is a matter not merely of sound but of all aspects of understanding and perception, including the visual. The eye, indeed, the mind, functions like a turning kaleidoscope that repeatedly makes and loses designs. Stephen Dedalus attempts a definition of rhythm that is characteristically pretentious, but that nonetheless signals its importance in this section of the novel: "—Rhythm, said Stephen, is the first formal esthetic relation of part to part in any esthetic whole or of an esthetic whole to its part or parts or of any part to the esthetic whole of which it is a part"(206).

It is difficult not to read this passage as Joyce mocking his hero, especially given the fact that it is said to the inattentive, lumpish Lynch. Nevertheless, it calls attention to the idea that rhythm is more than a pleasing technique, that it has an essentially relational function in artistic composition, that is is not external or static but an intrinsic, infinitely variable indicator of aesthetic integrity.

Joyce, who rarely speaks as a conventional nineteenth-century author-narrator commenting on his characters and engaging in direct address to the reader, nevertheless establishes modes of communication with the reader that are separable from those of his protagonist. Stephen may attempt a definition of rhythm, but it is Joyce who establishes the pulselike beat that gives life to his hero's designs and alternates solemnity with mockery, prose with song lyrics, obvious allegory with undecipherable dream, language as signifier and language as its own content, protagonist as hopeless prig and as surrogate artist. In other words, it is clearly Joyce who gives balance and measure to the narrative, who directs the reader's attention not so much to where Stephen is going, but to *how* he goes. It is he who provides a sense of order that does not correspond to a static geometric shape, a line or a square, but to a movement to and fro, a circulation and recirculation that never stop.

In a gesture as different from Stephen's pompous and abstract definition as it could be, Joyce provides his own commentary to the reader on rhythm. The one image that recurs in various forms throughout the episode in which Stephen encounters his school friends is that of a ball. In one sense, the continually changing image is a Joycean stunt, a verbal juggling act in which he demonstrates to the reader a control over language that almost looks like a control over things. Though it does not call attention to Joyce, the author, in any personal sense, it does call attention to his artistry and provides a counterpoint to the merely personal history of Stephen Dedalus. The ball has its story, too. Like meter in poetry, it reveals to the audience a controlling presence that affects the meaning of the composition and at the same time is independent of it.

As the ball appears and reappears with modifications throughout the episode, the reader can take it as a kind of pure punctuation, a periodic release from the density and otherwise unrelieved significance of the section. That is, he can take it as a repeated series of outlets or escapes from Stephen's history. Or he can put it to more practical use as an additional means of interpreting the narrative, special because it is not earned or argued about by Stephen but freely given by the unobtrusive author.

It has been clear throughout Stephen's dialogues with his school friends that he has been attempting to extricate himself from their affectionate but, to him, stultifying ways by means of abstraction. Paradoxically, it is the conjunction of his formal manner and habit of speculation with the comparatively formless but concrete nature of his friends and surroundings that brings about his most creative moments. Through the imagery of the ball, Joyce illustrates this point with a subtlety and wit that balance his hero's earnest attempts at willing himself into being an artist.

The first mention of the ball begins with an abstract lesson on the geometry of shape in the mathematics class. The professor's lame attempt to give concreteness to his definition by means of the line from *The Mikado* ("elliptical billiard balls") is quickly improved upon by Moynihan's joke about the cavalryman whose "balls" are "ellipsoidal," presumably from too much riding, and who because of this fancies himself particularly attractive to the ladies. That the joke is not explained in these terms but is simply a rapid-fire juxtaposition of "ellipsoid," "balls," "cavalry," and "chase me, ladies," underlines the connection between the geometric ellipse and the grammatical definition of "ellipsis." "Getting" the joke means being able to supply the missing terms. For the artist, unlike the mathematician, any form, whether ellipsoidal or something else, must also imply content—or be implied by content—in order to complete itself.

But as with the joke, if vitality is to be preserved, if meaning is not to be lost, the act of completion must be performed by the reader rather than by the artist. In this episode in *Portrait,* we witness Stephen's reaction to Moynihan's joke. He not only gets the joke—"his fellowstudent's rude humour ran like a gust through the cloister of Stephen's mind"— but a loosening of the sterile hold of the classroom enables his imagination to come alive with the liberated images of the entire faculty: "the forms of the community emerged from the gustblown vestments . . . the squat peasant form of the professor of economics, the tall form of the young professor of mental science . . . ambling and stumbling, tumbling and capering"(192). Beyond the immediate, trivial joke, the meaning for Stephen—the invigoration of the imagination through the detachment of form from familiar content and its reapplication to new raw material—has far-reaching artistic implications. He is learning and, through him, the reader learns, how formula is transformed into art.

In contrast, Cranly's references to the handball as a globe and a soul are not so much jokes as worn-out Metaphysical conceits. What were once conceived as radical revisions of old linguistic formulations are themselves subject to *rigor mortis.* At times, the effort to recover the vitality of language, like Stephen's effort to free himself from the constraints of friends and family, seems hopeless, no better than the games of handball and billards that Stephen so scrupulously avoids.

Yet if the reader sees Stephen sometimes as ridiculous, unconvinced and unconvincing, no better than the small objects his friends bounce against walls or knock into pockets, he also sees him in wonderful moments of brilliance and control. The key to his self-mastery is not in a particular symbol or metaphor but rather in his growing realization that the recurrence of gain and loss can be the very rhythm the artist embraces and absorbs into his creation rather than trying to avoid. When Stephen begins composing a villanelle, his mind turns back to the ball, which takes its significance not so much from its shape as from its capacity for movement back and forth from the breast of the priestlike artist to the heavens: "Smoke went up from the whole earth, from the vapoury oceans, smoke of her praise. The earth was like a swinging smoking swaying censer, a ball of incense, an ellipsoidal ball. The rhythm died out all at once; the cry of his heart was broken"(218).

Several times the rhythm seems to die out and the heart's cry is broken, but, in fact, the poem is completed and written down. It is a pleasant though hardly a great poem.[3] The great work is obviously *Portrait* itself, which incorporates into its own rhythm the broken cries, the incoherences out of which coherence is born, the irritating ball disappearing in an intoxicatingly beautiful "smoke of praise" and reappearing near the end as the letter "o," the vowel kissed by the "full carnal lips" of Father Ghezzi when he pronounces "risotto." It is not Joyce's way to portray his hero as the author of a perfectly "achieved" poem but rather to portray the making and unmaking of poetry, much as he shows the continual making and unmaking of a character. Friendship itself is subjected to the same rhythmic treatment, the word as word and the word as signifier, the uninterpreted, richly ambiguous experience and the selective formulation. Friendship is one of the "nets" over which Stephen wishes to fly. But even the neatness and solemnity of that metaphor do not stand unchallenged. An unexpected "Stevie" or "ellipsoidal balls" or "flaming yellow excrement" can blow through the "cloister of [his] mind" and bring Stephen and the reader back to earth, where independent flights of imagination begin and end.

In a deliberate act of sacrifice—like that of the young Ignatius leaving Loyola—Stephen eventually leaves Ireland and his friends in order to serve art. Joyce, of course, did the same. But what time and his will abbreviated, his art paradoxically prolonged: youth perenially verging on maturity, dependence striving for independence, youthful ties forever about to be broken and forever resisting. In the "progress" from the entanglements of friendship to the aloofness of art, the reality of the rejected friends remains palpable enough to embrace.

L AWRENCE, unlike Joyce, was not satisfied with catching reality on the rebound. As with other relationships, he pursued the idea of friendship directly and in the flesh. His artistic heroes do not seek to manage their friends by turning them into abstractions; they tend to the concrete, to capturing experience in the body. This approach is not necessarily simpler or more successful than Dedalus's habit of disembodying what he cannot assimilate. Ideas may fade, change, be replaced or interrupted; but bodies also undergo the transformations of time. If Dedalus needs the earth to supply him with the materials of his flights, Lawrence's heroes need the elegance of theory to give shape and coherence to the instincts of the flesh. Stephen tries to rid himself of his friends by assigning meanings to each of them. He ingeniously tries to interpret them out of existence and almost succeeds. But just as nature survives artists and texts survive readers, Stephen's friends survive Stephen. By showing us this, Joyce almost manages to convince us that he, like no other artist, can trap nature and set it free all at once.

Lawrence's heroes, no more satisfied than Stephen with the uncertain middle distance of friendship, try to eliminate the problem by trying to eliminate the distance, to unite with the friend. What is fascinating is that, like Joyce, Lawrence explores friendship in a fashion that often parallels his thinking about the relationship of an artist to his subjects, including considerations of perspective, integrity, and significance.

One of the most interesting and extensive accounts of friendship in Lawrence's fiction occurs in *The White Peacock,* which is also his only major work with a first-person narration.[4] The plot is structured in a familiar Victorian pattern, around two neighboring families in the rural Midlands, each with a marriageable son and daughter. The most obvious and frequently discussed grounds for union and conflict are class and temperament. George and Emily Saxton are the robust and handsome offspring of tenant farmers, while Cyril, the narrator, and his sister, Lettie, live in modest middle-class circumstances with their widowed mother. The main story line traces George's attraction to Lettie, his failure to overcome the shyness and inarticulateness of his class, her failure to overcome ambition and snobbery, and their unhappy marriages to partners they do not love. The mild and friendly flirtation of the narrator and George's sister, Emily, leads nowhere. In the end, Emily marries happily within her own class and the narrator remains alone.

On the surface, there is an almost Austenian symmetry of relationships amplified with Lawrence's sense of the landscape and the physical makeup of his characters. But though George's love for Lettie and her unsettled and sometimes cruel toying with his feelings make for some very good scenes, they do not stand well alone. Nor are they balanced by the tepid relationship between the narrator and Emily, or, indeed, by any other pairing in the novel except the one between the narrator and George. The friendship of the two is frequently mentioned, but its depth and intensity, and therefore the parallel pathos of its coming to nothing, are approached only indirectly.

The technical crudity with which Lawrence handles the narration of this novel is explained partly by its coming at the beginning of his career. He himself was particularly troubled by the characterization of Cyril and wrote to Blanche Jennings, "I will . . . stop up the mouth of Cyril—I will kick him out—I hate the fellow."[5] But he neither "stopped up" Cyril's mouth nor kicked him out of the story, nor did he resolve the difficulties his role created. The technical problems—the overheard conversations, the coincidental encounters, the repeated sense that the narrator is *de trop* in dramatic situations that clearly call for only two—reflect more than Lawrence's inexperience in the craft of story-telling. The confusions and inconsistencies in regard to the narrator reflect ambivalence about the author's relation to his fictitious characters and their relationships with one another.

In the first place, Lawrence could not decide whether to make the narrator a surrogate figure for himself, or the main character of the story, or both, like Paul Morel and Rupert Birkin. Insofar as the main plot holds the key to this problem, it must be said that the narrator—beyond his function as witness—plays a minor role. He does nothing of significance, he makes no choices, he drifts like a mist from scene to scene, and he appears no different and certainly no clearer at the end of the book than at the beginning. When he does call attention to himself, it is typically to lament that he has no purpose in his life, no direction, no recognizable character. He periodically cries out to nature—as if to the author who made him—to take notice of him, to rescue him from the vaporous limbo between seeing and being:

> I wished that in all the wild valley where cloud shadows were travelling like pilgrims, something would call me forth from my rooted loneliness.(151)

> I felt like a child left out of the group of my playmates . . . I wanted to be recognized by something . . . I wandering alone, felt them all, the anguish of the bracken fallen face-down in defeat, the careless dash of the birds, the sobbing of the young wind . . . I alone among them could hear the whole succession of chords.(347)

The complaint might be that of a figure in a Romantic lyric—a silhouette against a Wordsworthian horizon—begging to be put into a story, given speeches to make, characters with whom to associate, a destiny to fulfill, asking to be delivered from the heartbreaking beauty of a singular moment into a prosaic but significant continuum.

As a character, observed by the reader among the other characters, Cyril remains insignificant. Yet as a consciousness, as a projection of the authorial imagination, his significance is total, he encompasses and makes possible whatever occurs and has meaning in the narrative. The narrator's complaints about loneliness, seen in this light, are not those of an abandoned character but those of an author who realizes with pain that the artist's ambition and special privilege isolates, perhaps even alienates, him from the life he is peculiarly able to witness and render.

In discussing this phenomenon in the brilliant opening chapter of *Romantic Image,* Frank Kermode observes that Lawrence, "who certainly earned the right to understand it," perceived the ambiguous situation of the artist who "must be lonely, haunted, victimised, devoted to suffering rather than action" precisely because of the "enormous privilege" of possessing a powerful imagination.[6] Unlike many other critics, Kermode sees how this view of the artist links Lawrence with Joyce. "The artist who is vouchsafed this power to apprehend the Image—to experience that 'epiphany' which is the Joycean equivalent of Pater's 'vision'—has to pay a heavy price in suffering, to risk his immortal soul, and to be alone, 'not only to be separate from all others but to have not even one friend.' "[7]

As surrogate author, Cyril's primary task is to get on with the story of the two families, especially the relationship between George and Lettie and the sad course of their lives once they have parted ways and married. This he does with industry and care, if not originality, through the greater part of the book. But the most distinctive and therefore the most interesting aspect of his own character is not philosophical sympathy (in the tradition of George Eliot) or ironic detachment (in the tradition of Hardy)—that is, not the qualities of a good observer of other people's lives. Rather, it is his preoccupation with George, which repeatedly disrupts conventional narrative progress and threatens to stop the story altogether.

The novel opens with the narrator musing, Narcissus-like, by the side of a pond, but it is not his own form that is lovingly described—we never actually *see* him at all—but rather that of his young neighbor: "I was almost startled into the water from my perch on the alder roots by a voice saying: 'Well, what is there to look at?' My friend was a young farmer, stoutly built, brown eyed, with a naturally fair skin burned dark and freckled in patches"(13). George asks the question and answers it with his own presence. What there is to look at is himself. His appearance startles Cyril into life and speech; despite the conventional courtship plots that occupy much of the narrator's time, it is George's magnetic presence that fascinates his imagination.

Nearly all of George's appearances cause Cyril to forget his narrative responsibility and to enter into the situation with feelings of his own that he is unable to connect with the story he is supposed to be telling. The scene in which we are first shown Lettie and George together illustrates the confusion. Cyril and Emily are sitting by the window talking seriously about books when George enters and asks Lettie, who is at the piano, to "play something with a tune in it": "He had come straight from washing in the scullery . . . and he stood behind Lettie's chair unconcernedly wiping the moisture from his arms. His sleeves were rolled up to the shoulder and his shirt was opened wide at the breast. Lettie was somewhat taken aback by the sight of him standing with legs apart, dressed in dirty leggings and boots, and breeches torn at the knee, naked at the breast and arms . . . 'A tune?' she echoed, watching the swelling of his arms as he moved them, and the rise and fall of his breasts, wonderfully solid and white. Then having curiously examined the sudden meeting of the sun-hot skin with the white flesh in his throat, her eyes met his, and she turned again to the piano"(27).

The description of male beauty is not unusual in Lawrence. What is remarkable in this scene is the narrator's attribution of a response to another character when it is so clearly his own. An omniscient narrator who is everywhere and nowhere in his own story can, of course, "see" and "feel" whatever he wishes on behalf of his characters, so long as he is consistent in his discriminations. But a narrator who is a character in his own tale, who is sitting across the room in conversation with another character, inadvertently calls attention to himself *as character* when he describes with such relish and in such detail the physical charms of his sister's lover. Insofar as we think of Cyril as a figure in his own narrated scene, we can only imagine him breaking off his conversation with Emily and gaping at George. In addition to the extreme closeness of his observations, Cyril reveals that the attraction to George is as much his own as his sister's when he speaks of his breasts as "wonderfully" white and solid. However observant the brother may be of his sister's visible response—the movement of her eyes, her blushing—the word "wonderfully," since he is not omniscient, can belong only to him.

As narrator or surrogate author, Cyril expresses the part of Lawrence that organizes experience—even the private experience of love, affection, and desire—within a social and historical continuum. It is this special gift for seeing the "connectedness of things" that places him, as F. R. Leavis has so frequently asserted, in the great tradition of English moralists along with George Eliot and Hardy. But when Cyril falls to gaping, letting the story hang in suspension, he is betraying not merely the young Lawrence's reticence and inexperience as a writer, but a deep and persistent impulse in him to resist the conventions of the novel, to resist sequence and purpose and social relevance in deference to isolated moments of intense experience—possibly beautiful, but unassimilated and unusable. This tendency has its source in Romanticism, but Lawrence is most modern in his oddly stubborn refusal to accommodate these moments to moral generalization and, in some cases, to his own "primary" plots.

The White Peacock is too early and unsophisticated a work to justify the claim that Lawrence was incorporating an antinovel within its traditional frame. Yet Cyril's preoccupation with George has the effect of being an obstacle to the narration. Even after the unique character of the relationship between the two men is openly acknowledged, as it is in the chapter "A Poem of Friendship," there is nothing to be done with it, nowhere to go with it. And since their bond can lead nowhere, it seems to remain almost literally outside of the novel, a phenomenon with which not only the narrator but also the narration cannot deal.

This chapter, in which the friendship asserts itself as the main subject of interest rather than as an intrusion on another story, is set, for the most part, on an island, physically apart from the rest of the action. It is late June, and Cyril, who has been helping George in the fields, has risen early and walked down to the pond.

The two men swim together and later, while they are drying themselves, Cyril looks at and describes George's "handsome physique" with unconcealed pleasure. "He saw I had forgotten to continue my rubbing, and laughing, he took hold of me and began to rub me briskly, as if I were a child, or rather, a woman he loved and did not fear. I left myself quite limply in his hands, and, to get a better grip of me, he put his arm round me and pressed me against him, and the sweetness of the touch of our naked bodies one against the other was superb. It satisfied in some measure the vague, indecipherable yearning of my soul; and it was the same with him . . . We looked at each other with eyes of still laughter, and our love was perfect for a moment, more perfect than any love I have known since, either for man or woman"(257).

Cyril's final comment is without parallel in the novel. Nothing else that he or any of the other characters says has the emphatic, unqualified weight and certainty of that statement.[8] In a narrative that is not outwardly about the narrator at all, that in itself is remarkable. The episode is given further significance, not merely in contrast but in opposition to the main courtship plot, through the use of the richly sensuous convention of the lovers' "bower." Though the treatment of landscape is one of the most consistently successful aspects of the entire book, none of the love scenes between the heterosexual pairs is garlanded with such Spenserian luxuriance as this one is. Cyril's emphatic summary, the fantasy lushness of the natural setting, and the explicit eroticism of the two friends' naked bodies touching have no counterpart in the main plot. Still, for all its joy and honesty, the episode remains an island, a separate world, a "poem" in the midst of a novel. The moment is "perfect" and, in its perfection, complete. The experience has been represented with more forthrightness than the narrator has been capable of hitherto, though the "yearning" that is in some measure satisfied remains "indecipherable."

The chapter concludes with an escape into music and poetry: "As the day grew older, and less wistful, we forgot everything, and worked on,

singing, and sometimes I would recite him verses as we went, and sometimes I would tell him about books." Art is escapist because it provides
an alternative to the world of everyday responsibility, of brothers and
sisters, husbands and wives. Yet it is also truthful in the sense that it celebrates even if it cannot contain, decipher, or convert the shared experience of the two friends.

With George's marriage, Cyril returns to the business of narration
with few of the lapses that characterize the earlier section of the novel.
The plot takes on an almost melodramatic sharpness and pacing. A clear
moral viewpoint dominates the action. George's failure to summon up
courage and propose to Lettie at the right moment is taken as a fatal
flaw in his character, a weakness that expands with Hardyesque momentum as he turns from dissipation to dissipation, gambles, drinks,
beats his wife, loses his money, his self-respect, and, of course, his good
looks. "His arms seemed thin, and he had bellied, and was bowed and
unsightly. I remembered the morning we swam in the mill-pond."

One might simply say that the main plot—with its social and moral
patterns—has reasserted itself, that the book is finally about choices in
life, their consequences, and the consequences of vanity and indecision.
Lettie's neurotic maladjustment to marriage and high society and
George's physical and moral decomposition are the unfolding in time of
the flaws in their characters. This reading of the book, though consistent
up to a point, leaves Cyril out of the picture, despite the fact that he interrupts and participates in the story in addition to telling it.

The closing scene of the novel does not involve Lettie at all, but dwells
rather on a visit by Cyril to the sick and broken George, who has been
taken in by his sister, Emily, recently married to Tom Renshaw, a
steady, honest young farmer. Cyril coaxes the pale, self-pitying George
outdoors where they watch Tom and his younger brother, both tanned
and healthy, stacking sheaves of corn: "The two men worked in an exquisite, subtle rhythm, their white sleeves and their dark heads gleam-
ing, moving against the mild sky and the corn"(367). The scene is an
unmistakable reminder of the golden days when Cyril worked with
George in his father's fields, the summer of their island idyll and the
height of their friendship. It brings on the only cruel remark made by
Cyril in the entire narrative: "I turned to George, who was also watching, and said: 'You ought to be like that.' "

Cyril's rebuke and George's self-pitying reply—"I shall soon be out of
everybody's way"—bring together the surface plot and the subterranean
one in an extraordinary fashion. George's decline follows, with some
thread of logic, from his indecisiveness as a man, specifically from his

failure to conquer and marry Lettie. But the extreme nature of his debasement, the catastrophic quality of his collapse, and prophecy of his imminent death seem more in keeping with the nonnarrative digressions in which Cyril celebrates George's beauty.

Cyril's instrusions have, from the beginning, had the appearance of being uncontrollable and extreme in their irrelevance to the main story. His George, the perfect friend, never did belong in the main narrative any more than Cyril did as a character. Yet stories, if not idylls, must have an end. When Cyril turns, it almost seems in anger, to George and says, "You ought to be like that," it is as though the friend is berating his beloved for deserting him and returning to the world of time and change, that is, to the main plot. The severity and distaste with which George is treated at the end seem to derive from a combination of the wrath of an abandoned lover and the frustration of an author-narrator unable to incorporate his main characters—himself and his friend—into his story as well as from George's intrinsic moral flaws. The last line of the book is ostensibly about George: "He sat apart and obscure among us, like a condemned man." The metaphor of an idyllic island has been turned into one of alienation and exile. As a detached narrator of a moralistic tale, Cyril is drumming George brutally out of the story. As a character with sympathies and problems of his own, he might as well be describing himself, since insofar as the book is about friendship, the failure and isolation are his as well as George's.

I N H I S relation to Cyril, as in Cyril's relation to George, Lawrence inadvertently reveals the "penalty" imposed on the man of artistic vision. The creative act is seen to require not a selfish but a generous— even sacrificial—detachment; the artist is free to create, give independent life and order, only if he relinquishes the right of possession and subjective identification. Lawrence could not see a way to "stop up" Cyril's mouth without stopping up his own. Until he found a means of distancing himself as an artist from some of his strongest personal impulses, those impulses could not be expressed except as part of a muddle.

Women in Love is, of course, a later, much greater work than *The White Peacock*. Though in detail and execution it differs from the earlier novel, the basic structures and themes of the two books bear some interesting resemblances. Once again, the narrative is concerned with two couples simultaneously trying to understand the meaning of love and to work through to a possibility of mutual commitment; once again, one of the men is a specimen of masculine beauty who is destroyed at the end of the book; and, once again, the character whose viewpoint is most closely aligned with that of the author is deeply attracted to his male counterpart. Technically, an important difference is that Rupert Birkin does not narrate the story and though his is the perspective most consistently and elaborately shown and his vision is a major part of the narrative, they do not encompass it. The friendship between the two male characters is presented not as a flaw in the narration or the narrator but as an experience that does not lend itself to conventional novelistic treatment. If the major episodes involving Birkin and Gerald interrupt the main narrative flow, as they most certainly do, it is not, in this case, because Lawrence or his characters are uncertain or afraid of the subject, but because the relationship is being faced head-on and shown to be in violation of certain literary as well as social and moral norms.

Since Birkin and Ursula talk about getting married, their relationship can be accommodated to the narrative mode that imitates the historical chronicle. They think of themselves as having a past and a future, and even their relationship itself assumes much of its character in time; it is said to be growing, to be developing toward a state of maturity, of balance. And though, like all lovers, especially Lawrentian lovers, they unite and part with equal and recurrent passion, even their eroticism has a familiar sequential plot of preparation, foreplay, climax, and anticlimax. In short, though it may be told over and over, their love affair makes a good "story" in that it is organized and paced in a fashion as familiar and satisfying fictionally as it is physically.

Nearly everything in the book appears to participate in an accelerating movement toward "natural crisis" and a subsequent relaxation. Even the broader social patternings of the novel—Hermione's gatherings, the water party, the Bohemian huddles in London, the miners tracking to and from the pits—derive their movement from an erotic rhythm, what Lawrence calls a "pulsing, frictional to-and-fro which works up to culmination." Only the friendship between Birkin and Gerald occurs, as it were, between parentheses, in moments out of time. The four major encounters between the two friends take place in rooms sealed off from the world—in a train compartment, in Rupert's bedroom, in Gerald's study, and, finally, in the darkened hotel room that serves as a mortuary for Gerald's frozen body. Thus enclosed, the friends have only the language and conventions of the outer world with which to try to express the bond they both feel but cannot easily act out or put into words. The failure to integrate the friendship with the main plot is not a sign of moral and aesthetic uncertainty. It is not a problem with the structure of the book, but a problem with which the book concerns itself and which determines its structure as a series of rhythmic movements periodically interrupted by static parenthetical pauses.

In a letter written in 1913, Lawrence observed that "one is kept by all tradition and instinct from loving men, or a man—for it means just extinction of all the purposive influences." Birkin's harangues against "purposive" life and the world of progress are placed in contextual perspective by a narrative he does not control, but they are also reinforced by Lawrence, especially in the scenes with Gerald, as they expose the limitations of the narrative conventions by means of which the world is typically represented. The sealed-off compartments in which Birkin and Gerald meet provide alternative contexts to the outside world and a basis from which it is criticized. They also provide an alternative to and commentary on the main narrative. They are not merely digressive interludes but contrary schemas, counterstructures that call into question the validity and value of the formal conventions, the movements to and fro, the frictions and climaxes of the story of two men and two women.

Each of the major scenes between Birkin and Gerald is a partial undoing of all that has preceded it and an undermining of what follows. Meeting on a train to London, the two men sit opposite one another and discuss the need for social reform. Lawrence appears to have chosen the journey—one of the most common metaphors for the progressive narrative form—only to demonstrate its insignificance to his characters and its inappropriateness as a structuring device for their relationship. The meeting is accidental; the trip itself has no particular importance; indeed, space, time, and other passengers are ignored while the narrative concentrates wholly on the two men, locked in position, facing one another across a small table, focusing their attention with increasing intensity on one another. Gerald declares that he is a "purposive being" and seems to identify himself with the train advancing relentlessly toward London. But Birkin, earnest, moralistic, purposive in his own way, challenges Gerald's mechanical, businesslike manner. Birkin looks out the train window, not so much seeing the passing landscape as imagining its obliteration and the passing away of mankind. In his imagination he undoes the journey or, more precisely, dissolves the world in which journeys are made. Indeed, as the train draws nearer to London, Birkin begins reciting lines from Browning on the ruin of ancient civilizations, " 'Where the quiet colored end of evening smiles / Miles and miles—.' "

The two friends make perfunctory plans to meet in London and then part. Nothing dramatic has occurred between them; there has been no development or change in their relationship. Even their discussion of reform, the love of women, and mystical hatred is dispassionate. In sharp contrast with famous travel scenes in Tolstoi, Flaubert, and Dickens, this journey has provided neither the occasion nor the parallel for "progress" in their relationship. Whatever has occurred between them has not occurred as part of a linkage or transition, as a track from one place to another, or as a discernible connection from one chapter to another. If they have made contact in some fasion, it is as much despite the purpose and nature of the journey as it is despite the purpose and nature of the main narrative. What is important is that the meeting takes place neither here nor there, not that they are moving from one point to another. They encounter one another outside of the life both normally live and outside of the dramatic sequential rhythms of the main plot.

Even their dialogue—which occupies most of the chapter—does not provide an adequate form for their experience of one another, though, like other forms in the book, it defines by exclusion a realm outside itself, a silence, a margin within which one can imagine what is not actually said. Gerald is only mildly interested in what Birkin is saying; he is drawn by Birkin's words not toward their real content but toward Birkin himself. His insensitivity to Birkin's ideas is felt by Birkin as a flaw, an aspect of his unwillingness to give himself fully to his friend or to anyone. But this fault is all the more poignant because, in Lawrence's terms, Gerald's instincts are so good. His unconscious attraction to Birkin and his natural ability to "read" the life and the warmth of his friend in his words are revelations of a spirit in himself from which he takes pleasure and knowledge, but which he does not ultimately trust.

Birkin's experience of Gerald is also conveyed between the lines rather than through them. Though he argues with Gerald and tells him that he sometimes hates him, he is also drawn to him: "He saw too how good-looking he was. Gerald was attractive, his blood seemed fluid and electric. His blue eyes burned with a keen, yet cold light, there was a certain beauty, a beautiful passivity in all his body, his moulding"(53). Just as Birkin's wild ideas are enchanting to Gerald partly because they are beyond him, so Gerald's cold passivity, while infuriating to Birkin, contributes to the beauty he finds compelling. The failure of this friendship to take root and grow in the lives of these two men is usually blamed on Gerald, his conventionality, his machinelike willfullness, his distrust of his own imagination, his fear of emotion. But Birkin is not so simple a surrogate of Lawrence as to be exempt from all culpability. Not only does he have Gerald classed socially and typed physically from the beginning, but it is very much the stereotype, partly of his own creation, the peculiarly British combination of northern beauty and businesslike practicality, that he loves. Furthermore, precisely because he is so much less inhibited than Gerald, he is more concretely aware of the difficulties of finding the appropriate expression of the friendship they both feel.

As he gazes out of the train window, half wishing the world would be destroyed, Birkin thinks of Sodom. And as the train approaches its destination, the lines he recalls from Browning are not merely about ruins but about "Love among the Ruins," a rather sentimental romantic love, "a girl with eager eyes and yellow hair" waiting for a tryst amid the rubble of a great empire. Neither the narrator nor Birkin makes much of these allusions. But if one takes the core of the chapter to be not the journey or the dialogue but the powerful attraction between the two men, their placement and meaning become clear. Confronted with Gerald and his own strong but unfamiliar feelings toward him, Birkin casts his mind to two extremes of "love" and to the cultural and literary representations of them, one in the form of an institutional taboo and the other a sentimental jingle that mocks institutional power. Nothing is said to link these references, but the silence—as so often in this novel—speaks volumes. Not the kinds of love evoked nor the Old Testament or Victorian attitudes toward them nor the literary forms through which they are expressed seem even remotely appropriate to Gerald and Birkin.

The problem, as glimpsed by Birkin and presented with consistent clarity by Lawrence, is much greater than the disposition of Gerald. Both men are extraordinarily and, as it turns out, tragically isolated by the uniqueness of their bond. Their habits of mind and language do not equip them to express it; their literature and culture do not help them understand it; their own society denies it or, like Bloomsbury, trivializes it. Indeed, the fundamental biological rhythm of their lives and the texts that try to imitate it cannot incorporate it except in rare moments when time and motion seem to have stopped and life and the plots of novels stand still.

The second scene in which Gerald and Birkin are shown alone for a fairly sustained period is in the chapter entitled "Man to Man," when Birkin is ill. In the "frictional to-and-fro" of the main plot, several crises have occurred since the meeting on the London train. Hermione has tried to kill Birkin with a lapis lazuli paperweight, Gerald's sister Diana and her fiancé have drowned, Ursula has fallen passionately in love with Birkin, and Gudrun has slapped Gerald in the face. Since Ursula's love is described as almost insanely possessive and the drowned woman is discovered with a stranglehold on her dead lover, each of these crises is a variation on a single theme: the destructive power of women. Aside from a general neglect of himself, Birkin has no particular reason to be ill except exhaustion with the main plot and his own feverish efforts to figure out his relationship with women in general and Ursula in particular.

Before Gerald enters the sickroom, Birkin is ruminating resentfully on the nature of woman: "Always so horrible and clutching, she had such a lust for possession ... Everything must be referred back to her, to Woman, the Great Mother of everything" (192).

Once again the dialogue is mostly nonchalant; they talk about Birkin's health or their problems with women (Gerald describes being slapped by Gudrun). Yet each man acknowledges to himself with an almost startling directness that he loves the other: "Gerald really loved Birkin"; "Of course, he had been loving Gerald all along, and all along denying it." When Birkin tries to find a form for their friendship, when he proposes a solemn oath of unselfish, unfailing love, a *Blutbrüderschaft* without the blood, Gerald becomes embarrassed and draws back. Though we know that this episode is drawn from Lawrence's life and that his sympathy is with Birkin, it seems clear that his imagination is larger than his sympathy. He sees as an artist, even if he does not accept with his heart that the limit on absolute, unselfish, perfect love is not merely a limit of Gerald's character, that there may be deeper, wider restrictions on all human character and circumstance that make such perfection impossible.

Another way of putting the problem brings it even closer to the artist's dilemma as an imitator of reality and a creator of a new order. In discussing education, Gerald uses the metaphor of being "brought into line":

". . . you can't live unless you do come into line somewhere."

"Well," said Birkin, "I begin to think that you can't live unless you keep entirely out of the line. It's no good trying to toe the line, when your one impulse is to smash up the line ... For special natures you must give a special world."

"Yes, but where's your special world?" said Gerald.

"Make it. Instead of chopping yourself down to fit the world, chop the world down to fit yourself. As a matter of fact, two exceptional people make another world. You and I, we make another, separate world."(197)

Birkin's final assertion is an ideal stated as a fact. He wants a unique world of friendship between himself and Gerald much as Lawrence seems to want to "smash the line" of his own main story from time to time in order to create a new kind of novel, one no longer concerned with "Do I love the girl or don't I?" or "Am I pure and sweet, or am I not?" The language Birkin uses to characterize the uniqueness of his friendship with Gerald is analagous to the language Lawrence frequently uses in his critical writings about the novel, which he says must present "new propositions ... new feelings ... a whole line of new emotions which will get us out of the emotional rut . . . instead of snivelling about what is and has been, or inventing new sensations in the old line, it's got to break a way through, like a hole in the wall."[10]

The novel, Lawrence repeatedly insists, has a future. And, as in the friendship, the realization of that future implies a rupture that leaves past and present in a shambles. Here again, the artist's imagination in Lawrence is more comprehensive and farsighted than his critical impatience or his sympathetic treatment of Birkin might lead one to believe. The world of past and present do encroach on the scene in Birkin's bedroom, not only because of Gerald's conventionality but because the making of another, altogether "separate world" is as difficult for artists as it is for friends. Even without the intrusion of outsiders into the closed room where Birkin and Gerald meet, the furnishings and situation call attention to a world of signs outside the one the two men try to create for themselves. There is simply no getting away from the fact that this is a bedroom scene, that it is a particular kind of pause in the main action, that it reveals Birkin mentally active as always, but off-guard, physically vulnerable, and attractive in a new way to Gerald as he "came near the bed and stood looking down at Birkin whose throat was exposed, whose tossed hair fell attractively on the warm brow."

By selecting such a strongly evocative setting, Lawrence seems to want to expose the dishonesty and prurience of past associations and, at the same time, make a new context of it for his own purposes. But he cannot do one without slightly diminishing the effect of the other. To remind us of the bad old world only to be able to smash it is still to remind us of the bad old world. A complete separation of the sort Birkin seems to be talking about when he says two people can "make another world" or the sort Lawrence the critic is talking about when he anticipates the novel of the future is an impossibility that Lawrence the novelist recognizes and depicts. When Birkin criticizes Gerald for never being able to "fly away from himself," he is, in a sense, making a confession that applies to himself and the artist as well.

The scene of Birkin's and Gerald's coming together in which their relationship reaches a climax is "Gladiatorial," the chapter in which they strip down and wrestle until both are exhausted.[11] Like other scenes between the two friends, this one, which takes place at night in Gerald's locked library, is peculiarly insulated from the world of the rest of the novel. Also, once again, both men meet after a specific disappointment with a woman. Gerald has been rebuffed after what he had considered his manly rescue of Gudrun from an angry rabbit: "He felt again as if she had hit him across the face." And Birkin, who has just proposed marriage to Ursula, has been told that she does not wish to be "bullied" into answering. Without at first discussing their women, the two men decide to work off their "boredom" by hitting one another "in a friendly kind of way." In the most obvious sense, the "fight" between the men reverses the signs of their relations with women in which courting and lovemaking are, in fact, occasions for bitter conflict. If men and women show their antipathy while supposedly making love, the male friends will fight in order to demonstrate their love.

The boldly dramatic irony acted out in this reversal of signs is one of the many ways Lawrence comments on one of his favorite topics, the battle of the sexes. There is something healthy and therapeutic about an open contest, he implies, in contrast with the sarcasm, spitefulness, and covert hostility that characterize the heterosexual relationships in the book. But the "fight" is not only a dramatic and ironic comment on the men's difficulties with Gudrun and Ursula; it is also a ritualization of the male friendship. By containing elements of both drama and ritual, the "fight" represents the two major opposing tendencies in the novel, which are played out in the alternating focus on male-female and male-male relationships. The wrestling match is dramatic insofar as it mimics and criticizes courtship and marriage and points beyond itself to the "main" action of the novel, in which struggles lead to resolutions and choices and then on to new struggles. But, as always in the scenes between Birkin and Gerald, there is another element, a tendency that runs counter to purpose, progress, and resolution.

It would be hard to miss that the contest between the two friends is described in language so highly charged with sexual imagery that it suggests sexual intercourse as much as it does an athletic contest. But to read the chapter as an example of displacement, as a thinly disguised excuse to portray an encounter that is primarily sexual, is to misunderstand Lawrence's narrative method. For Lawrence, all serious human encounters are in some way sexual. Furthermore, there is little reason to believe that Lawrence saw sexual intercourse in itself as any simpler or easier an expression of Gerald's and Birkin's friendship that it is of the heterosexual relationships in the novel. Sexual love is not the unexpected and daring reality for which the wrestling match is a metaphor. It has been a powerful ingredient of the friendship throughout the novel, and it is brought into the "fight" in concentrated form in conjunction with a shared spiritual detachment from the world and a magnetic intellectual polarity. Part of the ritual quality of the combat, in addition to its gratuity, its enclosed and special setting, and its solemnity, depends on its capacity to hold a variety of impulses and needs in tension without resolving them. Ritual is a mode of expression, not a way of solving problems. It may give the appearance of dynamism, but it is essentially static. It can be repeated over and over again without changing anything. It represents a truth; it does not do anything about it.

What the two friends give one another, as has been hinted at throughout, is an experience of otherness that takes its cues from the familiar social, moral, and religious world, if only by way of contrast, but does not belong to it or its language. In a real sense, the scene does not belong in the novel. It is the solemnization of play. Since the friends have not had sex, planned or promised anything, hurt one another, or given or taken anything of substance, there can be no moral or social consequences to what they have done, no guilt or pride, no contract or breach. They have temporarily cut off or at least weakened their ties with past and future. By allowing this, by including it in his design, Lawrence unsettles the apparent momentum and purpose of his own novel.

The final major encounter between Birkin and Gerald takes place in the last chapter. After a quarrel with Gudrun, Gerald has wandered out into the mountains, fallen, and frozen to death in the snow. After seeing the body brought in and laid out on a bed of his hotel room, Birkin returns three times, as if magnetized and in a trance, to his friend: "Birkin went again to Gerald. He had loved him"; "Birkin went home again to Gerald. He went into the room and sat down on the bed. Dead, dead and cold!"; "But when he went in again, at evening, to look at Gerald between the candles, because of his heart's hunger, suddenly his heart contracted, his own candle all but fell from his hand, as, with a strange whimpering cry, the tears broke out"(471). Ursula is horrified and repelled by Birkin's grief. In a way, her reaction parallels that of the reader, whose attention may be so fixed on the main action (the male-female plot) that he takes little notice of the Birkin-Gerald friendship except as a minor eccentricity that detracts from the structural and thematic integrity of the novel.

There is little question that the relationship of the two men disrupts the novel, understood in a particular way as a narrative about two sisters, "women in love," and their efforts to work out their individual destinies in relation to social convention, especially marriage. If, indeed, the novel is only about that and follows the formal patterns of courtship and marriage narratives—encounter, attraction, union, break, and resolution in either final reunion or separation—then the recurrent and almost obsessive concern with male friendship, a relationship without moral framework or social significance, has no place in the book. It is not a formative subject but an author's problem, a psychological tick, an artistic flaw. Viewed in this way, Ursula seems right in her objection to the extremity of Birkin's reaction to Gerald's death. If not exactly a "perversity," as she calls it, the book's ending does seem to be an extraordinary act of self-indulgence on Lawrence's as well as on Birkin's part.

In fact, the friendship, what it is in itself and what it stands for as a statement about the nature of human experience and the narrative mode, has been a major element in the novel from the beginning. Gerald and Birkin's last discussion of marriage recapitulates the theme and epitomizes the problem. Gerald asks Birkin's advice about marrying Gudrun:

> "If I were you I would *not* marry: but ask Gudrun, not me. You're not marrying me, are you?"
> Gerald did not heed the latter part of the speech.
> "Yes," he said, "one must consider it coldly. It is something critical. One comes to the point where one must take a step in one direction or another. And marriage is one direction—"
> "And what is the other?" asked Birkin quickly. (344)

As always, marriage is associated with "direction," purpose, a line of action, and, for Gerald especially, "an acceptance of the established world . . . the established order." Birkin's impatiently ironic remark about his friend's "not marrying" him goes unnoticed by Gerald, but Lawrence's intrusion ensures that it will not be missed by the reader. The "other way," as is pointed out later, is for Gerald "to accept Rupert's offer of alliance." But the "offer" is finally no clearer to the reader than it is to Gerald.

That a special tie exists between the two friends is no longer in question. But how to act on it, label it, and incorporate it into life remains a problem. And the problem is not merely Gerald's; it is Birkin's as well. Not marrying, not pursuing a particular direction or purpose, not accepting the established order, may be the only way to discover a new life and a new order, one richer, more comprehensive, better integrated than what is known. But it may also be mere negation, a sacrifice that leads not to new life but only more quickly to death. Whatever his theoretical statements may be, both possibilities remain vividly alive for Lawrence the novelist.

Throughout the book, Birkin senses something deathlike, frozen, passive in Gerald. It is this quality in his friend to which Birkin is attracted but from which, he believes, he wishes to save him. His effort is frustrated by Gerald's reticence, but also by something more than that, something that is relevant to Lawrence's dilemma as an artist. The scene with the most paradigmatic resonance for the friendship and the composition of the novel is the one in "Water-party" when Gerald's sister and her fiancé are thought to have drowned. Gerald who has been diving unsuccessfully to search for them insists on waiting and watching by the lakeside as the water is drained. Birkin tries to convince him to leave the scene and save himself the horror of seeing the dead bodies:

> Gerald looked up at him. Then he put his hand affectionately on Birkin's shoulder, saying:
> "Don't you bother about me, Rupert . . ."
> "Very well. But you spoil your own chance of life—you waste your best self."
> ". . . Waste it? What else is there to do with it?"
> "But leave this, won't you? You force yourself into horror, and put a mill-stone of beastly memories round your neck. Come away now."
> ". . . God, you've got such a telling way of putting things. Rupert, you have."
> Birkin's heart sank. He was irritated and weary of having a telling way of putting things.
> "Won't you leave it? Come over to my place." . . .
> "No," said Gerald coaxingly, his arm across the other man's shoulder. "Thanks very much, Rupert—I shall be glad to come tomorrow. . . . I want to see this job through. . . . I'd rather come and have a chat with you than—than do anything else. I verily believe. Yes, I would. You mean a lot to me, Rupert, more than you know."
> "What do I mean, more than I know?" asked Birkin irritably.(180–181)

On the surface, Birkin's invitation is merely a sign of friendly concern, but the urgency of his words and the network of associations both between them and similar ones in literature and between this situation and similar ones in the book give them special weight. Birkin's "come away" and "leave this" have the intensity of a lover's summons in lyrical poetry. As a summons away from a scene of mortality, proffered by one with "a telling way of putting things," the episode also suggests a familiar theme of Romantic poetry, that of the poet being lured by a songbird, his muse or imagination, away from the impermanence of his own life. Since the couple is eventually discovered with the woman's "arms tight around the neck of the young man, choking him," the invitation to escape death is also linked with a call to escape involvement with women. After what amounts to a gruesomely repetitious and fruitless baptism, plunging again and again into the water, Gerald hears himself called to follow a friend who wants to save him from the "mill-stone" (Christ's metaphor) of death through what sounds like a form of celibate love.

None of these associations is brought into sharp focus at the expense of the others. If Birkin's summons contains a hint of salvation, it is to be found not so much in a particular course of action as in an effort to reintegrate man's sexual, imaginative, and religious natures. Gerald, typically, does not understand any of this; he prefers to stay on course, to "see the job through," much as he plays out his role as gentleman, industrialist, and lover according to his notion of duty and the established order. Yet something in him does respond to Rupert despite his refusal. Even his stilted "verily, I believe" unconsciously echoes the religious solemnity of Birkin's call and his clichéd "you mean more to me than you know" expresses a profound truth.

Birkin may be more open and adventurous, more articulate and reflective than Gerald; his understanding may go deeper, but he is not in full command of himself or the situation, either. He may resemble Lawrence, but he is not the author of the book. Both Gerald and Ursula remark on his unreliability. Gerald: "There is always an element of uncertainty about you . . . You can go away and change." Ursula: "He says one thing one day, and another the next—and he always contradicts himself." The same can be said of Lawrence as well, but only when we are thinking of him as a moralist or philosopher, as a polemicist. As an artist, at his best, his control is certain and his consistency flawless; he is never totally converted by his own dogmatism or that of his protagonists. He can make Birkin's love for Gerald credible because part of him is attracted to "seeing the job through," even in a willful, blind, self-destructive way. Approval or disapproval is almost beside the point since this aspect of human nature appears to have a nonhuman source and energy that can be recognized and wondered at without being rationalized.

One of Birkin's first thoughts after viewing Gerald's dead body is: "Whatever the mystery which has brought forth man and the universe, it is a non-human mystery, it has its own great ends, man is not the criterion"(469). Man can either give way mutely and unconsciously to this nonhuman mystery, as Gerald does, or else try to humanize it by weaving it into a friendship, a marriage, a life, as Birkin does, or into a story, as the artist does. For Lawrence, such efforts are more than vital; they are sacred. Birkin's words never parallel Christ's more exactly than when he is lamenting over Gerald's corpse and recalling the warm hand clasp after their wrestling contest. "If he had kept true to that clasp, death would not have mattered. Those who die, and dying still can love, still believe, do not die. They live still in the beloved"(471). These declarations, like Christ's, open limitless horizons, which place all systems and structures, literary as well as social and moral, in a perspective that sharply reduces their importance by vastly increasing the space around them.

Yet Lawrence allows a familiar pattern to reassert itself before the novel is finished. Ursula challenges Birkin's need for an "eternal" man friend and they argue. " 'You can't have it, because it's false, impossible,' she said. 'I don't believe that,' he answered"(473). It is frequently taken for granted that Lawrence is, at the very last, "with" Birkin. But to claim this is to ignore the rhythm and structure of the novel. He could have concluded with Birkin's Christlike assertion, but instead he returned to dialogue, to disagreement, skepticism, and negation. Lawrence is, after all, a novelist, not a mystic. He dares to bring the word "eternal" back into the novel without apology, but he is not Dante or Blake. He cannot fly away from himself to a sustained beatific vision. If immortality is to be experienced in his created world, it must be glimpsed through the cracks in the wall, in the pauses between words, in the silences between affirmation and denial, in dialogue with a woman who is more than wife, in the discovery and loss of a beloved friend.

FOR JOYCE'S Stephen Dedalus, friends, like parents, priests, and teachers, are an impediment to the destiny, or plot line, that he wishes to pursue alone. Had he chosen to remain in Ireland with his schoolmates, the shape and content of his story would have been different. Lawrence's Birkin takes part simultaneously in two plots, each of which challenges and undermines the other. What he wishes but fails to do is integrate the two in his own life, to satisfy opposing tendencies in his own being. In both cases, the idea of friendship is linked with a conception of experience and literary narrative as dialectic. Having or not having an intense and intimate friendship is a choice that conflicts with other choices and may even eliminate them. The protagonist is faced with the decision about whether or not to act out a part of his own character. Like the author he resembles, he must decide what path to follow, what set of possibilities to pursue, and which, by implication, to let alone.

In *The Waves*, Virginia Woolf tries to imagine what it is like not to make such a decision.[12] Friendship in her novel is not treated as an alternative, either conventional (as in Joyce) or unconventional (as in Lawrence), but as a necessity, a given, a starting place of consciousness, like nature and language. Her characters—Jinny, Susan, Rhoda, Louis, Neville, Bernard, and Percival—are born into a world in which other shaping structures—family, religion, nationality—may or may not be important. For the most part, they seem not to be. But friendship, the intermittently intense and casual association with a particular group of peers, is universal and essential. One does not choose it or deny it any more than one chooses that the sun should rise and set, the tide come in and go out, or words be spoken and written.

When Bernard, the writer of the group, tries to remember his first awakenings to life as an infant, the sequence is not sounds, words, story, and father, as in the case of Stephen Dedalus, but sights, sensations, words, and friends: "In the beginning, there was the nursery, with windows opening on to a garden, and beyond that the sea. I saw something brighten—no doubt the brass handle of a cupboard. Then Mrs. Constable raised the sponge over her head, squeezed it, and out shot, right, left, all down the spine, arrows of sensation. And so, as long as we draw breath, for the rest of time, if we knock against a chair, a table or a woman, we are pierced with arrows of sensation ... All these things happen in one second and last forever. Faces loom. Dashing round the corner, 'Hullo,' one says, 'there's Jinny. That's Neville. That's Louis ... That's Rhoda' ... Neville did not melt. 'Therefore,' I said, 'I am myself, not Neville' "(342–343).

The very basis of the realization of self is sense impression, utterance, and repeated contacts with others who are similar to but not identical with the self. Without the background of institutional potency and ideological constraint that provoked both Joyce and Lawrence into rebellion, Woolf tended, in her fiction, to discount institutions and "ideas" rather than oppose them. Friendship, as a major theme and organizing principal in *The Waves,* is not flaunted in the face of Church and state, nor is it proposed as an alternative to marriage. Family life, professional careers, creeds, and philosophical systems continue to occupy the characters, but they are faded and fragmentary; they appear to be incapable of providing coherence except in an extremely narrow sense. Still, the characters do not rebel against conventional pursuits; rather, the narrative consciousness, especially as expressed through the character of Bernard, the storyteller, places them in the background while focusing on the comprehensive and fundamental, but loosely structured and dimly understood, subject of friendship.

What provides drama in Woolf's fiction is not the tension between a "relaxed" structure and social and literary rigidities inherited from the past, but rather that between a relaxed structure and none at all. The threats to the characters in *The Waves* do not come from demanding families, dogmatic religions, or strict political ideologies, but from nullity, absence of meaning, incoherence. Narrative complexity is a consequence not of a parodic juxtaposition of incompatible texts, as in Joyce, or of the alternation of antithetical ones, as in Lawrence, but of the continual movement of minimal coherence toward and away from absolute nothingness. The conception of friendship in *The Waves* serves, in its fashion, the same formative function it does for Joyce and Lawrence. It provides an essential context for major characters' self-definition and a relational model for the pattern of the narrative.

Friendship, for Woolf, is neither an old trap nor a new mystical bond, neither a chorus of too-familiar voices nor an invitation to an untried dialogue. Like nature and language, it is a loosely knit fabric forever in danger of coming unraveled. But however vague and unpredictable friendship may be, it appears to be the most tangible, reliable, and authentic indication of the existence of a self and of a reality outside, with which the self can establish occasional contact. Friends are modestly consoling reminders that the world exists in some form that can be approached, touched, described, even addressed, if not entirely understood. In *The Waves,* the friends' speeches to one another—"Come in," "Sit down," "Tell me a story"—are variations on the childish exclamations about shape, color, and sound—"I see a ring," "I see a slab of pale yellow," "I hear a sound"—with which the narration begins. Friends stimulate the individual consciousness and provoke utterance, but they are superior to sunshine, water, and trees because they can talk back, not necessarily in a way that produces a meaning or a conclusion, but in the soothing, even occasionally harmonious, way of instruments tuning up for a performance.

Both Joyce and Lawrence use friendship, thematically and formally, as an emblem of an extreme: for Joyce, the stereotype of prosaic confinement; for Lawrence, a unique possibility of liberation. The value of friendship as a literary subject and structuring device for Woolf lies in its resistance to extreme formulations of any kind. It is her secular substitute for the Church of England, her middle way, undogmatic, undemanding, unassuming, quite as comforting for what it is not as for what it claims to be. The extremes from which friendship saves her characters and her text are love and isolation, either a total fusion with or separation from others, both of which amount to a form of death, a silence, an end to the kind of experience that requires language.

Early in *The Waves,* these two extremes are approached, as they will be repeatedly throughout the novel, and shown as radically threatening to the survival of the characters and the continuation of the narrative. In a childhood love scene, Bernard and Susan momentarily lose their distinctiveness: " '. . . when we sit together, close,' said Bernard, 'we melt into each other with phrases. We are edged with mist. We make an unsubstantial territory' "(185).

The "unsubstantial territory" is explored, and, though the words of exploration are Bernard's, they evoke neither his character nor Susan's. They do not hint at dialogue, even a lopsided one. The two characters have temporarily melted into one another and into the natural world, which is described not as "seen" or "felt" but rather as if all space, all distance, has been removed and they are gradually becoming indistinguishable from their surroundings. The exploration becomes a kind of drowning—"we sink," "the waves close over us, the beech leaves meet over our heads," "we have fallen"—a metamorphosis, a dying to the self and intermingling with the inarticulate world of nature. As the language begins to wind down to an almost nonsensical repetitiousness, "That is a woodpigeon . . . The pigeon beats the air; the pigeon beats the air with wooden wings," Susan recovers herself and speaks: "You have escaped me." Her words break the spell, but not because she challenges Bernard or disagrees with him. The gesture is much simpler and more radical than one of disagreement: she reasserts her separateness and withdraws from the "mist" by saying bluntly that she is no longer with him; he has "escaped" her.

One of the things the reader realizes in his relief at Susan's interruption is that this "love story" has been far too short and successful. The lovers meet and die into one another at once, without plot or problems, without impediment or separation. All the longing, misunderstanding, awkwardness—that is, all the varieties of space between the lovers that language tries to fill—have been removed. Neither lovers nor words have anything left to do, and the prospect is horrifying. Susan, however, returns to herself, refuses to understand or comply, and one has the reassuring sense of ground regained, the possibility of further discussion, another exploration to engage in, another friend to meet. Filled, like Lawrence, with a sense of the intense reality of ecstatic experience, Woolf wishes to render it truthfully and still retain enough control to be able to escape it and return to the resting places of discourse and sequence.

At the opposite extreme from ecstatic love, the total immersion of the self in another, is an isolation so complete as to make everything outside of the self appear to be unrelated and unrelatable. It is an idea of "detachment" utterly different from Joyce's, since, for him, it is associated with self-control, steadiness, and clarity of vision, a triumph over the twists and turns of one's materials. For Woolf, detachment carried to the extreme means loss of control, random shifts in perspective, a vulnerability to fragmentation that brings on panic. When in *Ulysses* Stephen Dedalus is shown in a classroom helping a pupil with arithmetic, the transformation of the numbers into dancing figures and descendants of ancient mathematicians saves Stephen from sentimentality and opens the small schoolroom momentarily into a vast dimension of space and time. The detachment from the immediate situation is not a drifting into incoherence, but a distancing that allows for the establishment of new and unexpected networks of coherence.

A parallel scene in *The Waves* reveals an important difference in Woolf. In this case, the lesson is seen from the point of view of one of the children, Rhoda, whose incomprehnsion of the figures separates her from her friends. " 'Now Miss Hudson,' said Rhoda, 'has shut the book.' Now the terror is beginning . . . She draws figures, six, seven, eight, and then a cross and then a line on the blackboard. What is the answer? The others look . . . with understanding . . . But I cannot write. I see only figures. The others are handing in their answers . . . But I have no answer. The others are allowed to go. They slam the door. Miss Hudson goes. I am left alone to find an answer. The figures mean nothing now. Meaning has gone. The clock ticks. The two hands are convoys marching through a desert . . . I begin to draw a figure and the world is looped in it, and I myself am outside the loop . . . The world is entire, and I am outside of it crying, 'Oh, save me, from being blown for ever outside the loop of time!' "(188–189).

For Joyce, the ability to move out of a given system of coherences (such as adding and subtracting) is a liberating act of the imagination, a grace note to the artist's creative power, puzzling at first for readers unused to it, but consistent and logical in its own way. True, Rhoda is a neophyte rather than an initiate, but it is characteristic of Woolf to present even the simplest conventional systems as they might look to one without a key. It is difficult to feel liberated from structures to which one has never been bound. That the numbers can be seen as isolated markings with no apparent connection with one another is a terrifying reflection to Rhoda of her nonrelationship with teacher and friends. Filling the blank with images—the clock hands as desert convoys—is no help, since the imagination appears to come up with insanely random pictures that are no help in drawing things together. Thus detachment is associated either with emptiness or with a chaotic proliferation of imagery. It points to a human situation, one's friends walking out of a room, and an expressive one, an inability to add, an incapacity to discover the sums of things. For narrative fiction, as for life in the world, this kind of distance is another form of death.

The presence of friends, their words and gestures, dilute the purity of self and distract the ego from its peculiar preoccupations. In cases when the individual experiences an isolation and blankness bordering on madness, both the dilution and the distraction are obviously welcome. What is important to realize is that, though the specific situation in the classroom is peculiar to Rhoda, the syndrome is common to all. Her momentary sensation of being outside of time and system is experienced by all the characters in their own way. And all are saved or at least temporarily returned to communion by their friends, whose function is at the same time important and modest in its manifestations. Friends are like magnetic particles, salutary and necessary in their ability to attract and move, dangerous only when their pull is strong enough to threaten absorption.

The movement of *The Waves,* more than any other of Woolf's novels, follows a recurrence of attraction and repulsion, a pulsation that marks individuation and reunion with the whole, as the waves separate themselves into shapes "like logs falling on the shore," "like turbaned warriors," like "horse's hooves on the turf" and yet always return to the placid and immense sea "indistinguishable from the sky." This movement is associated with birth and death, a coming into individual being and returning to the universal shapelessness of sea and sky, but for Woolf it is not only about the beginning and end of physical life or even the beginning and end of each day or season or year. The movement that concerns her is that of conscious life in its every moment, a throbbing like that of the waves on the beach repeated hundreds of times in a single day.

The way the human consciousness experiences this repeated tossing back and forth between individuation and absorption is the subject of *The Waves.* Friends and art (especially the arts of language) make it tolerable. Since they, too, are subject to the force of recurrent change, however, they ease, sustain, and delight without ultimately providing a means of escape. The attempt to turn a friend into a hero or a god, a source of permanent stability, is as futile and false as the attempt to represent life by means of a story, by lining up events in a sequence that promises a meaningful conclusion. Friends, like sentences, are necessary but vulnerable sources of coherence.

Bernard is the character most given to telling stories as a way of composing himself, establishing contact with friends, and avoiding his own version of Rhoda's blankness: "I must make phrases and phrases and so interpose something hard between myself and . . . the stare of clocks." But though he is acknowledged for his entertaining stories and for his ability to collect his school friends around him, Bernard's power often falters. On one occasion, when his friends become bored and begin to wander away, Neville observes, "Among the tortures and devastations of life is this then—our friends are not able to finish their stories." The comment is not merely an idle criticism of Bernard's ability to hold an audience but a deeply serious and universally applicable expression of life's refusal to conform to narrative convention. Friends cannot finish their stories because their audiences and their subjects are forever dispersing.

B E R N A R D is never entirely successful in his efforts to compose a continuous narrative; inspiration fails him, he is interrupted, or his audience becomes bored. But his efforts do not fail totally, either. They parallel closely what Woolf herself does with story line in *The Waves*.[13] The practice of linking one event to another is never completely dropped; there is a rough chronology, characters age, choices are made. A "wandering thread" is always visible and seems to provide a minimal semblance of familiar order to the lives being represented. Woolf does not eliminate the thread, but she radically alters its significance for the reader, as well as for her characters, by rendering experiences of great moment to individual characters that either do not belong to anyone else's story or else contain elements that contradict the story being told.

It is rarely the story itself but more frequently the interruptions it suffers that make the heaviest demands on the reader. When Bernard stops his own narrative in order to make declarations and ask questions, reader and author are drawn in by the powerful vacuum created when recognizable story and character are suddenly removed. The reader becomes involved in Bernard's momentary loss of individuality not simply because the words invite him to, but because the props and links of the fictitious world disappear and give him nothing else on which to concentrate. Furthermore, in a gesture that parallels Eliot's echo of Baudelaire's "mon semblable, mon frère," Bernard addresses the reader as an aspect of himself: "But *you* understand, *you,* my self, who always comes to a call (that would be a harrowing experience to call and for no one to come; that would make the midnight hollow, and explains the expression of old men in clubs—they have given up calling for a self who does not come)"(227–228).

By drawing the reader so deeply and fully into the experience of Bernard's diffusion of identity, Woolf not only creates a peculiarly sympathetic attachment between reader and character; she also reminds us dramatically of our responsibility in the reconstruction of the book.[14] The more nearly individual identity is associated with utterance, the more obviously important is the role of the responsive listener. The reader has very much the same function as the friend, for without him, authors are like the "old men in clubs . . . calling for a self who does not come."

For all the obvious drawbacks of names, stories, and labels, they, like critical interpretations of complex works of art, are the necessary means of revitalization, not because they are right—since, in some way, they are always wrong—but because they provide the new order of a revised discourse. Moreover, by their very inadequacy, they reveal dimensions of character or art that require contrasts in order to be seen. As a student, Bernard is rescued from his fragmentation of self by Neville, whom he encounters sunning himself on the banks of the Cam. Neville is lost in reverie but begins to collect himself as Bernard approaches. "How curiously one is changed by the addition, even at a distance, of a friend." The mere presence of the other provides each young man with a view of himself, distorted, perhaps limited, but reassuringly comprehensible and clear. In the peculiar fashion of the book, Bernard addresses Neville in his thoughts. "I will tell you what I feel, under the compulsion of your clarity. I feel your disapproval, I feel your force. I become, with you, an untidy, an impulsive human being whose bandana handkerchief is forever stained with the grease of crumpets"(232).

The friend's value obviously does not lie in flattery or even necessarily in the accuracy of his viewpoint, but in the fact that, through the narrower scope of his lens, the self is delineated and brought into focus. The frame and focus may need adjustment, but they provide a point of departure that the self cannot locate without help from outside. As always in this book, the meeting of friends is a temporary release from confusion, a recapitulation of identity, and the beginning of a new story: "I feel your distress acutely," thinks Bernard. Bernard builds on Neville's view of him to tell a story that will show his character in a favorable light. Although the motive may be defensive, he is grateful to his friend for the opportunity and sensitive to the need to return the favor: "Let me then create you. (You have done as much for me.)"

The height of rapport between the two is reached when Neville, in a gesture of respect and trust, gives one of his poems to his friend to read and criticize. After Neville leaves, Bernard reacts with emotion, "O friendship, how piercing are your darts . . . That confidence I shall keep to my dying day." But though deeply touched by his friend, Bernard recognizes that the gesture is ultimately a reductive one. "To be contracted by another person into a single being—how strange." The word "contracted" perfectly unites diminution and binding. The friend is one who holds us in a firmer and steadier grip than we can keep on ourselves, but the price paid is a contraction of being. The more time has intervened since Neville's departure, the happier Bernard is to be alone, to allow his sense of himself to exceed and contradict the judgment of his friend. "We are not as simple as our friends would have us to meet their needs . . . Now the stab, the rent in my defences that Neville made with his astonishing fine rapier is repaired. I am almost whole now; and see how jubilant I am, bringing into play all that Neville ignores in me . . . (We use our friends to measure our own stature.) My scope embraces what Neville never reaches" (236–237).

The process of contraction and of individual delineation is reversed as Bernard allows his imagination to wander in new directions; his being expands and fills spaces unknown to Neville. The affectionate "dart" becomes in his mind a "rapier" that wounds and pins down, preventing freedom and change. Yet neither friendship in general nor this particular friend is being rejected. The friends have served each other well, but their function as simplifiers and clarifiers has its value only as a periodic pause in the larger ebb and flow of being and perception. Friends provide modulation and rhythm to what might otherwise become a roar or a monotonous beat. "They retrieve me from darkness . . . They drum me alive."

IF ANY character in *The Waves* is the likely center of a story, it is Percival who seems to embody the best qualities of English youth. Certainly Bernard tries valiantly to make the most of his heroic potential, but he cannot find a plot that will stick. The would-be hero does not act badly, shame his legendary ancestors, or mock his potential; he simply eludes literary definition by repeatedly and abruptly quitting the scene, thus making it impossible to go on talking about him except in a fragmented, repetitious way. Percival's failure to take his "proper" place in a conventional heroic narrative is not a moral failure on his part or on the part of those who witness his life. The difficulty is epistemological. If the model of an author is the observant friend, like Bernard, rather than an omniscient god or prophet or historian, then the knowledge he can record is subject to the same limitations we all experience in our efforts to know one another. The trouble with Percival, for his friends and for the honest writer, is that he is forever moving out of reach.

Insofar as the novel can be said to have a central episode, it is the friends' reunion in a London restaurant on the eve of Percival's departure for India. Though the external setting is sketched in, the scene is primarily rendered through the internal meditations of those present. The actual moment of reunion, the dinner and the friendly conviviality, is almost lost in the prolonged anticipation of Percival's arrival and the sustained afterglow when the friends emerge from the restaurant onto the darkened street. Percival, as usual, says little and, in any case, his words and thoughts are not recorded. His entire existence, for the reader, depends on the responses he produces in his friends. He is the counterpart of the loquacious Bernard, the objectification of what is rendered subjectively through Bernard's consciousness, individual life given its contours and coloration by the affectionate artistry of friends: "We are drawn into this communion by some deep, some common emotion. Shall we call it, conveniently, 'love'? Shall we say 'love of Percival' because Percival is going to India?" (262–263).

The association of an imaginative construction of character in a given moment of time with communion and love is a crucial one for Woolf. Without this insistence on something emotionally valuable, almost transcendently significant, the scene might be taken as a mockery of human relationships, an instance of failed sympathies and thwarted communication even more disappointing than the final meeting of Stephen and Leopold in Bloom's kitchen. After all, the friends are filled with contradictory and divisive thoughts; they are all egocentric and anxious about themselves; they fashion their own images of Percival, which alternately idealize and trivialize him. As usual, Bernard puts the extremes into narrative form. His mind drifts to a vision of Percival as a hero of the Empire in a Kiplingesque India: "I see the tortuous lanes of stamped mud that lead in and out among ramshackle pagodas . . . I see a pair of bullocks who drag a low cart along a sun-baked road . . . Now one wheel sticks in the rut, and at once innumerable natives in loincloths swarm around it . . . But they do nothing . . . But now, behold, Percival advances; Percival rides a flea-bitten mare, and wears a sunhelmet. By applying the standards of the West, by using the violent language that is natural to him, the bullock-cart is righted in less than five minutes. The Oriental problem is solved. He rides on; the multitude cluster around him, regarding him as if he were—what indeed he is—a God" (269).

The passage has all the elements of mock-heroic with some additional touches that prevent it from having a simple effect. The opening sentences are a bit too good as imitations of descriptive romantic prose to produce obvious parody. But, more important, the qualifying "what indeed he is" in the final sentence breaks upon the surface of pure mockery. The reader is brought back from Kipling to Bernard, to the circle of friends and their complex but genuine adoration of Percival. The mockery fails to take hold completely since Percival's "heroism," in some objective sense, is not really at issue. The subject is the composite perception of the friends, focused for this moment of reunion, rather like the perception of the "swarming natives," on Percival. The perceptions evoked by Percival, whether "accurate" or not, are vitally true to the minds that form them and therefore undeserving of mockery, even if not entirely invulnerable to it. Percival cannot be blamed for what his friends "make" of him.

When Bernard tries to bring his own fantasy down to earth and, by implication, to present a neutral portrait of Percival undistorted by friendly interest, he produces another near-parody, this time of naturalistic prose: " 'The handsome young man in the grey suit, whose reserve contrasted so strangely with the loquacity of the others, now brushed the crumbs from his waistcoat and, with a characteristic gesture at once commanding and benign, made a sign to the waiter, who came instantly and returned a moment later with the bill discreetly folded upon a plate.' That is the truth; that is the fact, but beyond it all is darkness and conjecture"(275).

This "slice of life" is not entirely laughable, any more than the imagined episode in India, partly because we recognize some truth in it and see the necessity of balancing even the most radically subjective rendering of experience with a dispassionate registering of concrete detail. Though Woolf does not carry the process to the same extreme as Joyce, we are not so far from the world of *Ulysses,* in which layers of parodic language serve not so much to diminish characters as to expose the absurd limits of subjective styles pretending to omniscient objectivity.

Neither the romantic version of Percival in India nor the description of him brushing crumbs from his waistcoat is ludicrously or outlandishly false, because no single portrait of him is more reliable or more substantial. Woolf does not step in, nor does she permit Bernard or any other surrogate to step in, with a "better" or richer rendition. The reader is made to experience the inadequacy of single renderings of character and therefore to rely more and more, as do the characters themselves, on composite versions of everything. We are led to conclude that we can know about Percival only through his friends, as they know themselves only through one another. In this circle, the way to the center is the circumference.

What comes through most powerfully in the reunion scene is not a "fact" about Percival or any of the friends as individuals, but a conviction expressed with the intensity of drama that, at its deepest core, life and its reflection in art are social phenomena. The point being made is not simply that friends—those we can love, admire, even adore—are pleasant additions to life, comforting and consoling appendages to what is essentially a private affair, but that we cannot locate our being or find our words without them. That Woolf should so insist on this essentially classical idea is partly a sign of her disillusionment with one kind of Romanticsm and partly a strikingly modern effort to locate a common source of value and comprehension without the supporting structures of an integrated religious and political culture.

Like most modernists, Woolf was all too convinced by Romantic subjectivist psychology. And though she could depict characters reveling in their freedom to invent their own worlds, she had a horror, rooted in devastating experience, of losing touch with the world beyond self. It is no joke, therefore, to say that Percival is like a god, since he possesses the power, momentarily, to draw his friends out of their isolation into a world of meaning—that is, of *shared* experience. That their pictures of him are not identical does not matter; he provides them with a reason for gathering, a release from themselves, an occasion for talk. Their conversation is like prayer: its meaning is to be found not in its content but in its form as an act of faith in the presence of another.

As the evening draws to a close, Bernard sums it up. His language is once again subject to ironic interpretation because of its presumption, yet oddly touching in its effort to infuse this commonplace social event with the significance of a sacred adventure. "We have proved, sitting eating, sitting talking, that we can add to the treasury of moments. We are not slaves bound to suffer incessantly unrecorded petty blows on our bent backs. We are not sheep either, following a master. We are creators. We too have made something that will join the innumerable congregations of past time. We too, as we put on our hats and push open the door, stride not into chaos, but into a world that our own force can subjugate and make part of the illumined and everlasting road"(277).

It is plain that this meal is not the Last Supper nor a feast at Arthur's Round Table, yet the apostolic and chivalric language is not entirely false or silly. Percival is godlike in a particular sense, but he is not a master or creator or shepherd. In Trinitarian terms, he is more like the Spirit than the Father or the Son. His presence is an enabling one, a gift of verbal coherence and self-confidence. What is invisible in him is made visible in his friends. They will remember and talk about this moment, as the apostles and knights of the Round Table did about theirs, making of it an island of light and harmony. And in remembering the moment, and even more in recording it, they will enhance it and stabilize themselves through links with other islands, successions almost apostolic, "innumerable congregations of past time."

The association of friendship and art with tradition, a coherent structure outside the rapid flux of time, is made more and more explicit as the book moves toward its conclusion. In the chapter following the reunion, Neville receives a telegram from India announcing the accidental death of Percival. For Neville, as for all the other friends, whose lives are bound up with one another, the death is experienced vicariously as their own. "Why try to lift my foot and mount the stair?" he asks himself. As for Bernard, Percival's death does not simply deprive him of a companion, an object of affection; it deprives him of a way of seeing, a focal point: "About him my feeling was: he sat there in the center. Now I go to that spot no longer. The place is empty." The concept is reminiscent of Lily Briscoe's struggle in *To the Lighthouse* to complete her painting by one stroke of the brush. In graphic terms, the "center" is not necessarily the primary object of interest, but rather the element that brings all the others into place and gives rest and symmetry to disparate parts.

As Bernard walks through the streets of London with his thoughts of Percival, he turns for consolation not to a church but to the National Gallery, to "submit myself to the influence of minds like mine outside the sequence." Art, for Bernard, is like religion, not, as the Victorians said, because of what it teaches, but because of what it does and refuses to do. "Mercifully these pictures make no reference; they do not nudge; they do not point. Thus they expand my consciousness of him and bring him back to me differently. I remember his beauty. 'Look, where he comes,' I said"(283).

Woolf rarely comes closer to Joyce in articulating a theory of artistic equipose than in this passage. The paintings—Venus among her flowers, saints and blue madonnas—provide a meeting place for the abstract and the concrete, vivid temporality and the eternally passive. They capture a moment, yet themselves are never-changing. They insist upon nothing. Great art does not seduce or repel the viewer, it does not necessarily prompt him to action, but it imitates the function of great friends by gratuitously presenting a point of view that lifts him out of chaotic isolation and provides him with a new measure of himself.

As Neville, Rhoda, Percival, and the others have done so often, the paintings give life back to Bernard by confronting him with a perspective: "Now through my own infirmity I recover what he was to me: my opposite. Being naturally truthful, he did not see the point of these exaggerations, and was borne on by a natural sense of the fitting, was indeed a great master of the art of living so that he seems to have lived long, and to have spread calm round him, indifference one might almost say . . . A child playing—a summer evening—door will open and shut, will keep opening and shutting, through which I see sights that make me weep. For they cannot be imparted. Hence our loneliness; hence our desolation. I turn to that spot in my mind and find it empty. My own infirmities oppress me. There is no longer him to oppose them. Behold then, the blue madonna streaked with tears. This is my funeral service"(284).

Art, like religion, transforms loneliness, desolation, infirmity, tears from the realm of private grief to that of universal, because communicable, experience. Particular sights may not be "imparted," but the sorrow that comes of not being able to impart them can be shared and therefore made bearable. Similarly, Percival's death is the ultimate sign of his separateness from his friends. Yet, though they cannot follow him beyond the grave, his crossing over into permanent nonbeing does enter their consciousness. When Bernard says, "I turn to that spot in my mind and find it empty," he implies a bereavement that cannot be simply located in an event of the world outside. The loss of Percival is simultaneously an internal loss, the disappearance of a dialectical opposite that helped to strengthen and define his own being. "This is my funeral service," is more than a way of saying Bernard's visit to the museum is his own version of a church ceremony. The death of the friend is a dying in himself.

As the book progresses, the gift of self, whether through friendship or art or some combination of the two, is treated in more and more obviously sacramental terms. An aging Bernard, alone in a restaurant, addresses a stranger (the reader?) in an attempt to sum up his life: "If it were possible, I would hand it you entire. I would break it off as one breaks off a bunch of grapes. I would say, 'Take it. This is my life' "(341). The liturgical echo is not literally religious, but, as before, it is not simple mockery either. Sharing one's life—whether through words or, as for Percival, through quiet presence, however fragmentary or frustrating—is the nearest thing to salvation and immortality one person can offer another, the only means of experiencing otherness, of expanding consciousness, of extending time.

The final pages of the novel, given over almost exclusively to Bernard, are a long, lyrical meditation on art, both its limitations and vulnerabilities in the face of death and its mysterious resilience as a sign of collective resistance to the inevitable. As the meditation progresses, Bernard, who is aging and slowly dying, loses touch with his friends and with himself and finds it harder and harder to tell stories or complete sentences. Though his art becomes less conventionally narrative, less concerned, even in patches, with stories, it increases in musicality; its rhythms grow more insistent, its tones more richly modulated. In a fashion reminiscent of Woolf's favorite poets of the sixteenth and seventeenth centuries, Bernard does battle with death by alternately confessing the weakness and falsity of art and boasting of its power. But he sings either way, revealing harmonies and correspondences, glimpses of beauty and shafts of wit, as manifold and unexpected in form as the intrusions of death itself.

Pugnacity is often associated with Renaissance writers and with Joyce and Lawrence. They thumb their noses at death; they are willing to take on the world. But Woolf should not be excluded from this company, since, from the beginning, it was one of her strengths as a writer to include in her fiction so much that seems inimical to it. *The Waves* contains not only strange unnovelistic elements but all the stated reasons why it was an impossible book to write. In one of his many despondent moods, Bernard thinks, "But if there are no stories, what end can there be, or what beginning? Life is not susceptible perhaps to the treatment we give it when we try to tell it"(362). But, as always, Bernard rouses himself, starts a new sentence, tries another tone: "I jumped up, I said, 'Fight.' 'Fight,' I repeated. It is the effort and struggle, it is the perpetual warfare, it is the shattering and piecing together—this is the daily battle, defeat or victory, the absorbing pursuit. The trees, scattered, put on order; the thick green of the leaves thinned itself to a dancing light. I netted them under with a sudden phrase. I retrieved them from formlessness with words."

As elsewhere in this novel, the reader recognizes a tone—in this case, a Tennysonian bravado—that is almost laughable in the literal context—here that of an aging man sitting in a restaurant. But other echoes sound as well: Stephen Dedalus's *"Non serviam"* as he shatters the lamp and Aaron Sisson's "I believe in the fight which is in everything." Each instance has its potential for comic irony. But the laughter is subverted by quick and subtle shifts in identification. Like the characters themselves—especially Bernard—the reader has threaded his way through the novel moving back and forth from detached observation of a seemingly objective world to imaginative identification with another consciousness. As that consciousness becomes more frequently that of Bernard, the teller of stories, the reader feels not simply the problems of interpretation but the frustrations and satisfactions of composition as well. "Perpetual warfare" includes the task of finding the right words to express the perpetual warfare. The reader who has been taken into the artist's confidence in a rare and extraordinary way, who has been shown his or her doubts and despondencies, is also carried into the celebration of achieved form. The triumphant note is not lightly or ignorantly sounded. Few readers will have come this far in the book without being ready to consent to and share the writer's (Bernard's and Woolf's) brief exultation over the recovery from formlessness.

If art is capable of great moments of clarity and beauty, despite death, it is also capable, in a more sustained way, of balance. It does not dismiss chaos or deny the internal disorder of insanity. In fact, it dares to mimic them and place beside them, by way of magnificently arrogant contrast, the artist's own invention, what Sidney called "in effect another nature . . . making things either better than nature bringeth forth, or, quite anew."

Woolf demonstrates the power of mind together with the power of friendship by giving the reader a portrait of Bernard as he is seen in the world, with a particular body, voice, profession, address, niche, and as he is in his own imagination, protean, androgynous, infinitely expansive.[15] He recognizes his biographical self and the figure he cuts for his acquaintances, but he makes a claim to a larger, more complex being as well: "When I meet an unknown person, and try to break off, here at this table, what I call 'my life,' it is not one life that I look back upon; I am not one person; I am many people; I do not altogether know who I am—Jinny, Susan, Neville, Rhoda, or Louis: or how to distinguish my life from theirs"(368). Later, as he is about to cross the street, he imagines himself taking the arm of Rhoda, who has committed suicide, and trying to convince her that all men are her brothers: "In persuading her I was also persuading my own soul. For this is not one life; nor do I always know if I am man or woman."

These acts of love and identification, so manifold and contradictory, have no way of being lived out except in the imagination and, through the imagination, in art. Bernard really does give himself most fully to his friends in words. Even when he feels his own life ebbing away, feels himself "a man without a self . . . a dead man," he imagines his dissolution as an intermingling with his friends. "Here on my brow is the blow I got when Percival fell. Here on the nape of my neck is the kiss Jinny gave Louis. My eyes fill with Susan's tears. I see far away . . . the pillar Rhoda saw, and feel the rush of the wind of her flight when she leapt"(377). The language is of the sort one associates with mythical heroes who are simultaneously capable of dispersing their spirits among their people and of containing within themselves the sum total of human experience. The artist possesses a divine gift, which often seems like a curse, the imaginative capacity for experience well beyond his mortal power to act out in life.

Bernard is a kind of composite of Stephen Dedalus and Leopold Bloom whose imagination soars and droops; he sees himself as a mythically capacious soul or a pathetic body—an eternally young and adventurous spirit like Percival or "an elderly man, rather heavy, grey above the ears." His final soliloquy is a rising of the wave within him, a challenge to death, the enemy, and an exhilarating impersonation of the heroic young Percival "when he galloped in India." "I strike spurs into my horse. Against you I will fling myself, unvanquished and unyielding, O Death!" And against this deliberately literary and formal battlecry from Bernard, Woolf places the inarticulate death blow, "the waves broke on the shore."

That the echo of Donne and the vivid recollection of Percival form

Bernard's last thoughts before the final breaking of the waves strikingly reaffirms the alliance of art and friendship against death. Essential to life, to self-knowledge, and to the knowledge of worlds beyond the self, formative, freeing, gratuitous, both provide an entry into experience and, paradoxically, the only dependable relief from it. Neither demands choices as lovers or spouses do or as religion does. Their headquarters is not the office or the bedroom or the sanctuary, but the imagination and the memory.

The Waves is a deeply contemplative book. "How much better is silence," thinks Bernard after his lifetime of trying to string the right words together. The book itself, though composed largely of quotations, contains very little direct discourse or speech, since nearly all of what is "said" by the characters is said to themselves, even when it paraphrases or refers to conversations they have had with others. The effect of this method of rendering character and situation differs from that of Conrad or James, for example, in which elaborate internal dramas ultimately explain or at least point to moral actions. However complex and tortuous they are, however much they monopolize space, the inner probings of these writers are always in some sense motivational. They refer to choices and to plot.

Though the outlines of a kind of plot, a chronological sequence of happenings, is always visible in *The Waves,* the long internalized meditations have no causal relation to them. How or why the characters choose their spouses or professions is a matter that involves conscience or duty or common sense—considerations prominent in nineteenth-century novels but barely mentioned in this work. The inner world explored by Woolf is truly "another nature," that of the imagination, inseparable from the external world but not tied to it in functional ways. The imagination, for Woolf, is the faculty of mind that does not have to choose. It absorbs, accumulates, extends, refashions, or refines, but its primary characteristic is capaciousness. It shapes but does not exclude. When Bernard says, "I go to my friends," he is describing an action that is susceptible to treatment in a linear plot, a matter of choice and direction; when he says, "I am my friends," he is asserting a truth of the imagination that is nonsense in the world of describable external nature. Friendship is the link between the doubtful world that is and the certain one that never can be.

T H O U G H clearly different in important ways, the friendships explored by Joyce, Lawrence, and Woolf have significant similarities. In each case, the friend or friends represent a threat and a comfort to the surrogate author-hero. Dedalus, Birkin, and Bernard are all smarter and more articulate than most of their friends, yet susceptible to their physical and emotional charms. Each sees the friend he most loves (Davin, Gerald, Percival) as a masculine archetype of his nation, a personification of characteristics that both attract and repel him. Out of intellectual disapproval of his friend, the protagonist builds his own independent character. Through affection, he retains a sympathetic awareness of whatever it is in human nature that resists typing by artists as well as by society. The friend helps the artist define and criticize himself.

In each case, the separation from the friend—Stephen's departure from Ireland, Gerald's and Percival's deaths—is experienced by protagonist and reader as inevitable, morally appropriate, and, at the same time, irremediably sad. There seems no doubt that Stephen must distance himself from the provincial backwardness of Ireland or that Birkin and Bernard must detach themselves from the arrogant Philistinism of England. Yet, as Lawrence so often said, novelists cannot think merely like historians or moralists or philosophers. The challenge and opportunity of their genre is to treat the whole person. What the novelist must show—as no one else could or would—is the heartbreaking truth that the appalling types of national character are also the beloved brothers and friends of those who describe them and distance themselves from them.

The friend is no simple allegorical figure of the nation; he is as often an intimately experienced, palpable, yet mysterious presence, another self that comes disturbingly close but never unites with the protagonist's self. Nothing is more striking, in contrast with their treatments of marriage, than the tendency in Joyce, Lawrence, and Woolf to introduce ritual into their representations of friendship. In attempting to see marriage in a fresh way, each author is at pains to detach it from its institutional trappings. Betrothals and weddings are either not shown at all or shown from an oblique angle: Gerty MacDowell's fantasies; Ursula and Gudrun talking outside the church where a wedding is taking place; Peter Walsh's romanticized recollection of his proposal to Clarissa. The result is that marriage is returned from the realm of social and religious convention—part sacrament, part business contract—to that of the biological, psychological, and moral rhythms of particular men and women living in pairs.

In a reverse manner characteristic of their treatment of a great variety of social and artistic forms, Joyce, Lawrence, and Woolf subject friendship, that relationship least formalized by society, to moments of highly structured, ritual formality. Stephen's conversations with his friends occur in part during slow, deliberate, processionlike walks through

Dublin—"like a celebrant attended by his ministers"—and culminate in the writing of a poem that celebrates feminine beauty in terms of the exclusively male rites of incensing and the consecration of the Eucharist. After a series of set scenes in which they are closed off from the world, Birkin and Gerald engage in a ritual combat, a pantomime of attraction and opposition. When Gerald is dead, and his body set between candles, Birkin visits him three times, as if returning to a shrine. On the eve of Percival's departure for India, Bernard and his other friends entertain him at a supper that is repeatedly referred to and remembered as a communion. It is as though the experience of friendship—purposeless and difficult to classify yet intensely felt—is best represented in a tableau that fixes contraries in an eternal symmetry but does not resolve them.

The friend is always near and far, unique and typical, a twin and an opposite, an easy simile and a strained conceit. Once physically away from his friends, each protagonist resorts once again to language. Stephen writes a poem, Birkin argues with Ursula, Bernard tells stories to strangers. The absent friends may or may not be included in the new verbal forms. They certainly are not sentimentalized by them. But their remembered presence makes a new language possible, a language that is not merely a tool for advancing plot or proving a point; instead, it is a reflective vehicle circling back to an experience that can be reenacted like a contest or celebrated like a Eucharist better than it can be explained or justified. A work of art can be a "friend to man," providing harmony, beauty, and permanence in a world of suffering and change. A friend can also be like a work of art, simultaneously warm and cold, deep and shallow, vital and lifeless, silent and capable of calling the ego beyond itself. The subject of friendship can grip a narrator and still elude his narration; it seems to epitomize that element of life that "is not susceptible perhaps to the treatment we give it when we try to tell it."

FIVE

The Tendency toward Drama

Actor and Audience

Drama has to do with the underlying laws first, in all their nakedness and divine severity, and only secondarily with the motley agents who bear them out.

JAMES JOYCE, *Drama and Life*

All that is sayable, let it be said, and what isn't, you may sing it, or act it.

D. H. LAWRENCE, *Collected Letters*

The play is poetry, we say, and the novel prose. Let us attempt to obliterate detail, and place the two before us side by side . . . Then, at once, the prime differences emerge; the long leisurely accumulated novel; the little contracted play; the emotion all split up, dissipated and then woven together, slowly and gradually massed into a whole, in the novel; the emotion concentrated, generalized, heightened in the play.

VIRGINIA WOOLF, *Notes on an Elizabethan Play*

T HE GREAT MODERNISTS had an ambition and talent for drama far surpassing that of the Romantics. "Everything, even individuality itself, depends on relationship," wrote Lawrence.[1] Joyce and Woolf agreed, so much so that both subjected their most prized and hard-won of literary trophies—their incomparable narrative voices—to an increasing range of counterpoint, contradiction, mockery, and cacophonous abuse. In her essay "Notes on an Elizabethan Play" Woolf argues, as Joyce does elsewhere, that "the great artist is the man who knows where to place himself above the shifting scenery."[2] But if it has been the writer's practice, following the Romantic convention, to include an artist figure, a surrogate self, at the center of his work, placement "above the shifting scenery" becomes a neat trick. The figure may be emptied of significance, released from its special tie to the author, and allowed to drift aimlessly like Dickens's poetic fops and Thackeray's bohemian quacks. Or the reader may be treated to the much more intriguing spectacle, more reminiscent of the Elizabethans than of the Victorians, of the author distancing but not detaching himself from his representative, placing his own capacity for being described, classified, and dismissed on stage with everyone else's. By exposing a version of himself that is subject to the buffets and contradictions of a world of many voices, the author escapes his limitations by acknowledging them—an act that unites humility with supreme authority.

Joyce, Woolf, and Lawrence began to discover the world beyond self through their sensitive mimetic awareness of utterances like but not identical with their own. As they pursued certain accents, tones, habits of voice, they moved back and forth from a sense of themselves as individual creators, controlling things from behind the scenes, to a view of themselves as members of a large audience, listening, watching, judging, and generalizing. In their mature fiction, indeed in Woolf's and Lawrence's last novels, the three writers introduced drama not simply in the form of dialogue and conflict, but as a theatrical event with a ritualistic stress on gesture, movement, and costume, on the recurrence of action and on the individual's resemblance to a type. They continued, like their Romantic predecessors, to pursue self-knowledge, but the pursuit became a more and more expansive process. The personal self did not disappear, but the individual psyche became less easy to separate from the collective unconscious, personal history from cultural history, the fate of the individual from the destiny of the race.

The introduction of some form of dramatic performance into a novel depersonalizes both the characters and the reader's relationship with the author. The narrator either disappears or takes on a relatively unimportant role during the stage action. With the narrator go many of the details of mind and body that help to create an illusion that the reader has an intimate knowledge of certain characters. Figures we may have seen informally and off-guard are suddenly on stage, in costume, limited to expressing themselves through gesture, dialogue, and declamation. The reader is further distanced by the appearance of a fictitious audience, a crowd of onlookers whose reactions are often so silly or sheeplike as to discourage identification.

The movement from fictional narrative, with its accumulation of concrete observed detail, to drama—the spectacle of distilled speech and movement—is a movement from analysis to contemplation, from description to reflection. A play within a novel, like a play within a play, is a new layer of artifice that gives perspective and credibility to the created environment from which it draws the materials it transforms. It provides a clue to the artist's tricks and to the relationship between experience and art, or, more precisely, between the levels of formal refinement to which man subjects all experience.

But the play within the novel does more than this. It is a vehicle of understanding not merely more stylized and concentrated than the one from which it grows, but of a different order. The novel is a product of a scientific and secular mentality. Its method is descriptive, moralistic, and analytical. Drama is in its origins religious and mysterious, a presentation in sound and gesture of recurrent human needs, fears, compulsions, and joys. Though there may be a chorus or wise characters, no one in a play is so privileged as the narrator in a novel to speak for the author. Reading a novel is a silent and private affar, which occurs only between the reader and the book. Witnessing a play is a participation in a public, sometimes noisy, event. Just as a proper reading of a novel requires a certain loss of self-awareness, attendance at a play imposes a dual awareness of actors and audience, a combined sense of self as performer and observer, yet not wholly either. To read a novel is to become another self, to identify with the narrator, to become his child, companion, or friend. To watch a play is to suspend the self between the observed and the observing, to join the author and God temporarily in knowledge that is both internal and external, subjective and objective, here and there.

To move from the novel to the drama is to move from a way of perceiving the world and the self that is rationalistic, empirical, verbal, individualistic, and indirect to another, very different way, which is sensuous, intuitive, physically symbolic, universal, and direct. By maintaining the superstructure of the novel or a prose narrative while inserting a significant dramatic interlude composed of more or less the same characters and situations, the modern writer requires the reader not merely to see in a new way but to engage in a continual readjustment of perspective. As we witness the elasticity of fictional characters and circumstances, we experience, as though with the author, his capacity for transforming himself by means of his own creative activity.

H O W E V E R difficult and mannered the other sections of *Ulysses* may be, it is the Circe episode, structured like a dramatic script, in which the reader is assisted least by any semblance of a narrative guide. Still, to read a play is not necessarily difficult. A playwright can help a reader in a number of ways to locate himself in relation to the main characters and actions of the piece, that is, help him imagine himself as a member of an audience. One of the first curiosities of the Circe episode is that the narrator's vanishing act seems to involve taking the audience, as a stable, identifiable entity, with him. From the earliest sections of the book, Stephen Dedalus and Leopold Bloom have been observers of themselves and their surroundings, and their actions and thoughts have been sufficiently prominent to form focal points for the reader's attention and that of the minor characters who witness them.

The episode opens with a crowd of grotesques, stunted men and women squabbling, bodiless voices calling and answering—a muddle of actors and observers—and a burlesque figure of the absent narrator, "a deafmute idiot with goggle eyes"—the author as the most hopelessly lost member of his own audience, watching all, able to explain nothing. When asked by the children, who turn Isaiah's proclamation into a question—"Where's the great light?"—the idiot answers, "Ghaghahest." It is a garbled reply that mingles the sounds of foolish laughter with "guest" and "guess." Either Joyce is perversely refusing to take responsibility for his own creation, or he is suggesting that authors, like readers, are guests in the worlds they imagine and that the act of explanation is sufficiently different from that of invention to make his interpretations "guesses" like ours.

The peculiar structure of the Circe episode suggests that the latter view is neither arrogant nor frivolously humble, but a serious comment about the relationship between creative activity and observation. The roles of creator and observer are continually explored, interwoven, and confused in the section. Creativity is seen not to be nearly so independent and "active" as is often supposed. Dreams, memories, fantasies—racial, historical, and religious—drift unbidden through Bloom's and Stephen's minds and force their way into gesture and word. Similarly, watching is not nearly so passive as is supposed, since, as in Bloom's Odyssean case, it involves pursuing a hazardous course and actually undergoing metamorphoses, changes in identity, as each turn in the journey demands. A great dramatist must be able to place himself in the dark with the least sophisticated members of his audience. A good observer and reader changes as he watches and therefore cooperates at the deepest level with the author's creative act.[3]

The first of the major characters who appears in Nighttown is Stephen Dedalus, but his role as actor-artist is indistinct. Though in ambition, eloquence, and conceit, he is one image of an artist, his originality is strictly limited by his background and surroundings. His flourishing of his ashplant walking stick and his recitation of the paschal introit *"vidi aquam,"* asserts his self-image as mocker, magician, priest, writer, and lusty young buck. His ashplant is his spear (which in the liturgy is said to have brought forth water from Christ's side), his wand, his aspergillum, his pen, and his penis. His gesture suggests that he will challenge the divine, heal old wounds, open new ones, write masterpieces, and make love. In fact, he does none of these, not even the last, though he is in a whorehouse. Even his learned and blasphemous recitation of the introit is far from an act of pure rebellion. As the day began, Stephen watched Buck Mulligan perform a mock mass; though at the time he disapproved, he is trying another version of the same thing here, a case of an observer remembering what he has seen and turning it to his own inventive use. Furthermore, the play on the image of the ashplant is anticipated by a ditty, half bawdy, half childish, sung by the whores about the leg of the duck:

> I gave it to Molly
> Because she was jolly
> . . . . .
> I gave it to Nelly
> To stick in her belly (430)

The brazen phallus, the blasphemous spear, the rebellious sword and inspired pen—emblems of enormous pride and satisfaction to those who wield them—are, in fact, well-worn instruments, creative, but communal property, tossed about like an old joke or a familiar customer by a flock of whores. This is not to say that Stephen and his artistic preten-

tions are merely mocked in this episode. Though young and imperti-
nent, Stephen is not greatly different from anyone else who defines himself primarily in creative terms. His emphasis is only half right. The
reader who sees Stephen as an imitator can correct the imbalance without despising his art or his ambition.

Far more prominent in the Circe episode is Bloom, whose course the
unseen author traces much more closely than he does Stephen's. Yet for
the reader in search of help, Bloom makes a troublesome guide. He is
neither Dante nor Virgil in this Inferno; he certainly does not know his
way around, and he is in no position to ask searching questions and re-
peat the answers for the reader's benefit. A wanderer and misfit, he appears to belong in Nighttown even less than in other quarters of Dublin.
He has drifted into the district in vague pursuit of the drunken Stephen
and his friend Lynch, though he has no very clear motive for seeking
them. Insofar as readers rely on him at all—and to a large extent we
must, since Bloom's mere prominence makes us cling to him as we would
to a guiding narrator or hero—we do so at first as though he were another observer like ourselves, following a sequence of words and events
he has not made and is not at all sure he understands.

In the absence of an apparent author and a hero whose actions are significant and motivations clear, we follow Bloom into Nighttown as
though he were a personification of an audience projected into a scene it
is witnessing. As Bloom enters, his first experience is not an action but an
observation; he sees a composite portrait of Nelson, Wellington, and
Gladstone in a hairdresser's window and various distorted reflections of
himself in a concave and convex mirror. If we eliminate Bloom's dream
fantasies and trace his actual behavior throughout the episode, we can
hardly avoid being struck by his passivity. He is a bystander, an onlooker extraordinaire: he watches the street people, the police, the English soldiers, the whores, Stephen and Lynch, and, as his mirrored entrance suggests, he watches himself as a guilt-ridden witness to his own
would-be daring as an interloper in Nighttown. Indeed, his mere presence there carries with it a complex guilt since he is ashamed, before his
ancestors and children, to be there at all, and embarrassed, before the
whores and their madam, not to be there on business.

But observation is not an isolated phenomenon. The guilt-ridden
Bloom imagines himself arrested for "unlawfully watching and beset-
ting," though what he has actually done is feed a stray dog. But watching *is* an "arrestable" offense in the nonjuridical sense that its purpose is
fulfilled, it comes to a stop, when the self is found in the spectacle being
observed. The point is not a solipsistic one. For Joyce, the ego is not all.
On the contrary, the human world outside the self is so densely rich, so

thick with complexity, as to provide a continuing challenge to the ego to find a link, however frail, and a place, however meager, within it. The links are as often trivial and humiliating as they are significant or satisfying, yet finding them is an essential human act, an embrace of living reality. Joyce never seriously deviated from his early conviction that "we must accept [life] as we see it."[4] Bloom looks until he finds himself *with* others; he is a lost spectator until he plays a part in the drama.

Bloom's seeing himself in the distorting mirrors as he enters Nighttown is not mere mock-heroic debasement. It lifts him (and with him the reader) from the role of passive observer to that of a reflected image, part of the passing scene of creatures made and diminished by the vision of others. When Bloom imagines himself apprehended by the police, appropriately called "the watch," it is as though he changes places with them and is transformed from one who watches and witnesses to one who is watched and witnessed against. As he tries different accents, languages, and costumes (the fez of von Bloom Pasha, the dinner jacket of a squire, a sporting suit, workman's overalls, Don Giovanni's hat) he deserts his place in the audience and becomes, with outlandish abandon, an actor, a player of roles, a speaker of lines, and, most significant of all, an inventor of alibis. To move from the irresponsibility and ignorance of the audience onto the stage is to assume "a face," a reason for being, in the shape of a gesture or speech.

Superficially, Bloom's fancy disguises are travesties of art and manhood, nearly as demeaning as his moments of inarticulate defeat. But it is the movement from role to role, not particular disguises in themselves, that provides the key to Joyce's art and Bloom's vitality. Whenever Bloom changes from a curious and puzzled observer to an actor in a drama, he moves from a condition of shadowy identity to a state of caricature sharpness and simplicity. He becomes the pantomime lecher, cuckold, buffoon, lover, victim, king, savior. Each of these roles calls forth a certain kind of speech from him, an appeal to his accusers, a political harangue to his followers, a prophetic sermon to his adorers. No longer a member of the crowd, he himself commands an audience, attracting attention and strong feelings.

Bloom's imagined roles are absurd, but they do provide a clue to his character and an equally revealing clue to the world of spectators to whom he plays both in fancy and in reality. To the extent that the crowd demands an explanation, provokes self-justification or confession, and looks from its own haze for clarity, the audience creates the fool. Bloom's quick costume changes, his attempts at ventriloquism, and his speech-making are comments on his own anxieties and desires, but they are also comments on the nature of communication. Man betrays himself with speech, both in the sense that he exposes himself but also in that, in the process, he simplifies, diminishes, or exaggerates his potential.

Bloom's dreamlike fantasies are deeply rooted in his own life, his family and race, the particularity of the day he has just passed; thus they place him *in* humanity, not apart from it, as he was as a silent and brooding observer. His feelings and thoughts are his own, unique, until he exposes and expresses them. The public gesture, especially the spoken word, however pathetic, absurd, ordinary, or obscure, creates a world to which Bloom belongs. He does, in wildly rapid and shifting pantomime fashion, what all but the totally solitary or mad do: he imagines parts for himself and communicates through them.

O F A L L the characters, Bloom is most like an artist, not because of particular skills but because he is the most transparent in his shifts from contemplation to action, from complex silences to simple utterances, from awesome potentiality to ridiculous actuality. He moves imaginatively from character type to character type, but, more important, he moves from vantage point to vantage point, from being one who sees to being one who is seen. For Joyce, the artist loses his personality not simply in a varied cast of characters, but in the spaces between those who perform and those who watch until they see themselves in the performance; then, like Bloom, they are "arrested" in their watching and join the performers in being adored and crucified. When Bloom is questioned by the watch, he gives his profession as that of a writer: "Well, I follow a literary occupation. Author-journalist. In fact, we are just bringing out a collection of prize stories of which I am the inventor, something that is an entirely new departure. I am connected with the British and Irish press. If you ring up . . ."(458).

Bloom's insistence on the originality of his "art" and the factual basis of his story underscores his guilty awareness of the weak ground he is treading. Yet there are fragments of truth and originality in his words. He is connected with a newspaper, and his imitation of Philip Beaufoy, author of *Matcham's Masterstroke,* which he read and wiped himself on that morning, is an amusing satire on the self-importance of third-rate writers. He imagines Beaufoy on the telephone with Myles Crawford of the *Freeman's Urinal and Weekly Arsewiper,* accusing him of plagiarism. "A plagiarist. A soapy sneak masquerading as a literateur. It's perfectly obvious that with the most inherent baseness he has cribbed some of my bestselling books, really gorgeous stuff, a perfect gem, the love passages in which are beneath suspicion." When Bloom snickers at this, Beaufoy hurls out his worst insults: "Youre too beastly awfully weird for words! . . . [you've] not even been to a university." Bloom replies (indistinctly): "University of life. Bad art." And Beaufoy, in his ultimate gesture of outrage, shouts "foul lie" and holds up his ill-used story, "damning evidence, the *corpus delicti,* my lord, a specimen of my maturer work disfigured by the hallmark of the beast."

The exchange, all of which takes place in Bloom's mind, reveals much about Bloom—the fertility of his imagination, and the extent to which he at least realizes he is a fake—and even more about the foolish claims sometimes made about art. Both Bloom's and the imaginary Beaufoy's claims of originality are misplaced, since art, as *Ulysses* continually demonstrates, is inherently derivative and parodic. The difference is that some authors know it and others do not. Beaufoy's ungrammatical attempts at elegant locution, his use of high-toned clichés, and his horror at the thought of his works being defiled are a caricature of the artist who defines his vocation as an avoidance of the merely human. That Bloom could be "too beastly awfully weird for words" is, in the aesthetic world of Joyce, more an admission of artistic impotence than an insult. Furthermore, when Bloom associates the "university of life" with "bad art," Beaufoy assumes that he is criticizing his work again (which is one possibility) rather than making a connection, if only a poor one, between life and art. The final indignity, Beaufoy's shit-smeared story, bearing "the hallmark of the beast," may be a low form of art and humor, but it is an unmistakable emblem of fiction being rubbed in the stuff of human nature. Insofar as Bloom has accomplished that both in fact and in his imaginary dialogue with Beaufoy, he has acted out in farcical burlesque fashion what the invisible author has been doing throughout his book.

Bloom is also seen as a literary man in the Circe episode when he is accused by three ladies of writing them indecent letters making sexual propositions. Each lady remembers her particular letter vividly enough to be able to paraphrase it with sufficient accuracy to suggest Bloom's style as well as his intentions: "He lauded almost extravagantly my nether extremities, my swelling calves in silk hose drawn up to the limit, and eulogized glowingly my other hidden treasures in priceless lace"(466). One recognizes the voluptuous euphemisms that Bloom so relishes in the romantic pornography he buys for Molly and the analogous pleasure the disapproving ladies take in repeating Bloom's lewd descriptions. In a sense, the imaginary act of seduction is welcomed, as they recognize themselves in Bloom's allegedly outrageous and illicit prose. All forms of communication may involve a kind of seduction, an invitation and response to another's imaginative version of things. The reaction of the ladies, both their pleasure and their disapproval, stems from the recognition of their own fantasies in Bloom's writing. Like many writers, he presents them with a picture of themselves that they find privately fascinating and publicly unacceptable.

Reading the indecent propositions in Bloom's letters is an act of literary interpretation in which the recipients, in this case the three ladies, place themselves imaginatively in line as the objects of the writer's interest. The artist selects from nature and makes an expressive gesture; the reader cooperates with the artist and joins in his selectively creative impulse by a further process of selection, in which she herself figures. But if art can offend by being too pointed, it can also offend by failing to be pointed enough. The three ladies, who become more and more angry with Bloom, even threatening to scourge and flay him, may, as they claim, be upset by his rude suggestions. Or, like the Maenads who tear Orpheus to pieces, they may be angry because his art has little directly to do with them. Orpheus pines for Eurydice, and behind all of Bloom's erotic fantasies is a preoccupation, amounting to fidelity, with Molly.

Bloom, the letter writer with an unforgettable style, cannot win. Whether or not the ladies are the direct object of his interest, they are outraged. To be overlooked is even more insulting than to be singled out. Bloom's art, like Joyce's, is constantly subjected to the accusation that it means too much or too little. The same artist may be rebuked simultaneously for indecent exposure and for needless obscurantism, for being obtrusively present or annoyingly absent from his work.

If Joyce shows Bloom "playing" imaginatively at life, he also shows him, with mixed effect, "playing" dead. Alternating with Bloom's literary alibis are moments when he tries to avoid the snares of language altogether by assuming the role of a man of wide and varied experience who is unable to tell anything about himself. The barrister J. J. O'Molloy defends Bloom on the grounds that he is foreign, a child, physically ill, mentally retarded—a compilation of all those who cannot make themselves understood. After several references to travel and shipwreck, O'Molloy asserts that "if the accused could speak he could a tale unfold one of the strangest that have ever been narrated between the covers of a book." The barrister argues that Bloom is "not all there, in fact." If Bloom the plagiarist and letter writer has been a seriocomic figure of the writer in action, Bloom the idiot Odysseus, who can only speak pigeon Chinese-English ("Li li poo lil chile"), is an absurdly pathetic figure of the writer in potential, the tongue-tied antithesis of expressive man.

In a similar moment of humiliation, Bloom is challenged by Bella Cohen to tell the "most revolting piece of obscenity" in all his career: "Tell me something to amuse me, smut or a bloody good-ghost-story or a line of poetry, quick, quick, quick! Where? How? What time? With how many?"(538). Bella wants Bloom to be a poet or storyteller, to entertain her with fictitious facts, but the most he can do in his slavish pig-like state is to grunt a vague self-condemnation, "I rererepugnosed in rererepugnant . . ." He cannot be a Homer on demand to recite his travels or those of his heroic ancestors, since, literally, he was not "all there" with them. Yet his ancestors, cultural and genetic, are in part present in him. Like his erotic fantasies, which Bella tries to tap, they possess the promise of a very good story if it only could be told. But the once talkative Bloom is made to feel the weight of inexpressible experience, of happenings that clog the brain and thicken the tongue.

In Bloom, through his buffoonery and transparency, Joyce combines a confession and an observation, a subjectively felt emotion and a critically detached analysis, and turns them into a dramatic spectacle: tongue-tied Bloom in the witness box, stuttering Bloom under the heel of a whore mistress. It is in such contexts of mute impotence that Bloom's flamboyant costumes and magniloquent alibis take on a significance beyond gusto and quick wit and become emblems of creativity and heroic resistance to the living death of silence and paralysis. *Ulysses* has frequently been praised as a fictional encyclopedia of the arts; it is equally exhaustive in its display of those impediments, the varieties of *rigor mortis,* internal and external, that ought to make art impossible.

The only one not caught "dead"—permanently in the mirror—is the artist, not merely the craftsman, but everyone in his capacity as maker. He does not have a simple escape, a stable perch above and beyond it all, but he has the flexibility to move between watcher and watched; he is, moreover, unwilling to take his place fixedly with either. Like Shakespeare, he can see into and out from the mirror, stage, or mind. He can internalize, brood, make all concrete and lyrical, or he can break away from himself in gesture and dialogue and create a universal drama. For Joyce, the artist, modern or ancient, who combines these perspectives surpasses those, whether neoclassical or Romantic, who accentuate one at the expense of the other.

T HE A R T I S T as rebel and disrupter of conventional order is one of Joyce's favorite characterizations, but he presents with similar energy a number of portraits of art as a balancing act between the chaotic extremes of life and the blank vacuity of death. Since all forms of human expression, whether self-revelation or narrative description, are limited and ultimately self-defeating, the artist can no more afford to be complacent in his authorial role than the actor can in the parts he chooses to play. Parody is another side of the silly or grotesque human caricatures that result from the simplification and stiffening of moral and psychological traits. Both demean the potential forms they appear to promise but do not deliver.

Bloom dons voices and modes of speech as quickly and frequently as he does costumes. Sometimes his mode is direct and emotional, but often he adopts the manner of a storyteller, calm and uninvolved, relating the "facts" of his life as though narrating the plot of a work of fiction. Just as certain of his fantasies are greatly exaggerated self-caricatures, these imagined narrations are networks of familiar understatement. By reciting the external details of his life in the most banal of phrases, he provides a contrasting dullness to the glitter of his far-fetched tales; he plays down what is played up by his most fearful and hopeful self; he retreats into timid conventionality, into plot, seen as a sequence of uneventful domestic episodes with all strands neatly tied together, from ritual drama, a reenactment without end of the recurring crises of the race.

One of Bloom's most prosaic moments as a teller of his own tale precedes his first claim to being a literary man. He tries to convince the jury of his respectability by saying, "I am a respectable married man without a stain on my character. I live in Eccles street. My wife, I am the daughter of a most distinguished commander, a gallant upstanding gentleman, who do you call him, Majorgeneral Brian Tweedy, one of Britain's fighting men who helped to win our battles"(457). Here Bloom follows the conventions of realistic narration: he provides the jury with names and places, identifies his family with national interest, and allows his wife to "speak" for herself. He gives the appearance of providing accurate information while, as the reader sees, revealing nothing of any importance to him. His dull, respectable understatements are finally as inadequate and misleading as expressions of identity as his wild fantasies of himself as von Bloom Pasha, the Emperor Leopold I, or a white slave girl in captivity in Bella Cohen's brothel.

That Bloom's attempts at self-justification and definition by means of conventional narration fail to do him "justice" in his own estimation as well as in that of the jury and reader is suggested by the fact that, each time, he abruptly departs from his own dull text and plunges imaginatively into a more controversial and interesting literary persona, that of the plagiarist-defiler and offensive seducer. He moves from tedium to adventure, from the greater deception of prosaic narration—pretending to simplicity, clarity, and completeness—to the lesser deception of dramatic dialogue, which admits ambiguity, obscurity, and imperfection. In one case, language appears to claim a functional transparency for itself, an unassailable instrumental honesty; in the other, the language of conversation is primarily an expression of the human imagination, eternally open, like poetry, to interpretation.

In the world of Nighttown, the artist who presents himself as a complacent storyteller, a benign historian and placid grammarian, certain of his chronology and syntax, is a failure and a fraud like everyone else, only less entertaining. However, the literary man who is at the same time accused of plagiarizing and defiling, honoring with imitation, and insulting with earthy additions to the text, is a tantalizingly ambiguous figure, one who admires what he finds but cannot help adding something of himself to it and thereby changing it forever. Similarly, the letter writer who both attracts and repels the ladies balances seemingly opposite traits.

In the crowd of voices and roles he adopts, Bloom is most Bloom when he is equivocal. He resolves the conflicts within himself, not through pursuing any of the political, religious, or sexual extremes that so often lead to violence, but peacefully, playfully, and, under some circumstances, bravely, through language. Bloom's characteristic speech is a gesture of respect for the freedom of the person he is addressing. Even in his imaginary seductions, he plays games with language that tantalize with possible unspoken meanings, add the pleasures of the imagination to the pleasures of the flesh, yet force nothing on the one being addressed.

Meeting an old sweetheart in Nighttown, Bloom recalls a childhood word-substitute game and uses it to flirt with the woman and resurrect "the dear dead days beyond recall": "(*Meaningfully dropping his voice*) I confess I'm teapot with curiosity to find out whether some person's something is a little teapot at present." To which Mrs. Breen answers: "(*Gushingly*) Tremendously teapot! London's teapot and I'm simply teapot all over me"(445). The "meaningfulness" of this exchange is not to be found in discovering the "right" words with which to fill in the blanks, though the possibilities are fairly obvious and amusing. A kind of communication, typical of the entire book, has been established. It is not so much communication understood as exchange of information as it is a presentation of one imagination to another, a self-revelation that, despite the party game or perhaps because of it, is more direct and honest than a recitation of street numbers and family names. Mrs. Breen is "aroused" by Bloom's words in a way that parallels what Joyce may expect from his reader, an awakening of curiosity, which does not necessarily lead to a translation into other words or actions, but, rather, brings about an imaginative cooperation, a participation in the game.

Even Bloom's mistakes, his unconscious games with language, are dynamic and liberating in comparison with the fragments of closed and correct narration. His confusions usually seem closer to a larger and more complex truthfulness than the narrow recitations and explanations through which human beings have so often tried to connect their lives with the rest of the world. Bloom has attended the funeral of Paddy Dignam earlier in the day. His mind returns to the ceremony and to the dead man several times during the day and night. Finally, the ghost of Dignam appears and addresses Bloom.

PADDY DIGNAM
Bloom, I am Paddy Dignam's spirit. List, list, O list!
BLOOM
The voice is the voice of Esau.
SECOND WATCH
(*Blesses himself.*) How is that possible?
FIRST WATCH
It is not in the penny catechism.
PADDY DIGNAM
By metempsychosis. Spooks.
A VOICE
O rocks.(473)

The scene may expose confusion on the part of its players, but it is not itself confused. Two dominant themes of *Ulysses*—usurpation and the return of the dead—appear in illuminating ways. Bloom's identification of the voice is a literary error that contains a psychological truth. Esau, the older son of Joseph, was tricked out of his rightful inheritance by his younger brother Jacob, the prototypical usurper. Hamlet's father was murdered by his brother, who married his wife and usurped his throne. Bloom, as usual, can identify himself with more than one part in these dramas. Molly's voice is a reminder that his role as husband has that day been usurped by Blazes Boylan. At the same time, in his encounters with the ghosts of Dignam and his own father and grandfather, he experiences the guilt of the living who take the places of the dead. Metempsychosis, the exchange of souls, occurs within Bloom's imagination. His ambivalence is not mere confusion or passivity, but the personification of dramatic displacement, an act of perception and sympathy that does not lose touch with the self but connects it with the larger network of human experience beyond the individual.

The difference between the living Bloom and the dead Dignam is that Bloom, however unconsciously, can embody and express these connections, while Dignam, except through Bloom or some other survivor, cannot. Dignam attempts to tell about himself, but his mode, predictably, is that of a conventional realistic narration. "Once I was in the employ of Mr. J. H. Menton, solicitor, commissioner of oaths and affidavits, of 27 Bachelor's Walk. Now I am defunct, the wall of the heart hypertrophied. Hard lines."

Dignam's story has the one advantage of a clear ending. His lines are "hard," not difficult to follow, but rigid, unyielding to a variety of interpretations, the opposite of Bloom's party games and literary bloopers. Just before Dignam returns to his grave, Bloom imagines the cemetery caretaker calling him through a megaphone to return to his proper place. The narrative, now taken up by the caretaker, ends as it had begun with an address. "Burial docket letter number, U.P. Eightyfive thousand. Field seventeen. House of Keys. Plot, one hundred and one." The pun on "plot" is devastating, Joyce's equivalent of Lawrence's exasperation with stories that reduce, confine, and complete, that impose *rigor mortis* in the name of structure.

T HE T R O U B L E with plots is that they tend to treat human beings primarily as bodies with measurable contours and predictable conclusions. This is part of Woolf's argument in her essays "Mr. Bennett and Mr. Brown" and "Modern Fiction." One of the ways the writer can convey not merely an inner but a different rhythm of life is by disrupting the onward rush of events with which plot ordinarily concerns itself. As a primarily visual writer, Woolf developed a technique that was impressionistic and imagistic. The flow of time is continuously diverted into whirlpools and eddies, circles of light and substance that provide a movement of their own, not unconnected to the general tow but not entirely regulated by it either.

As a primarily aural writer, Joyce relied heavily on verbal configurations, which are in many ways the counterpart of his mythical superstructure. The *double entendre,* the play on words, especially word sounds, momentarily turns the reader away from the forward momentum of the narration toward a recognition of connections that are not sequential and diachronic but simultaneous and synchronic. The same tactic—an association by coloration, texture, and tone rather than merely by directional currents—is applied to characters.

Much has been said about the seemingly ironic inconsequentiality of Bloom's and Stephen's meeting in Nighttown. Certainly, according to the conventions of linear plot, the two characters have little cause to come together, almost nothing in common, and only the most casual motivations for being in the brothel in the first place. One might argue that their relative aimlessness binds them, but true as that may be, their relationship has other, more distinctive aspects. Both are dressed in black, giving them a priestly or rabbinical impression that is literally false but figuratively appropriate since their mourning dress—Stephen's worn because of his mother's death and Leopold's because of Dignam's funeral—signals a preoccupation with last things. Both are haunted by loss and by the various ways of responding to it and attempting to recover what is lost. Both behave, at least some of the time, as artists and think of themselves as "literary" men. Both are repeatedly "performing," acting out roles in their own minds or for the benefit of a chosen few, while refusing or failing to do what is expected of them in conventional social circumstances. In the traditional sense, Stephen is an undutiful son and Leopold an unobliging husband. And while in the brothel, neither "performs" in the manner expected of male visitors. In short, though little "happens" during their encounter, the reader is made aware of countless details of affinity, quite apart from the Odysseus-Telemachus parallel, that make their meeting seem inevitable.

The most profound and important link between Leopold and Stephen is the humanity that brings together their artistic, imaginative, ordering minds with their sensitive, active, responsive bodies. Despite the criticisms of Joyce as a writer who uses the imagination to flee from life, the varied interweavings of the characters of Leopold and Stephen dramatize a yearning for design and the never-ending need to immerse the design in animal nature. When Florry, one of the whores, asks Stephen to sing "Love's Old Sweet Song," the title that spells "loss" and that has been running through Bloom's mind all day, he refuses:

STEPHEN

No voice. I am a most finished artist. . . .

FLORRY

(*Smirking.*) The bird who can sing and won't sing.(518)

Not only does the title of the song recall Bloom, but Stephen's peculiar use of "finished" sounds like one of Bloom's revealing mistakes in which meaning is suspended between opposites. It seems as though Stephen wanted to make an excuse for not singing ("As an artist I'm through") and manages to make the alibi sound like a boast ("I am a most accomplished artist"). The brothel setting and Florry's ironical retort suggest a comparison between performing artistically and sexually. The rebellious Stephen will do neither on demand, any more than he would pray for his dying mother on demand. The genuinely artistic gesture, like the genuinely loving, moral, and religious act must be a free gift, an act of grace, not a mechanical performance of duty.

The association of the aesthetic and the sexual is not merely an idle joke, but a bringing together of mind and body, a refusal to dissociate the moral and imaginative life from the physical. Understood in this way, Stephen's rebellious negativity and Bloom's impotence are not altogether different: the mind, with the body, rebels against certain automatic expectations and, for all practical purposes, becomes incapable of expressing itself except in what appear to be negation and passivity. When Stephen is pressed about the song, he answers, "Spirit is willing but the flesh is weak," thus using his head to blame his body for failing to do what neither wishes.

Remarking on his black suit and possibly even recognizing the familiar Biblical quotation, Florry asks Stephen if he is from the seminary:

FLORRY
Are you out of Maynooth? You're like someone I knew once.
STEPHEN
Out of it now. (*To himself.*) Clever.

Stephen's "clever" repetition shows how the same words can have altogether opposite meanings, but here again the point is not in the idle play but in what it suggests about words and experience. The polar significance of "out of" as either "belonging to" or "not belonging to" demonstrates the capacity of the human brain, and therefore of the language it invents and uses, to sustain simultaneous antitheses. Stephen is in some ways—culturally and temperamentally—very much a seminarian, and in equally important ways he is not. His "out of it now" is analogous to Bloom's "teapot," an equivocation with the most serious of functions— to express the dynamic and precarious conflicts inherent in human nature in a fashion that provides form without destroying vitality.

Immediately following Stephen's reply, Philip Drunk and Philip Sober, two vaudeville dons, stage equivalents of Stephen's divided state of mind, perform a song and dance act with lawnmowers on the theme of Stephen's play on words. "Clever ever. Out of it. Out of it. By the by have you the book, the thing, the ashplant? Yes, there it, yes. Cleverever outofitnow. Keep in condition. Do like us." This imaginary fools' duet is Stephen's evasion set to music, an artistic expression as a projection of the equivocal but truthful state of its author's mind. Once again, the association of "book," "thing," and "ashplant" suggest a phallic (creative) and rebellious (destructive) role for the writer. But as the dons are "trimmers" and wear Matthew Arnold masks, they also expose Stephen's fear of compromise. The imaginary song and dance that emerges from Stephen's refusal to sing on request does nothing to advance the story. On the contrary, it helps to explain why it is so difficult for Stephen to act, that is, to behave like a character in an advancing plot. In this land of Circe, he is under as much constraint as Bloom when he imagines himself under the heel of Bella Cohen.

The particulars of Bloom's conflicts, though different in detail from Stephen's, reveal a comparable capacity to imagine a life outside the one that is given, to live in it intensely, to be both audience and actor, to multiply and reflect images of the self to the point of paralysis. The feminine and maternal side of Bloom alternately pleases and disturbs him throughout the book. When imagining a defense against accusations that he is a notorious seducer of women, he conjures up medical witnesses who testify that he is about to have a baby. For Bloom, the moment is a curious blend of shame and pride. But in the presence of the powerful and domineering Bella Cohen, the madam who becomes a master, he undergoes a sex transformation of unmitigated humiliation and servitude. In Bloom's dialogue with Bella, there are several analogues to the don's duet. One of the most striking occurs when he imagines Bella addressing him through her fan: "Is me her was you dreamed before? Was then she him you us since knew? Am all them and the same now we?"(528).

At first, this jumble of words seems pure nonsense, but the disorder suggests a new order. The three questions have very much the same effect on standard grammar and syntax as the structure of *Ulysses,* especially the Circe episode, has on standard narration. Linguistically, pronouns, verb tenses, and word order are confused. But the grammatical and syntactical confusion provides an accurate reflection of Bloom's mind, in which past and future are continually intruding on the present and other lives on the integrity of the self. The fan's garbled questions, like the "trimmers' " duet, has a design, artistry, and truth of its own. Nonetheless, it becomes clear that if the book were only fools' songs and grammatical jumbles, it would become unreadable. And if Bloom and Stephen were only locked in self-conscious inactivity, they would become like the characters in the later works of Samuel Beckett. But neither is allowed to happen. If drama—with its choral voices and heightened gestures—comes to the rescue of the plodding, fact-laden novel, the novel, in its turn, provides an escape from the timeless and static rituals of the stage. Drama provides an alternative to space and time; the novel comforts with local history. After spectacular visions of enthronement and persecution, the world in flames, and the heel of Circe, Dublin, June 16, 1904, seems a relief.

Another way of putting this is to say that *Ulysses* provides a dramatic interaction not only between words, grammatical and syntactical structures, character types, and authorial perspectives, but between genres. The play and the novel are themselves "characters" within the author's control. The spectacle does eventually wind down and give way to a simpler, more conventionally linear sequence. Bloom regains his sense of manhood and brushes off Bella, who tells Stephen at the pianola that "this isn't a musical peepshow." She demands to be paid, but Stephen prefers describing a Parisian pornographic show in mock pigeon-French, thus narrating what would have been shown earlier in the episode. In a quixotic act of rebellion (against God, the Church, his mother), Stephen smashes the chandelier and is hurried out of the brothel. In the street outside, he becomes involved in a drunken argument about Ireland and Edward VII with a British soldier who becomes angry and knocks him down. All these events are accompanied by distorted voices and gaping crowds, but Stephen is clearly at the center of a comparatively swiftly advancing story of a young Dubliner, a man very much of his time and place, engaged in a fight that brings history and politics sharply to mind.

What is even more important in terms of the return from the extremes of dramatic ambivalence to localized narration is the presence of Bloom as a witness to Stephen's actions and words. Bloom is technically not narrating this section since it is still presented in play form, but his presence as prime observer provides the reader with a vantage point, a sensibility through which he can watch and judge events. Bloom is finally playing the role he seemed about to play at the beginning of the episode. No longer shifting costumes and voices, he remains a relatively stable consciousness, a guide, a fellow reader of Stephen's story.

This return to recognizable time and place and to a narrator distinct from the protagonist is not a permanent phenomenon. Eternity is not conquered by time, mythic stature by biography, or gesture by narration. This is not that kind of battle of the books; it is a struggle born out of absolute and unending interdependence. The dramatic spectacles of Bloom and Stephen as they might have been in other times and bodies and as they are in their imaginations, gives immense power and poignancy to their narratable lives. The reader is made not only to see but vicariously to experience the spectacular causes for passivity, negation, and paralysis, the nightmare pantomime of conflict between desire and guilt, ambition and timidity; he then returns with Bloom and Stephen to a narrated episode on a Dublin Street with a greatly heightened sensitivity and respect for the least sign of reason and generosity wrested from that universal hell.

According to the linear narrative, the one action performed by Bloom that is distinct from wandering, dreaming, and observing is his coming to the aid of the unconscious Stephen. He guards his money, hat, and stick, and, when the others have all left, he bends down, calls softly to Stephen, brushes the wood shavings from his clothes, and loosens his waistcoat buttons so that he can breathe more freely. Considered in the narrative context exclusively, the action, while clearly generous, has little point beyond its own transient sentimentality. But, following as it does the apocalyptic vaudeville of the two characters' imaginations, the interlocked chorus lines of accusation and defense, motive and countermotive, the simplicity, directness, and gratuity of the act endow it with an extraordinary significance.

Once more, Bloom leaves his post as observer and enters the scene he has been watching. As he does so, the linear narration of external detail does not so much give way to an internal universal drama as blend with it in a new form, in which history and eternity, the body and the imagination, are no longer at absurd odds but coupled in a momentary harmony. Outside of *"ce bordel où nous tenons nostre état,"* where love is bought and sold, Bloom performs an act of unsolicited generosity. The fact that his action is relatively pointless in narrative terms, that it can "lead" nowhere is essential to its significance as a free gift.

Up to a point, Joyce's moral theology is unerringly orthodox. The good man is like the Good Samaritan coming to the aid of one with whom he has no apparent kinship.[5] Bloom, who has been so comical and pathetic in his various costumes, is not at all absurd when he takes up Stephen's stick and stands guard over his inert form. In the literal sense, he protects Stephen's identity, his belongings, and helps him to breathe. But as he does these things, he also creates Stephen in his imagination. He names him and fashions Stephen's half-conscious mutterings from Yeats into a poem of his own: "Face reminds me of his poor mother. In the shady wood. The deep white breast. Ferguson, I think I caught. A girl. Some girl. Best thing could happen him . . . swear that I will always hail, ever conceal, never reveal, any part or parts, art or arts . . . in the rough sands of the sea . . . a cabletow's length from the shore . . . where the tide ebbs . . . and flows"(609).

It does not matter that Bloom has mistaken the Fergus of Yeats's poem for a girl named Ferguson or that he has summoned up fragments of the Freemason's oath of secrecy in his promise not to reveal Stephen's unguarded confessions. Nor does it matter that he cannot reveal his "art or arts," since Joyce does that for him. Bloom's errors in detail, typically, convey truths beyond detail. By leaving his post at the reader's side as fellow observer, he participates in the scene in a way that demonstrates how we, like him, are reader-authors, putting together a bit of this, a bit of that, a rhyme here, a verse there, and fashioning from them a portrait—surely not an objective one, but more than merely our own reflections. In Bloom, we see ourselves in a responsive, creative relation to lives outside our own.

Bloom's sympathetic and imaginative act momentarily makes Stephen his son. The truthfulness of this newly created relationship cannot be tested by plot as in a Dickens novel, in which Stephen would leap to his feet, embrace Bloom, and go home to live with him as an adopted child. The point is not that it leads to a story about family life, but that it is an instantaneous, indelible, universally familiar realization of human relationship. Bloom is not rewarded with an adopted son. But in a recurrence of the kind of dramatic projection employed throughout the episode, his action toward Stephen produces a vision of his dead son Rudy. In the intersection of the dramatic and the narrative, the paradigmatic gesture and the syntagmatic act, Bloom recovers the past in the present, the dead in the living. In short, he reconciles what for all but God and the artist is irreconcilable.

F R O M most indications, Lawrence had little of Joyce's taste for the theater. Stage metaphors rarely figure in his writing, and he seldom mentions playwrights among the authors he most admired. When, as occasionally happens, characters in his fiction attend a theatrical performance, those most in tune with Lawrence's narrative voice tend to be bored or disgusted. In *Aaron's Rod,* for instance, a group of friends goes to the opera; Josephine, a woman evidently after Lawrence's own heart, is filled with "horror at the sight the stage presents." The obvious fakery of the production offends her artistic sensibility. "The sham Egypt of *Aida* hid from her nothing of its shame. The singers were all colour-washed ... to a bright orange tint. The men had oblong dabs of black wool under their lower lip; the beard of the mighty Pharaohs"(60).

The "shame" of such a production is that it does nothing to overcome, indeed it seems to wallow in, the discrepancy between craft and reality, art as technique and art as a genuine expression of human nature. It appears to be taken for granted that the might of the Pharaohs is beyond authentic representation. Paralleling this trivialization of an art form is the sexlessness of the performers. "But the leading tenor was the chief pain. He was large, stout, swathed in a cummerbund, and looked like a eunuch. This fattish, emasculated look seems common in stage heroes."

From this and similar episodes, it seems clear that Lawrence's distaste for the theatrical arts stems from his belief that, even more than the other arts, they had been tamed and debased by a bourgeoisie intent on preserving and amusing itself without interference. The Pharaohs, like Samson, are tolerated only without real beards. But Lawrence's dissatisfaction has other causes as well. In his essay "Indians and an Englishman," he complains of the theatricality, the "insistent drama" of the American Southwest, where each type—the Indian, the cowboy, the Mexican, the tourist—walks about in a different costume, at cross-purposes with every other type. In part, this is a foreigner's fairly typical first impression of unassimilated America, which "is all rather like comic opera played with solemn intensity." But biased and quick to judge as he was, Lawrence also tried to analyze and understand his own reaction. "Whatever makes a proper world, I don't know. But surely, two elements are necessary: a common purpose and a common sympathy. I can't see any common purpose . . . As for a common sympathy or understanding, that's beyond imagining . . . And so everybody smirks at everybody else, and says tacitly: "Go on; you do your little stunt, and I'll do mine," and they're like the various troupes in a circus, all performing at once, with nobody for Master of Ceremonies."[6]

Apart from what this tells us of Lawrence's view of America, certainly not unique in its characterization of the apparent chaos produced by too much individualism, it is revealing in its use of a "performance" metaphor in relation to a vision of a "proper world." The parading of differences may not be false in the way the performance of *Aida* was, but it is a pointless, empty form of self-revelation. As at the opera, there is no communication, no exchange. Despite the solemnity, real seriousness is absent. "Nothing is as farcical as insistent drama." Like a circus parade without a master of ceremonies, it has no order, no focus, and no resolution. The figures are liked fractured caricatures of genuine drama, in costume and always ready to leap at one another's throats, but unable to change or be transformed by the presences around them. It is drama short-circuited.

In these passages from the novel and the essay, Lawrence depicts the debasement of the dramatic impulse through what to him are two extreme social maladies, the complacent conformity of England and the unchecked individualism of America. He is no more explicit in defining his ideal drama than he is in describing his notion of a "proper world," but in two novels, *The Lost Girl* and *The Plumed Serpent*, he brings together cultures at odds with one another and, to an increasing extent, attempts to explore and resolve their differences in terms not merely conceptually "dramatic" but literally theatrical.

T HE FATHER of Alvina, the heroine of *The Lost Girl*, owns a cinema in the Midlands before World War I, when short silent films were often accompanied by performances of traveling vaudeville troupes.[7] The visiting artists are third-rate entertainers, jugglers, singers, acrobats, and dancers. Still, Alvina likes them better than the films because they are alive and present in the flesh. She realizes, however, that the audiences prefer the films because they identify themselves with the heroines and heroes. "They can spread themselves over a film, and they *can't* over a living performer. They're up against the performer himself. And they hate it"(144). Alvina's argument is an important one since it is tied to Lawrence's distaste for any theatricality in which an unbridgeable gap exists between performers and spectators. In its debased form, drama is a kind of self-indulgence that precludes the existence of others. The audience demands fake, emasculated, or nonexistent performers. They love films because "there isn't anything except themselves." Whatever else Lawrence may mean by authentic drama, it is plain that it cannot exist unless the audience comes "up against the performer himself."

The arrival in town of the Natcha-Kee-Tawara, a troupe of performing "Indians," is usually considered the weakest element in this novel. Lawrence does nothing to conceal the tawdriness and the ludicrous fakery of the small company of young Swiss, German, and Italian men and the Belgian Madame, who dance about the stage in a pantomime of North American Indians, a white prisoner, and a captive bear. The men are commonplace and uneducated, their mistress, a domineering middle-aged matron. Lawrence seems deliberately to have compounded the pretentions of opera, which he considers high-brow fakery, with the comic and pathetic vulgarities of a small company of down-and-out traveling players. In short, he seems bent on showing theatricality at its cheapest and worst.

At first, Alvina is filled with contempt for the company. But when she comes to know them and grows infatuated with the handsome Cicio, she watches their performance with unexpected pleasure. "Madame danced beautifully. No denying it, she was an artist. She became something quite different: fresh, virginal, pristine, a magic creature flickering there. She was infinitely delicate and attractive. Her *braves* became glamorous and heroic at once, and magically she cast her spell over them"(197). It must be remembered that this performance is described as Alvina witnesses it. The phrases indicate what is going on in her mind as she watches and "bangs the piano crossly," feeling "shut apart." Alvina's mood can be taken as a sign of her painful maturing and of the confusion caused by the performance's touching hitherto undiscovered chords within her. But if Lawrence throws himself unmistakably into his own narratives, as so often is claimed, takes sides with the traveling performers, and even identifies himself with the magically effective Madame, he is also able to remain outside the narrative, detached from the players and from Alvina and the other spectators, revealing dimensions and complexities that are visible neither from the stage nor from the audience.

For all the charm of the troupe in performance and the genuine manly appeal of Cicio, it is never completely certain that Alvina, who is lonely, repressed, and inexperienced, is not being taken in by raw and even brutal sex in the guise of cheap theatricality. Madame, who by some magic is able to appear virginal on stage, is in behavior as well as title a sensual woman whose hold on her young men is as much sexual as artistic. And though Cicio is able to show tenderness and affection to his male companions, his attraction of Alvina is often described as mixed with cruelty and a peculiar indifference. Eventually, Alvina succumbs to Cicio's pleading and goes with him to his remote farm in the Abruzzi to live as his wife. The countryside and the living conditions are primitive and wild beyond anything she has imagined, but the beauty and vividness in her harsh life make the monotonous gray respectability of her middle-class English existence seem unreal. "She had gone beyond the world into the pre-world, she had reopened on the old eternity"(372).

It seems, in passages like this, that Lawrence wishes to show Alvina as having left her position in the audience, gone up onto the stage, joined the pantomime dance, penetrated and survived its superficial vulgarity, and come through ultimately to a state of being with a permanence and truthfulness that make her old life appear trivial and thin, a poorer performance than that of the least accomplished of traveling players. Read in this way, the narrative shows that the function of drama, when it contains some shred of authenticity amid the crudest fakery, is to draw the audience out of itself into a life of pure gesture where the mind and body move together as one.

Even in her new life, however, Alvina suffers periods of skepticism, doubts about the value of the man and the world she has chosen and, even more, about her ability to travel the psychological distance necessary to be part of them. Despite moments of almost mystical union with her husband and the landscape, Alvina is often shown as a spectator, looking with a detached perspective at a life not entirely hers. In a sense, Cicio is still on stage for her, though the setting has changed.

At the end of the novel, Cicio is about to go off to join the Italian army and fight in the war. Alvina, who senses his restlessness, fears that he will never return. Their final exchange is a promise and a question: " 'I'll come back,' he said. 'Sure?' she whispered, straining him to her." As is true of the endings of most of Lawrence's fiction, nothing is settled by this conclusion. A statement is made and a question asked. If the two-penny pantomime, the cheap drama, has done anything for Alvina, it has not carried her through to a permanent state of joy and understanding but rather awakened her to the larger drama that is, for Lawrence, the natural dynamism of life.

I T I S characteristic of Lawrence to be disrespectful of the conventions of stage drama. Whereas Joyce tramples on them internally through the waking dreams and fantasies of Bloom and Stephen in *Ulysses,* shifting time, place, and costume at will, Lawrence prefers a more literal approach involving a social and cultural collision. He brings spectator and performer together in a manner that places enormous pressure on the conventional assumptions underlying the behavior and reactions of both. Lawrence loves the idea of a congregation in the wrong church, the spectacle of an audience and show utterly unsuited to each other. Since actual communication, coming "up against the performer," is essential to Lawrence's concept of drama, and since conflict is essential to his idea of genuine communication, performances that live up to all the expectations of the audience, confirm their prejudices, and lull their minds and bodies to sleep are mere mockeries of the real thing. If the only friction occurs on stage, the play has failed.

In *The Plumed Serpent,* Lawrence takes up many of the themes of *The Lost Girl* even more boldly.[8] Though more ambitious than the earlier work, *The Plumed Serpent* is an unevenly constructed book, cluttered with obstacles to a sympathetic reading. It alternates between extraordinary political and sexual obtuseness and dramatic insight, passages of prolonged tedium and pages of intensely realized vitality. The stark beauty of the landscape, the grace and latent power of the Indians, the pretentious superiority of European culture, are evoked with brilliant sensitivity. Furthermore, within and sometimes despite the artificial entanglements of the plot, Lawrence struggles seriously with many of the same problems that preoccupied him since the beginning of his career.

In this case, the Indians are not Europeans in fancy dress but Mexicans seen against the background of their own landscape. The heroine is a middle-aged Irish woman, twice married, sophisticated, and sensitive, not in the least a naive provincial girl. But the encounters between the main characters and the cultures they reflect are once again depicted in terms of public spectacles that contain powerful dramatic possibilities.

From the beginning, Kate is a tourist and spectator, out of her element, widowed and looking on at life without feeling there is a place in it for her any longer. She thinks of Providence as "the great Show-man" producing a variety of acts to which she must politely respond without really taking part. She is first seen with her American cousin at a bullfight in Mexico City. He takes it, in the spirit of the tourist, as a colorful event, an "experience," a foreign rite to be seen but not judged and certainly not to be entered into emotionally. Kate, however, is already filled with distaste for the other spectators and contempt for the matadors; she is appalled by the sight of the wounded bull goring the horse of the picador. "Kate had never been taken so completely by surprise in all her life. She had still cherished some idea of a gallant show. And before she knew where she was, she was watching a bull whose shoulders trickled blood goring his horns up and down inside the belly of a prostrate and feebly plunging old horse"(13).

After a few more minutes, Kate leaves the arena, revolted and shaken by what she has seen. What is interesting about the episode, in addition to Lawrence's graphic depiction of the spectacle, is that Kate's reaction is shown as a sign of strength rather than of feminine weakness. She is a true spectator in that she, unlike her cousin, actually sees what is happening, rather than allowing herself to be lost in a haze of festival and local color. And she sees a living creature debased and tortured in an obscene gesture that combines murder with rape. The excitement of the crowds, the brassy music, the dandy toreadors in "tight uniforms plastered with silver embroidery" do nothing to distract her from the central action. She is undeceived by the decorative surface and unswayed by the enthusiasm of the other spectators. Her response to the performance is direct, penetrating, personal. She is a sound interpreter, a reliable reader of events, not merely because she is intelligent, but because she has the heart and imagination to place herself in a living relationship with what she sees. It is too simple to say that she identifies herself with the stricken horse. While that is partly true, she also sees and feels the cowardice and savagery of the performers and spectators. Her leaving the scene is a measure of the extent to which she has been present in it.

If the bullfight is morally repulsive, it is also bad art, as false in its pretensions to order as in its display of courage. One of the conventions of the bullfight is to create an illusion of strict order and authority: the stages of the spectacle and the hierarchical ranking of the performers are determined by tradition. The seating—in the sun or the shade—divides people according to class, and there is a special box for officials, judges, and state dignitaries, whose place as controlling figures in the society is mirrored by their honorific role in the spectacle. But, as Kate notices, even this illusion of order and control is thin. "In the seats of the Authorities were very few people, and certainly no sparkling ladies in high tortoise-shell combs and lace mantillas. A few common-looking people, bourgeois with not much taste, and a couple of officers in uniform. The President had not come."

Just as the opera at Covent Garden and the parading of egos in a Southwestern town reflected the peculiarities and, for Lawrence, the flaws in British and American society, the chaotic savagery under a thin veneer of traditional pageantry provides a "show" in concentrated, almost burlesque fashion, of the social and political turmoil of Mexico. Immediately after leaving the arena, Kate meets Don Cipriano, a Mexican general who is a follower of Don Ramón, the leader of a new nationalistic sect; his aim is to replace Christianity with a revival of the ancient religion of Quetzalcoatl and the corrupt system of bourgeois democracy with a benevolent dictatorship.

Don Ramón is the master of ceremonies in every sense. As a political and religious leader, he guides his followers; he embodies—or thinks he embodies—the divine on earth; he provides, through Cipriano, his right-hand man and surrogate, a haven for Kate; and he is composer, choreographer, and star performer in the rites that are meant to fulfill the people's need for religion, art, and community. Much more even than Madame in *The Lost Girl,* Rawdon Lilly in *Aaron's Rod,* or Ben Cooley in *Kangaroo,* he is a forceful leader whose hypnotic hold on his followers is part craft and part sex, a weaving together of a natural force with a strong will determined to bring about a new order.

Though the reader may be filled with disgust for Ramón's pretentions and skeptical of the outcome of his theories of government, we are given little chance, except by projection, to test the social and political value of his ambitions in the narrative itself.[9] They are spoken of in only the most general and metaphorical of terms. Ramón is seen most frequently at the center of increasingly elaborate ritual spectacles of his own invention. In the terms established by the novel in the first powerful scene at the bullfight, the reader is led, like Kate, to judge Ramón and the world projected by his imagination through the performances in which he "shows" himself to an audience.

T H E F I R S T and most striking of these ceremonies occurs in a chapter entitled "Auto da Fé," in which the religious images in the local church are carried out in solemn procession, taken by boat to an island, and burned. Part of the effectiveness of this episode may be called genuinely dramatic in that it is an acting out, as in Joyce's mock masses, of an emotional and intellectual conflict in a highly stylized, concentrated form. The procession, so common in Catholic countries, is repeated with new actors and a new destination. The old outlines are still visible, the cadences still audible; but, though they retain some of their magic, the reader actually witnesses them losing it in the progress of the performance. A transformation takes place not merely in the mind but in the objects the mind contemplates. "The strange procession made its way slowly under the trees, to the coarse sands ... Folded serapes on naked, soft shoulders swung unevenly, the images rocked and tottered a little. But onwards to the edge of the water went the tall crucifix, then the flashing glass box. And after, came Jesus in a red silk robe ... Mary in lace that fluttered upon stiff white and blue satin. But the saints were only painted; painted wood"(310).

The contrast between the artificial, fussily decorated statues and the natural motion of the strong and partially undressed Indians is sharp. But what adds particular power to the scene is the solemnity and reverence with which the old images are treated. This is not a Cromwellian smashing of icons, but a respectful funeral service for a dead religion. There is a hymn entitled "Jesus' Farewell," and the young priest, faithful to his obligations, "staggers" under the crucifix and perspires in his vestments until the fire roars and he can strip himself of his old garments and join the new sect, once the relics of the old one have been dutifully cremated.

At the beginning, the procession and ceremony are seen through Kate's eyes or, more precisely, from the place where she is standing. "With a parasol lined with dark blue," Kate joins the crowd standing outside the church, listens to the slow, insistent drumbeat, hears the singing, and watches as, one by one, the images are carried past. But when the boat is filled and the statues taken to the island for burning, she is left ashore while the narrative continues to follow the ritual—as though telling itself. In fact, the action seems no longer to depend on an audience or actors, but advances with a momentum that appears intrinsic to things in themselves and that cannot be stopped. Predication becomes more and more impersonal and the passive voice is used with increasing frequency. "Slowly the procession went up the bank of the dishevelled island. ... In a rocky hollow at the water's edge, tall stones had been put up on end, with iron bars across, like a grill. Underneath, a pile of faggots ready ... The images, the glass box of the great Dead Christ, were laid on the iron bars ... The crucifix was laid against them ... Beyond the water, beyond the glare, the village looked like a mirage"(313). Obviously, the mirage effect is not visible to Kate, who has remained behind. If a new vantage point has been reached and, with it, a new reality that makes the old world look false, the reader has been transported to it in a generalized trance, not through the clear vision of an identifiable character and guide.

If Kate's role has been to lead the reader to the ceremony and then abandon him to it, Don Ramón's part is comparably important, unobtrusive, and incomplete. Since he is the leader of the sect, Ramón's will is behind the entire ritual, yet his public role is one of restraint. He appears only after the crowd has gathered at the church doors; he removes his hat in a gesture of respect as the priest hands over the keys. Ramón unlocks the church, leads the procession himself, carrying the front pole of the bier of the "dead Christ of Holy Week," and it is he who silently lights the funeral pyre. Crucial as these actions are, they are performed without flourish. In the detailed, rhythmic, almost monotonous description of the procession, Ramón is not otherwise mentioned. As the fire burns, he is indistinguishable from the other spectators. "Ramón stood aside and watched in silence, his dark brow quite expressionless."

At the climax of the ritual, which occurs in "a little amphitheatre" of rocks, the personal identities of Kate and Ramón are similarly dispersed. As two surrogate figures of the author—Kate, the reasonable, observant, narrative guide and Ramón, the mysterious godlike manipulator—they merge into the event that, in different ways, they have made possible for the reader. For a moment, the performers and the audience have overcome egotism and self-consciousness. Passive observation, mere perception, and active, manipulative creativity blend indistinguishably in an event that seems inevitable and self-generated. Even emotion is poised and impersonal, balanced between exhilaration and pity, relief and regret. The movement from narration to dramatic gesture has momentarily succeeded.

But Kate is still waiting on the shore; the world of narratable reality, of choices, evaluations, and analyses, remains intact. The "auto da fé" has been not, as in *Ulysses*, a half-conscious nightmare to be overcome, but a challenge to be met, an alternative reality to be chosen or rejected. Kate is repeatedly urged to marry Cipriano, to join the sect, participate in its rituals, and asume the role of a kind of goddess. She goes along with most of this, after a fashion, but her "going along" is so equivocal, such a peculiar mixture of skepticism and submission, that it keeps the reader permanently on guard. Never again in the novel is the trancelike, rhythmic power of the "auto da fé" recaptured; never again are spectators and performers so much in harmony in witnessing and revealing an event.

Kate remains detached, observant, rather like a good Victorian Protestant witnessing a cannibal orgy or a beatification ceremony at Saint Peter's, gritting her teeth and trying to remember every detail to record for the enlightened reader at home. When she reenters the church for the enthronement of the old gods, she remarks that the interior design has changed: "The walls were vertically striped in bars of black and white, vermillion and yellow and green." Even when she is given a husband, a new name, and robes to wear, she is not transformed in the only way the reader can judge, in her manner of seeing and speaking.

But the fault is not exclusively Kate's. In this and subsequent ceremonies, Don Ramón plays a disastrously prominent role, in contrast with his earlier restraint. He preaches, chants, and gives traffic directions. " 'Hear me, people. You may enter the House of Quetzalcoatl. Men must go to the right and left . . . Women must go down the centre, and cover their faces. And they may sit upon the floor' "(371). He also produces "magical" effects as a boy might with a chemistry set. "Then suddenly he threw the contents of the bowl into the altar fire. There was a soft puff of explosion, a blue flame leaped high into the air, followed by a yellow flame, and then a rose-red smoke."

With this kind of detail, the potential mystery and inevitability of the ritual collapse. Ramón's religion seems to have entered its rococo phase early, and all the worst elements of the Covent Garden *Aida* reappear. Movement and gesture are reduced to stage directions, iconography to properties, and atmosphere to decor. Ramón himself takes on the attributes of the wooden idol he has had erected in place of the old altar. Enthroned, vested, pontifical, he loses all interest as a character, not because he has transcended his ego, but because he repeatedly and monotonously calls attention to it with such statements as "I am the Son of the Morning Star . . . I am Quetzalcoatl . . . I am the living Quetzalcoatl." Transformation, the point of genuine ritual and drama, is unrealized; instead, everything, in almost geometric order, points to the dead end of Ramón's self-assertion. The reader is left with an unmoved Kate and an unmovable Ramón, a static performance before an impassive audience, Lawrence's own definition of failed drama.

I T I S easy to dismiss Lawrence's failed drama as an instance of indulgence in his exaggerated infatuation with Mexico and primitive ritual, but even in its weaknesses, *The Plumed Serpent* is a more serious book than that. In some ways, it is one of Lawrence's most theoretical works. It is filled with ideas about religion and human experience that, when separated from the fake ceremonies and politics, are not so exotic or dangerous as they seem. Probably the single dominant idea behind the new sect of Quetzalcoatl is that religion should integrate all aspects of human life, the solitary and the communal, the physical and the spiritual, and that it should be an agent that brings people to their fullness.

Furthermore, despite his bare breast and incantations, Ramón often sounds a note with a strong Pauline, even Protestant, ring to it. When his wife dies, his "superstitious" Catholic sons believe she is in heaven up in the sky, but he corrects them like a benevolent pastor; "And there God is; and Paradise; inside the hearts of living men and women"(389). In discussing organization with his deputy, he stresses internal faith and spirit above external authority, saying, "It is the discipline from the inside that matters"(399).

One must not underestimate the seriousness with which Lawrence, through Ramón, urges the incorporation of physical, individual sexuality and the tangible culture of a society into religious expression. But the strong Protestant bias in Lawrence's thinking is curiously at odds with his longing for symbolism and ritual. The stress on inwardness, self-discipline, and self-sacrifice clashes with the exhibitionism of Ramón's ceremonies. The inconsistency at the very heart of these spectacles is neither resolved theoretically nor exposed dramatically, except in fits and starts.

Perhaps the best indication that Lawrence's artistic instinct is ill at ease with the manifestations of Quetzalcoatl, and that his own image of himself as an artist is not entirely in accord with the master of ceremonies, is that Ramón's rituals—geometrically patterned, tidily orchestrated, symbolically neat—bear almost no resemblance at all to the structures of Lawrence's own fictions. The novel—which Lawrence called "the one bright book of life"—with its concreteness, its bulk, its tendency to disorder, remains, even in *The Plumed Serpent,* a salutary corrective of fastidious visions. In this book, as in others, some critics have tended to identify Lawrence too exclusively with a single character. F. R. Leavis refers to "Ramón-Lawrence" and W. Y. Tindall claims that the novel "represents [Lawrence's] ideal state because he himself, under a splendid disguise, is dictator."[10] Surprisingly, such critics forget the dialectical and androgynous nature of Lawrence's imagination.

Though Ramón's first wife dies in a spasm of disgust with her husband's new religion, the element of dissent and subversion is continued in the character of Kate, even after she "joins" the sect and marries Cipriano. Late in the book, she bursts out with a direct energy that identifies her once more with the skeptical reader. " 'Oh! . . . For heaven's sake let me get out of this, and back to simple human people. I loathe the very sound of Quetzalcoatl and Huitzilopochtli. I would die rather than be mixed up in it any more. Horrible, really, both Ramón and Cipriano. And they want to put it over me, with their high-flown bunk' "(407).

Cathartic though it may be, Kate's outburst can, of course, be taken as a sign of her cultural and spiritual limitations, of her unreadiness to submit to Ramón and Cipriano. But this is precisely the point. She remains a character in a novel—talkative, imperfect, changeable, interesting—rather than a silent, passive, and dull goddess. It is clear through-

out that, despite her academic interest in their religious ideas and ceremonies, Kate's most authentic response to Cipriano and Ramón is sexual. She is constantly comparing them physically—Cipriano: small,
dark, quick; Ramón: tall, muscular, serene. She is more drawn to
Ramón, but it is not until Ramón has already married her to Cipriano
that her preference comes to the surface. " 'The wife of my friend!'
[Ramón] said, 'What could you be better?' 'Of course,' she said, more
than equivocal"(469).

And after a spiteful conversation with Ramón's second wife, in which
the two women debate the color of their ceremonial robes, Kate vents
her jealousy in a fashion worthy of a character in a Jane Austen novel:

> "And different women must have different husbands," said Kate
> "Ramón would always be too abstract and overbearing for me."
> Teresa flushed slowly, looking down at the ground.
> "Ramón needs far too much submission from a woman to please
> me," Kate added.(475)

Once again, Kate's jealousy and cattiness can be taken as flaws in her
character. From the point of view of the people of Quetzalcoatl, she is
showing her egotistical, possessive, bourgeois European colors. But if, as
is likely, the reader has not been converted to the viewpoint of the new
sect, she is demonstrating the same clear-sightedness she showed at the
bullfight, an ability to cut through façade and see to the heart of things.
Her choice is not the choice of a God, but the choice of a man.

After several lifeless ceremonies, including the marriage of Kate and
Cipriano and Cipriano's installation in the church-temple as the god
Huitzilopochtli, Kate witnesses one final "staged" event before reaching
her decision about whether to remain in Mexico or return to Europe.
This show, involving a bull and a cow, harks back to the opening scene
at the bullfight. It is not engineered by Don Ramón and does not resemble his wordy, elaborate and long rituals. Rather, it is swift, silent,
and intense, the work of a subtler, more remote master of ceremonies. "A
black boat with a red-painted roof and a tall mast was moored to the
low breakwater-wall, which rose about a yard high, from the shallow
water. On the wall stood loose little groups of white-clad men, looking
into the black belly of the ship. And perched immobile in silhouette
against the lake, was a black and white cow, and a huge monolithic
black-and-white bull. The whole silhouette frieze motionless, against the
far water that was coloured brown like turtle doves"(473).

The scene is neither confused nor excessively neat in its arrangement;
it is vibrant with contrasts held in precarious balance. To Kate, "it was
near, yet seemed strange and remote." The wall is like a stage platform

and the figures like characters in a tableau or a frieze. Yet poised against this artificiality are the two animals and the strikingly organic imagery of the "black belly of the ship" and the sea water "coloured brown like turtle doves." Caught in a moment of perception, all the figures seem strangely still, yet they are filled with an energy that propels them in the direction of the boat. The men strain against the animals and the animals resist until the very last instant, when they board the waiting boat. Over the entire scene is an intense silence, unbroken by sermons or chants, but it provokes in Kate a flow of thoughts and words altogether different from the dutiful recording of the details of Ramón's ceremonies.

Like the bullfight, this spectacle has its superficially colorful aspect— the black and red boat, an old Mexican in "fawn, skintight trousers" and a "huge felt hat heavily embroidered with silver." But, also as in the bullfight, a core event in this show, a central act is so obvious as to elude only the most hopelessly blind of viewers. The arena was filled with such blindness, since only Kate seemed to see the slaughter for what it was. Here again, Kate is the unsentimental, undeceived spectator, aware of costume and local color but not distracted by them from the sight of the irresistible force of life in the act of mating. The men and the animals form a "group of life," in contrast to those in the bullfight, who act out death. Kate "reads" the ship not as a prison but as a vessel that contains life but also carries it forward. As she watches, "the ship was going across the waters, with her massive, sky-spangled cargo of life invisible."

Though the apparent drift of events as the novel draws to a close suggest that Kate will remain in Mexico and submit to Don Ramón's "rule," a significant accumulation of detail indicates that if Kate stays at all, she will stay on her own terms, that she wants life and a man, not ceremony and apotheosis. As is so often the case in Lawrence's novels, this countertendency is an undertow rather than an outright contradiction. Don Ramón is not exposed as a Mexican Wizard of Oz whose power is a fraud. There is little doubt that he represents much that Lawrence and Kate admire in theory. Yet the sharp contrast between his ceremonies and the absorbing spectacles of slaughter and mating with which the book opens and closes exposes his radical limitations as a master of ceremonies. Furthermore, though Kate is seen at first as lonely and adrift, she is never a stupid or dull or naive character. She is not at all like the young heroine of a *Bildungsroman*. One feels not that she has much to learn but that she must figure out what to do with the rest of her life. Her sight is sharp and penetrating from the first moment at the bullfight. The question is where it will lead her.

Kate resolves to submit both to Ramón and to Cipriano, yet the final scene in the novel reveals a powerful counterforce to that resolution. She finds the two men together chanting, and instantly reacts ironically to their piety. "She had come to make a sort of submission . . . but finding them both in the thick of their Quetzalcoatl mood, with their manly breasts uncovered, she was not very eager to begin . . . 'We don't meet in your Morning Star, apparently, do we!' she said, mocking, but with a slight quaver"(486). Kate begins to cry and plead with Ramón to tell her whether or not she should stay in Mexico or return to Europe. Cipriano becomes jealous and angry; he tells her that Ramón is not the one to ask. And Ramón speaks his last and possibly most significant words in the novel: " 'That is very true,' said Ramón. 'Don't listen to me!' " With Ramón's exit, Kate gets what she apparently wants, not a ritual anointing or benediction, but a tender, erotic love scene with Cipriano:

> "Te quiero mucho! Mucho te quiero! Mucho! Mucho! I like you very much! Very much!"
> It sounded so soft, so soft-tongued, of the soft, wet, hot blood, that she shivered a little.
> "You won't let me go!" she said to him.

Evidently, the new religion is no more immune than the old from skepticism and heresy. Its harmonies, too, can be broken and its images expelled; its poems can be undermined by prose, its authority embarrassed by nature, its order disrupted by impulse, its answers challenged by new questions. And this opposition, for Lawrence, is where drama begins, not isolated on the stage or the altar, but in the encounter between spectator and actor in a gesture of love or rebellion, the movement within the consciousness between subject and object. The audience comes "up against the performer," seeking the flesh and blood behind the most ingenious inventions of the mind.

V IRGINIA WOOLF loved the theater. As a Londoner especially fond of the city in season, she frequently went to plays, operas, and ballets two and three nights in succession. Even as a young woman, she could be an acerbic critic: "Bernard Shaw kept us on the rack for three hours last night; his mind is that of a disgustingly precocious child of two."[11] But the thought of great drama, if not always the actual performances, stirred Woolf's imagination and her capacity for admiration. After reading *Cymbeline* at the age of nineteen, she wrote to her brother in Cambridge that she was among the "company of worshippers."[12] Though less interested in religion than Joyce or Lawrence and less inclined to use "sacred" terminology even ironically in her prose, she is like them in recognizing a mysterious, almost transcendent quality in drama, what she calls in "Notes on an Elizabethan Play" "the presence of the Gods."[13]

Woolf locates this "presence" (or its effect), despite all the bombast and artificiality of the genre, in its exposition of death. "The bell that tolls throughout the drama is death and disenchantment." It is not the macabre mood or grotesque plot that Woolf admires, but the acknowledgment of mortality that gives savor and perspective to the material existence depicted and endows even the most outrageous pieces with an ultimate seriousness. Elizabethan plays—including the second-rate— perform a function analogous to that of religious liturgies; they celebrate life while reminding the spectator of final things.

Woolf contrasts the absurdly unrealistic knights of some Elizabethan plays with the all too credible Mr. Smiths of Liverpool of the nineteenth-century novel and wishes "to join those territories and recognize the same man in different disguises." What is crucial to Woolf's thinking, what aligns her with Joyce and Lawrence, is that she does not wish to reject one idea of "reality" in favor of another; instead, she wants to "join" truths by making "the necessary alterations in perspective."

The novelists' task is not simply to be an accurate observer of nature or an imaginative visionary, but to be able to move between both perspectives, to mediate between fact and vision. Woolf's concept of authorial detachment, much like Joyce's and Lawrence's, provides the artist with a freedom of viewpoint, a mobility and balance unavailable to the author who is too aloof from or attached to her material. But perspective is not only a matter of distance. An artist must be able to move forward and away from her material, but she must also be free to change her angle of perception. She must be able to show her story as well as tell it, move from her position as narrator, guide, observer, and historian to that of showman and actor, thus helping the audience to use "the ear and the eye which the moderns have so basely starved, hear words as they are laughed and shouted not as they are printed in black letters on the page, see ... the changing faces and living bodies of men and women."[14] For Woolf, the drama is not a superior alternative to the novel, but a key to the liberation of the author from her fixed role as a narrator.

An early and extraordinarily successful attempt to use a theatrical performance as an occasion to shift perspective, not merely from one character to another but from one angle of consciousness to another, occurs at the opera in *Jacob's Room*.[15] The major characters are scattered through Covent Garden in various boxes, stalls, and rows. Woolf does not pursue the consciousness of a single character in her narrative line. Rather, she moves from ironic detachment, equally remote from audience and performers, to multiple identification with several members of the audience, and then to a passionately earnest monologue in which she uses the first person, as an actress alone on the stage might use it, in a direct address to the reader.

> But the difficulty remains—one has to choose. For though I have no wish to be Queen of England—or only for a moment—I would willingly sit beside her; I would hear the Prime Minister's gossip . . . the massive fronts of the respectable conceal after all their secret code; or why so impermeable? And then, doffing one's own headpiece, how strange to assume for a moment some one's—any one's—to be a man of valour who has ruled the Empire . . . or see in a flash, as the shepherd pipes his tune, bridges and aqueducts. But no—we must choose. Never was there a harsher necessity! or one which entails greater pain, more certain disaster; for wherever I seat myself, I die in exile: Whittaker in his lodging-house; Lady Charles at the Manor.(69)

Following, as it does, so rapidly after an opening paragraph of cool and impersonal detachment, this shift to exclamations and broken sentences conveys a powerful urgency, a rhetorical drama in which the narrative seems to be at odds with itself. The convention of authorial distance and formality is interrupted not in the direct address of an all-knowing complacent author, but through an outcry that binds audience and author in the words of a performer. The subject that provokes this dramatic turn and, in Woolf's terms, evokes the "presence of the Gods," is mortality, the limitation inherent in life. The pain of choosing is not relieved, as plots of novels often seem to suggest, by right thinking, by deciding on this suitor rather than that, this profession instead of another. Even sensible and virtuous choices are prefigurations of death, confinements, like stalls in a theater or coffins in a graveyard.

But if Covent Garden provides the setting for this meditation on death, it also provides a clue to the forms of art, in the aisles as well as on stage, that are most effective in temporarily cheating it. Through the imagination, the individual can escape exile and confinement and dwell momentarily with shepherds and queens. But the exercise of imagination involves more than inventing situations and characters; it is, as the entire episode demonstrates, a movement of mind and heart from one vantage point to another. It is not merely a multiplication of flat scenes, but an entrance into the dimensionality of experience beyond the self, a leap from the balcony to the stage, from silence to speech, from interval to action and back again.

WOOLF'S most sustained and complex use of the theatrical metaphor occurs in her last novel, *Between the Acts*.[16] The setting for Woolf's spectacle is characteristically modest, a country pageant for the benefit of the parish. There are two sets of characters, those in the pageant and those who watch it, notably, the host, old Mr. Oliver; his widowed sister, Mrs. Swithin; his daughter-in-law, Isa; and two early arrivals, the vulgar Mrs. Manresa and her homosexual friend, William Dodge. The amateur performance involves villagers and their children in cheap homemade costumes, seen against a background of pastures and grazing cattle; it is attended by polite but indifferent neighbors on an outing. Neither the grotesque and ribald humor of the Circe episode in *Ulysses* nor the ritual solemnity of Lawrence's Mexican ceremonies is present. Yet there are similarities deeper than setting and tone.

Like Joyce and Lawrence, Woolf plays with the mixture of the cheap and obvious falsehood of the show and the mysterious, almost sacred, aura created by the process of acting before an audience, even under the most restricted circumstances. She makes no attempt to force an illusion on the reader, no effort to conceal the tinsel and cardboard substituting for gold and silver or the scratchy phonograph in the bushes providing celestial music. Similarly, Joyce never covers Bloom's lies or the outlandish absurdity of his disguises; Lawrence moves backstage frequently in *The Plumed Serpent,* allowing the reader and the skeptical Kate to intrude on Don Ramón while he is fabricating his ceremonial hymns and rehearsing ritual gestures.

In Woolf's spectacle, as in those of Joyce and Lawrence, there are moments of unexpected beauty and authenticity and, more than that, a sense that, notwithstanding the irony directed at institutional religion, the theatrical event is a hallowed one. The first mention of the annual pageant sounds to one of Woolf's characters like "the first peal of a chime of bells." The old barn where tea is served during the interval is likened to a Greek temple, and the members of the audience are compared to "pilgrims" who had "bruised a lane on the grass." The point is repeatedly made that the coming together of audience and performers, the temporary cooperation of such a random and ill-suited company, is itself a miracle. During the Victorian section of the pageant, which recapitulates British history, a policeman recites a long list of nineteenth-century slogans and moral sentiments, including, most strikingly, a Biblical fragment with a Cockney twist, "wherever one or two, me and you, come together." The sentence is appropriately unfinished; if there is a divine presence in the performance, it is not understood as a personal God but found in the recognition, however brief, of a different order of being from that experienced apart from the show.

Like Joyce and Lawrence, Woolf plays with contrasting worlds by introducing a staged spectacle into her narrative. In *Ulysses,* much of the Nighttown script is a burlesque nightmare interacting but also sharply contrasting with the mundane waking world of Bloom wandering through Dublin. In *The Plumed Serpent,* the Quetzalcoatl ceremonies are ritualized utopian visions radically opposed to the bourgeois European world inhabited by Kate. Woolf's pageant is a vision of history compressed, flattened, rationalized, and ordered, in contrast with the apparently aimless, random, extenuated quality of everyday unrecorded life. Despite major differences in tone and ideology, each author employs the techniques of stage drama to subvert the linear, sequential, causal presentation of time ordinarily associated with prose narrative.

In one way, Woolf's tactic is close to Joyce's; she evokes eternity not through Miltonic swellings, but by making an utter mockery of history as a plot, with major and minor characters, introductions, climaxes and conclusions, moral tags, and readily decipherable meanings. At first, the audience thinks it quaint to see children and neighbors dressed up and speaking the "parts" of England, Elizabeth, the Age of Reason, the Victorian period, and so forth. Every now and then, seen from a distance, the costumes look surprisingly good for a moment, and the spectators are stirred with nostalgia or patriotism. But it is clear that they are not looking into the past at all. They are seeing a stylization of their own memories and imaginations, a gratifying conquering of time, threatened, as the ordering mind always is, by rain or passion or boredom.

If the past is apprehended in this novel, it is not so much in stories and costumes as in the landscape and characters, imprinted with hieroglyphic markings to be read and deciphered in terms of the present. Before the "historical" pageant begins, old Oliver, the owner of Pointz Hall on whose grounds the pageant takes place and a retired member of the Indian Civil Service, gives a clue to the recovery of the past. "The site they had chosen for the cesspool was, if he had heard aright, on the Roman road. From an aeroplane, he said, you could still see, plainly marked, the scars made by the Britons; by the Romans; by the Elizabethan manor house; and by the plough, when they ploughed the hill to grow wheat in the Napoleonic wars"(4). History is presented as a "scar," a mark of some human activity, roadbuilding or ploughing, that is familiar and functional and not necessarily interconnected in a single meaningful pattern. Like the earth, people are marked by the past, but not always in ways they recognize or understand. The errand boy who brings the fish for lunch has "to deliver right over the hill at Bickley; also go round by Waythorn, Roddam, and Pyeminster, whose names, like his own were in Domesday Book"(31).

When connections to the past are carefully selected, sorted out, and arranged according to some order, the result is a story with the capacity to "instruct by pleasing," in short, to satisfy the human hunger for pattern and meaning. The alternative is a glimpse—never a sustained scrutiny, which would be impossible—of connections so numerous they appear unending. This glimpse into infinite association is the contemplation of an absolute, like looking directly at the face of God or into the abyss.

In the terms available to a novelist, absolute harmony and absolute chaos are nearly indistinguishable. Both are beyond words and character to express except in temperamental nuances that themselves seem incidental and random. Mrs. Swithin (Mr. Oliver's sister), a religious old lady given to praying for good weather, is not for a moment taken in by the historicity of the pageant. In the interval after the Victorian scene, she is questioned by Isa about the past:

> "The Victorians," Mrs. Swithin mused. "I don't believe," she said with her odd little smile, "that there ever were such people. Only you and me and William dressed differently."
> "You don't believe in history," said William. (175)

Mrs. Swithin understands what the director, Miss La Trobe, is attempting in her spectacle as few of the other characters can. She does not see the pageant, even in its quaint and amateurish aspects, as a summary of British history or a glimpse into other times, but as the precise opposite; for her it is a relief from time, an ordered revelation of the possibilities unrealized in a single life. The pageant is not history but art, and, like the opera at Covent Garden, it momentarily relieves the spectators from the choices they have made, the "exile" of their own lives.

Mrs. Swithin's "madness," her abstraction and impracticality, stem not from rigid dogma, not from religion understood as a particular way of telling every story, but from her sense of the infinite number of untold stories and unlived parts. She defeats history by living, like an artist or saint, in an eternal potential and by responding to that in the people around her. What makes her "religious" is her faith that all lines—the stories told and untold, the idiot, cows, and kings—will eventually come together in harmony. When she caresses her cross and gazes vaguely into the distance, her skeptical relatives imagine her mental state. "She was off, they guessed, on a circular tour of the imagination—one-making. Sheep, cows, grass, trees, ourselves—all are one. If discordant, producing harmony—if not to us, to a gigantic ear attached to a gigantic head . . .

All is harmony, could we hear it. And we shall. Her eyes now rested on the white summit of a cloud. Well, if the thought gave her comfort, William and Isa smiled across her, let her think it"(175).

A more cynical rendering of contemplation could hardly be imagined, but it is important to notice that, despite the fact that William and Isa's attitudes correspond with what seems to have been Woolf's own view of religious faith, the irony and the viewpoint presented in the novel are theirs, not those of an authoritative narrator. Woolf is less interested in ridiculing piety than in demonstrating the ways people show themselves to others, in contrast to the way they see themselves. Using the pageant, as she used the opera in *Jacob's Room,* as the occasion to move back and forth from the consciousness of the actor to the consciousness of the viewer, she uncovers the richness of the imagination by continually exposing it to the inadequate judgments and interpretations, the verbal caricatures, that unsympathetic spectators impose on it. The reader need not share Mrs. Swithin's mystical faith to see that Isa and William have represented her superficially and that their failure is one not only of belief but of imagination. They have turned her into a "character," eccentric and lovable, easy to place and patronize—something Woolf, with exquisite tact, has refused to do.

L I K E Joyce and Lawrence, Woolf frequently lets her invented figures do a great deal of the narrative dirty work. They tag and judge other characters, make generalizations and easy connections, explain and interpret events in ways the author never would. The representations of life that are more nearly true and vital emerge, like the drama between the acts, in the spaces between the necessary falsehoods. Nearly all the characters are trapped by the way others see them as well as by the lives they have chosen for themselves.

Isa, Mrs. Giles Oliver, is seen by her neighbors as a lucky young woman, happily married to a handsome and wealthy man, the mother of two beautiful sons, the mistress of a fine house. But in her interior life, Isa is not at all what she seems, nor is she so different from her husband's pious aunt. Though skeptical and melancholy, Isa, too, dwells on unseen connections; she responds to the vulnerability of William Dodge, is impatient with stories, and longs for an absolute resolution to everything. For her, the point toward which things converge is death, not God, and though the difference does seem to affect the two women's dispositions, there are otherwise few observable distinctions between them in the untheological world of Woolf's novel. Death, like God, is absolute, omnipotent, unknowable, the solution to all possible problems, the eternal mystery. If taken into account with any real seriousness, it sheds a strange and pervasive light on human experience.

Isa, like Mrs. Swithin, lives in the "presence of the gods" because death is never very far from her thoughts. Mrs. Swithin's heaven is "changeless," the perfectly balanced equation where all is at rest; in the abstract, it bears a striking resemblance to Isa's vision of death. The difference is that what Mrs. Swithin contemplates with serenity and hope, as the final summing up, Isa experiences with gloom as infinite subtraction. " 'Where do I wander?' she mused. 'Down what draughty tunnels? Where the eyeless wind blows? And there grows nothing for the eye. No rose. To issue where? In some harvestless dim field where no evening lets fall her mantle; nor sun rises. All's equal there. Unblowing, ungrowing are the roses there. Change is not; nor the mutable and lovable; nor greetings nor partings; nor furtive findings and feelings, where hand seeks hand and eye seeks shelter from the eye' "(154–155).

As an expression of Isa's mental state, the passage is a curious mixture of blank sterility and lyricism, a pastoral elegy that blends a longing for peace with an anticipated regret for the loss of life. Neither woman is able to penetrate the curtain between life and death; thus each behaves as if she were a member of an audience witnessing the spectacle of earth and sky and trying, like all spectators, to see what lies behind. What they imagine—the end of change—is remarkably similar.

The contemplation of death and God plays absolute havoc with the two women's sense of time and place. The ability to experience imaginatively the end of time and place frees them from the illusion that years and situations are somehow fixed in order and significance. From the vantage point of eternity, hours and settings are curiously flexible and relative. Mrs. Swithin's servants and relatives take it for granted that her habit of transporting herself, while reading the *Outline of History,* to primeval forests of rhododendron growing in Piccadilly, is part and parcel of her being "batty." But the same imaginative freedom is what enables her to feel what the young homosexual William Dodge feels and to "heal" him with her attention. " 'We have other lives, I think, I hope,' she murmured. 'We live in others, Mr. . . . We live in things' "(70). When he gathers up the courage to tell her his first name, "she smiled a ravishing girl's smile, as if the wind had warmed the wintry blue in her eyes to amber." Mrs. Swithin's capacity for imaginative "dislocation" transforms both William and herself momentarily; she gives him his manhood and, through his grateful response, regains her youth for an instant.

Without realizing it, Isa repeats almost exactly Mrs. Swithin's gesture of sympathetic identification with William Dodge. She takes him to see the barn and they fall into natural and intimate conversation. " 'Perhaps because we've never met before, and never shall again.' 'The doom of sudden death hanging over us,' he said. 'There's no retreating and advancing'—he was thinking of the old lady showing him the house— 'for us as for them' "(114). Living in the presence of death is obviously not a matter of age but of mentality. Those who do—like Isa and Mrs. Swithin—have a bond with others that their age, sex, and station in life do not explain. But if this capacity to break out of the limitations of the external self has a healing and benevolent effect on others, it is a power that frequently brings pain to the one who possesses it.

Throughout the novel, Isa returns to the emotions stirred in her by a gentleman farmer to whom she has barely spoken but who once handed her a teacup and a tennis racket and whose "ravaged," "romantic" face she cannot forget. The difference between Isa's imaginative attachment and the flirtation between her husband and Mrs. Manresa during the intervals of the pageant is that hers is an "unacted part," a role that her mind envisions but that her circumstance and sense of duty prevent her from acting out even in that harmless and superficial fashion. The importance of Isa's romantic longing for the "man in grey" is not in the fantasy itself but in the extent to which its possibilities remind her of the fixed limits of her external life. "She sought the face that all day long she had been seeking. Preening and peering, between backs, over shoulders, she had sought the man in grey. He had given her a cup of tea at a tennis party; handed her, once, a racket. That was all. But, she was crying, had we met before . . . had we met, she was crying. And when her little boy came battling through the bodies in the Barn 'Had he been his son,' she had muttered"(208).

Isa is not so much looking for a lover as she is seeking a savior who will rescue her from the fixed scheme of her life. In subordinating plot, the history of external events, to the unrestricted life of the imagination, Woolf shows that in many lives there is more drama—conflict and heightened emotion—in enduring what fails to happen than in acting out what does. In the terms of the novel's plot, the sequence of the day's events, Isa and Mrs. Swithin are passive members of the audience watching the pageant. Their lives are settled; nothing occurs in the course of the day to change their circumstances; outwardly no decisions or choices are made. Yet, seen from within the two characters, a drama is composed, played out, and observed. Every gesture and word, every movement and revelation to the outside world, is forged, often at great cost and with enormous discipline, from the array of other possibilities, the most persistent and extreme of which is death. The acceptance of an ordinary role in life for those who can truly imagine themselves in either many roles or none is a concentrated act of affirmation and sacrifice.

PERHAPS the most obvious effect of Woolf's novel-cum-pageant is that it dramatically redefines drama. The "real" drama occurs not on stage—where the lives of the rich, the famous, and the excessively virtuous or evil are represented—but in the ordinary, unobtrusive, moment-by-moment lives of the audience as glimpsed in the intervals of the performance. But valid though this is as a partial description of the effect of the book, it does not entirely justify its peculiar structure. George Eliot long ago argued for the emotional richness and historical interest of the daily lives of "unremarkable" people, and she showed in most of her fiction how a novelist could tap this richness and interest without radically altering the structural conventions of prose narrative.

Woolf's insistence on the pageant, not merely as a background piece but as a literary invention in peculiar competition with the narrative, provides the reader with an experience not found in George Eliot. Speeches, plots, characters, and costumes are presented in detail and in sharp counterpoint to the comparatively unspectacular, even desultory, carrying on of the audience. The rapidity with which the pageant races through British history makes the spectators seem almost to be standing still in contrast. Furthermore, the compressed and complicated plots of the three scenes from plays typical of the Renaissance, the eighteenth century, and the Victorian age make it appear that, in comparison, nothing at all is happening in the lives of the audience. Superficially, the very reverse of Eliot's view emerges. Glamor and excitement do seem to belong to heroic ancestors, rather than to one's own life or those of the dull neighbors.

In fact, Woolf's concept of "dramatic interest," has to do with method of presentation rather than with subject matter, though she agrees with Eliot that fame, social status, and conventional heroism have little to do with literary merit. What the full-scale reproduction of the pageant shows with satirical sharpness, however, is the radical difference between exploring human character through plot and exploring it through moments of illumination loosely bound by circumstance. During the period scenes, each of which is a parody of the literary conventions of its day, the whole idea of plot is challenged by a member of the audience.

As the Renaissance revenge tragedy unwinds, for instance, Isa's mind rebels. "There was such a medley of things going on, what with the beldame's deafness, the bawling of the youths, and the confusion of the plot that she could make nothing of it. Did the plot matter? She shifted and looked over her right shoulder. The plot was only there to beget emotion. There were only two emotions: love; and hate. There was no need to puzzle out the plot"(90).

Isa's glance over her shoulder (presumably looking for the "man in grey") reminds her and the reader that the literal acting out of events is not the only way to "beget emotion." Beneath the story line of every life lie unacted parts and unnarrated plots with their own power over the heart. In seeking some means of expressing this potent inner life, Isa cuts through external variations to the core emotions themselves, to love and hate or their resolution in peace. She wants to strip down and simplify life even further than a stage play does. For her, the two shortest speeches in the play rather than its story come closest to the truth of life. *"Hail, sweet Carinthia!* said the Prince, sweeping his hat off. And she to him, raising her eyes: *My love! My lord!* 'It was enough. Enough. Enough,' Isa repeated. All else was verbiage, repetition."

Isa's exclamation betrays something more subtle than a sentimental susceptibility to romance. It is an expression of impatience with whatever distracts attention from the central reality. For Woolf, through Isa, the passage makes a literary point in a highly literary way. While allowing a genuine plea for plain and honest language, the author demonstrates that its aim is best achieved not through naiveté but through an informed grasp of the possibilities of language. While Woolf sympathizes with Isa's impatience with plot, she demonstrates at the same time how its tedious intricacies are the preconditions of her recovery of simplicity. Thus the passage is more than simple assertion or debate. It is an implicit dramatic dialogue, a presentation of conflict and a precarious resolution of complex "scenes." The title *Between the Acts* refers not only to what occurs during the intervals of the pageant but to the dramatic interaction between what is performed on stage and what is expressed or thought among the spectators.

For Woolf, art, in its highest form, combines the techniques of poetic drama and prose narrative; it mediates between the extremes of absolute simplicity—Mrs. Swithin's notion of God and Isa's of death—and absolute chaos. The work of art itself, rather than being fixed in a static and neutral ground between poles, continually moves back and forth between extremes; it best imitates life by repeatedly risking and surviving insane profusion and sterile economy, prodigious inclusiveness and arid selectivity.

When an entire scene is summarized for the audience during the presentation of the eighteenth-century comedy, Mr. Swithin is delighted. " 'How right! Actors show us too much. The Chinese, you know, put a dagger on the table and that's a battle. And so Racine ...' "(142).

Amidst the parody of an elaborately schematic eighteenth century play, Woolf intrudes with a similarly absurd caricature of Isa's—and in many ways, her own—irritation with plot. With her tendency for "one-making," Mrs. Swithin would reduce all theatricals to staring at an inanimate object, but she is interrupted by the down-to-earth Mrs. Manresa, who, "scenting culture," responds that "they," apparently meaning Racine, the Chinese, and other cultural snobs, "bore one stiff." Certainly, for the reader as well as for several members of the audience, the pageant would be much less interesting without Mrs. Manresa and her lack of cultured reticence and refined ideas. Once again, Woolf dramatizes an attack and a counterattack—not merely a disagreement between two spectators, but a clash between two radically different forms of literary expression, the economy of the drama and the prodigality of the novel, the taciturn Carinthia confronted by Moll Flanders.

During the rendition of a Victorian play of sentimental love and piety, another member of the audience finds another reason to wish the pageant were shorter and simpler. Isa wants pure emotional truth; Mrs. Swithin, unity; but old Mrs. Springett, who grew up in the Victorian period, wants something less like life as she has lived it. When one of the actors, in the role of a country parson, rises to say grace at a picnic, Mrs. Springett protests, "This is too much, too much." She feels vaguely that the imitation is somehow mocking her and her religion. Despite the stylization, she recognizes herself and her kind too easily.

The ultimate outrage to the audience, however, comes in the modern period, which is represented not by a play but by the entire cast holding up mirrors and broken fragments of glass to show, in moving and distorted flashes, the audience to itself. Aside from vividly identifying the audience with the spectacle, transforming the spectators into performers, as has been done in a variety of other ways from the beginning, this scene makes yet another comment on the mimetic nature of art. For once, the audience has been relieved of the burden of a plot, of a simplifying design, and the result is pandemonium, a confusion of outcries and laughter, grimaces and gaping. Miss La Trobe's "trick" has been to move the audience from its comfortable detachment during the early and highly formalized sections of the pageant to an unmediated vision of itself, not as wicked or ugly but as fragmented and insignificant. She has shown them with her cheap, amateur country spectacle how desperately they depend on even her art.

NEAR the end of the novel, when the pageant is over and the guests have gone home, Isa sits down with her husband and prepares to take up her role as wife and mother—that is, to sink for as long as she can into a plot. " 'The father of my children, whom I love and hate.' Love and hate—how they tore her asunder! Surely it was time someone invented a new plot, or that the author came out from the bushes"(215). The thought that the "author" of life's plots is hiding in the bushes parallels Stephen Dedalus's remark to a whore who tries to tell his fortune by looking at the lines in his palm: "I never could read His handwriting." To the modern artist, God as a prototype of the hidden author of obscure but repetitive plots is a curious blend of inspiration and disillusionment. On the one hand, the artist who is himself a reader incapable of deciphering the "big plot" is in no position to act, as his predecessors did, the part of oracle or interpreter. He cannot penetrate the motivation of God's mind or imitate its fertility. On the other hand, God in the bushes, the God with unreadable handwriting, endows humanity with a unique gift. In His act of abandonment, He leaves it peculiarly free. The artist need no longer imitate a particular kind of virtue or wisdom or omniscience, since the divine character who once seemed to possess them has left the stage.

The highest form of mimesis is no longer one that attempts to reproduce a grand design, a superstory with countless subplots and a foregone conclusion like that recounted by the Archangel Michael in *Paradise Lost*. Instead, its new form is dynamically relational, a tentative call and a free response, an incomplete gift that requires an active receiver; it is an utterance in constant need of fresh interpretation to become a word. At one point, Miss La Trobe, who frequently emerges from behind the bushes, wishes that she could produce a play without an audience. Literally, this is only a sign of momentary irritation with her dull spectators, but the absurdity of the wish is central to Woolf's conception of art. The play only becomes a play when it has an audience.

If there is something godlike in Miss La Trobe, it can be found not in her craft or her strong will or even in her obscurity, but rather in what she, with the help of the audience, can bring to fruitition. When Mrs. Swithin tries to thank Miss La Trobe for the pageant, her words are halting but the character of her gesture is clear:

> She gazed at Miss La Trobe with a cloudless old-aged stare. Their eyes met in a common effort to bring a common meaning to birth. They failed; and Mrs. Swithin, laying hold desperately of a fraction of her meaning, said: "What a small part I've had to play! But you've made me feel I could have played . . . Cleopatra!"
> She nodded between the trembling bushes and ambled off.
> The villagers winked. "Batty" was the word for Old Flimsy, breaking through the bushes.
> "I might have been—Cleopatra," Miss La Trobe repeated. "You've stirred in me my unacted part," she meant.(153)

When Mrs. Swithin mutters something about how she "might have been Cleopatra," Miss La Trobe repeats her words. In a rare authorial intrusion, Woolf adds to the exchange, placing the quotation marks in such way as to distinguish her own observation from those of the two characters, " 'You've stirred in me my unacted part,' she meant." The "stirring" of a new life, the glimpse into realities beyond the immediate and external is like a biological birth, the consequence of the labor of two.

In this case, Miss La Trobe's intentions in writing and directing the pageant are actually quite clearly stated, though they are swamped by the efforts of many in the audience who are looking for explanations and meanings of their own. In fact, the explanations, even when they are conventional and limited, like those of the vicar at the end ("we act different parts; but are the same"), contribute to the success of the drama. Their value is not so much in their accuracy, since as general statements they must always be different from the concrete spectacle itself, but in their responsiveness to the artist's appeal to create a new order and, by doing so, to overcome the inscrutability of nature. As the first interval begins, Miss La Trobe is exhilarated: "Hadn't she, for twenty-five minutes, made them see? A vision imparted was relief from agony . . . for one moment . . . one moment"(98). To ask what the members of the audience see is to pose the wrong question; as their musings during intermission reveal, they all see different visions according to their circumstances. The shared experience is "relief from agony." Visions may differ, but the agony of no vision is the same for everyone. Later in the pageant, when things seem to be going wrong and the audience is becoming bored, Miss La Trobe feels their discomfort with an intensity that links her with all other mortals: "Panic seized her. Blood seemed to pour from her shoes. This is death, death, death, she noted in the margin of her mind; when illusion fails"(180).

Together, author and audience rescue life from chaos and death. Neither can do it alone; each takes on some of the other's tasks while superficially maintaining a "primary" role. Miss La Trobe is not exclusively a mysterious presence in the bushes, a director behind the scenes. She, too, has a part in a familiar and tiresome plot. She is a lonely, eccentric spinster, suspected by the villagers of being a lesbian, and she drinks too much. The responsiveness, the momentary trust of the audience, relieves her from the bleak tedium of the role in which she seems to have been pointlessly cast. But if she is director and actor, she is also a spectator. From her hidden vantage point, she observes the audience as though they were the performers—as in the modern scene when the mirrors are held up to them, they briefly become. Her success as an artist, like the lives of Isa and Mrs. Swithin, depends on her capacity to shift perspective and to make connections that are unexpected, but recognized and accepted once made.

Miss La Trobe knows the value of illusion, because she knows the blank horror of its failure. When the pageant is over and she is leaving the grounds of the house, she undergoes a kind of "death" very much like Isa's, in which the landscape is seen stripped of life and change. "It was growing dark. Since there were no clouds to trouble the sky, the blue was bluer, the green greener. There was no longer a view—no Folly, no spire of Bolney Minster. It was land merely, no land in particular"(210). Miss La Trobe pauses and puts down her suitcase, and suddenly the barren deathscape becomes a stage. " 'I should group them,' she murmured, 'here.' It would be midnight; there would be two figures, half concealed by a rock. The curtain would rise."

This is, of course, a prefiguration of the last "scene" of the novel, in which Giles and Isa sit alone after everyone has gone to bed; for the first time in the long day, they are actually about to speak to one another and, in doing so, to create their lives again: "Then the curtain rose. They spoke"(219). Though this is a dialogue the reader will never hear, it is an anticipation of design that he has been prepared to evaluate with fresh sympathy. Woolf has made a unique identification with artist, actor, and audience. Like Miss La Trobe, she prepares to compose a new scheme against the barren landscape. But, as Isa demonstrates, this gesture of will and invention is not merely a craftsman's prerogative; rather, it is essential to acting out one's roles in life, to the player's as well as the author-director's function. Finally, Giles, who has seemed throughout the book more a member of an audience than an actor, is called upon to interpret and respond to his wife's words. "Before they slept, they must fight; after they had fought, they would embrace. From that embrace, another life might be born"(219).

The artist's gesture is godlike not because of its power or wisdom or virtue but because, against the backdrop of certain death, it imagines love and new life. Woolf's symbol of creative reconciliation, the anticipated embrace of husband and wife, parallels Bloom's protective gesture toward Stephen and the lovers' dialogue at the end of *The Plumed Serpent*. None of these is a conventional "happy ending." Each serves as a kind of culmination, but none is wholly conclusive or simple in its effect. Each moment of harmony is wrested from painful dissonance and presumably will yield to it again. The cooperating imaginations, like children, friends, lovers, and members of an audience, will disperse until "called" again into coherence. And beyond the numerous minor dispersals is the final one that, when recalled, seems to make all the momentary harmonies futile.

But the modern writer who lets dramatic spectacle intrude on fiction does more than remind the reader of death. By dividing consciousness between audience and actor, the author scatters his ego and forces the reader to do the same in an imagined loss of time and place, an interruption of plot and history, liberating to the point of vertigo, after which the momentary recoveries of limited order and understanding emerge like interventions of grace.

NOTES

Introduction

1. The view recurs among literary critics that it is all but impossible for the same reader to admire both Joyce and Lawrence and that totally different criteria must be employed in evaluating their work. See, for example: F. R. Leavis, *D. H. Lawrence: Novelist* (London: Chatto and Windus, 1955), p. 10; Arnold Kettle, *An Introduction to the English Novel* (New York: Harper and Brothers, 1951), vol. 2, p. 135; Leon Edel, *The Modern Psychological Novel* (New York: Grosset and Dunlap, 1955), p. 203; Hugh Kenner, *Dublin's Joyce* (London: Chatto and Windus, 1955), p. 140; Walter Allen, *The English Novel* (London: Phoenix House, 1954), p. 357; and David Daiches, *The Novel and the Modern World* (Chicago: University of Chicago Press, 1960), p. 185. For significant exceptions to this attitude, see Richard Ellmann, *Ulysses on the Liffey* (London: Faber and Faber, 1972), pp. 26, 73; George Ford, *Double Measure* (New York: Holt, Rinehart and Winston, 1965), p. 134; and Frank Kermode, *Romantic Image* (London: Routledge and Kegan Paul, 1957), pp. 1–2.

2. Quotations are from James Joyce, *A Portrait of the Artist as a Young Man* (New York: Viking Press, 1964).

3. *Phoenix: The Posthumous Papers of D. H. Lawrence*, ed. Edward D. McDonald (New York: Viking Press, 1976), pp. 379–380.

4. *The Collected Letters of D. H. Lawrence*, ed. Harry T. Moore (New York: Viking Press, 1962), vol. 1, p. 282.

5. Virginia Woolf, *The Moment and Other Essays* (London: Hogarth Press, 1947), p. 137.

6. Ibid., p. 138.

7. Virginia Woolf, *The Second Common Reader* (New York: Harcourt, Brace and World, 1932), p. 200.

8. Virginia Woolf, *Granite and Rainbow* (London: Hogarth Press, 1960), p. 19.

9. Virginia Woolf, *The Common Reader* (New York: Harcourt, Brace and World, 1925), p. 244.

10. Ibid.

NOTES

1. By the Beautiful Sea

1. The original idea for *The Trespasser,* or *Siegmund's Saga,* as it was first called, came from an episode in the life of Lawrence's friend Helen Corke. "The Freshwater Diary," the memoir she let Lawrence use in writing his novel, and her later reflections on the affair are contained in Helen Corke, *In Our Infancy: An Autobiography* (Cambridge: Cambridge University Press, 1975).

2. Quotations from D. H. Lawrence, *The Trespasser* (London: Penguin Books, 1975).

3. See the discussion of *Portrait* in Wayne Booth, *The Rhetoric of Fiction* (Chicago: University of Chicago Press, 1961), pp. 324–336.

4. Though most critics have dismissed *The Trespasser,* especially its Wagnerian allusions, Frank Kermode has noted that the tone is "qualified by irony since Helena is a neurotic Wagnerite" and that the book as a whole "has its importance" as an early expression of some of Lawrence's fundamental and persistent attitudes. See *Lawrence* (London: Fontana/Collins, 1973), pp. 14–15.

5. Quotations are from Virginia Woolf, *The Voyage Out* (New York: Harcourt, Brace and World, 1948).

6. Northrop Frye, *The Stubborn Structure* (London: Methuen, 1970), p. 34.

7. Quotations are from James Joyce, *Ulysses* (New York: Random House, 1961).

8. Quotations are from D. H. Lawrence, *Kangaroo* (London: Penguin Books, 1975).

9. Quotations are from Virginia Woolf, *To the Lighthouse* (New York: Harcourt, Brace and World, 1927).

2. Our Great Sweet Mother

1. In discussing Joyce's concept of the imagination in *Portrait,* Richard Ellmann observes, "Joyce was obviously well-pleased with the paradox into which his method had put him, that he was, as the artist framing his own development in a constructed matrix, his own mother." *James Joyce* (New York: Oxford University Press, 1959), p. 309.

2. For an excellent discussion of the mother in *Ulysses* and of Molly as one incarnation of the role, see M. Schechner, " 'The Song of the Wandering Aengus': James Joyce and his Mother," in *Fifty Years: Ulysses,* ed. Thomas F. Staley (Bloomington: Indiana University Press, 1972), pp. 72–88.

3. Of the many discussions of the mother-and-son relationship in Lawrence, some of the most provocative are Seymour Betsky, "Rhythm and Theme: D. H. Lawrence's *Sons and Lovers,*" in *The Achievement of D. H. Lawrence,* ed. Frederick J. Hoffman and Harry T. Moore (Norman: University of Oklahoma Press, 1953), pp. 131–143; Father William Tiverton, *D. H. Lawrence and Human Existence* (London: Rockliff, 1951), pp. 19–37; Mark Spilka, *The Love Ethic of D. H. Lawrence* (Bloomington: Indiana University Press, 1955), pp. 39–89; H. M. Daleski, *The Forked Flame* (London: Faber and Faber, 1965), pp. 42–73; Alfred Kazin, "Sons, Lovers, and Mothers," *Partisan Review* 29 (Summer 1962): 373–385.

4. Kazin, "Sons, Lovers, and Mothers," p. 384.

5. For a particularly brilliant exposition of this view, see Robert Alter, *Partial Magic: The Novel as a Self-Conscious Genre* (Berkeley: University of California Press, 1975).

6. Quotations are from D. H. Lawrence, *Sons and Lovers* (New York: Viking Press, 1958).

7. Quotations are from D. H. Lawrence, "Daughters of the Vicar," in *The Complete Short Stories of D. H. Lawrence,* 3 vols. (New York: Viking Press, 1961), vol. 1, pp. 136–186.

8. For a discussion of this aspect of the story, see Leavis, *D. H. Lawrence: Novelist,* pp. 85–112.

9. Quotations are from D. H. Lawrence, *Aaron's Rod* (London: Penguin Books, 1975).

10. D. H. Lawrence, *Psychoanalysis and the Unconscious* (New York: Viking Press, 1960), p. 31.

11. For psychoanalytic speculations on the parallels between Woolf's attitude toward her own mother and the relationship between Lily Briscoe and Mrs. Ramsay, see Phyllis Rose, *Woman of Letters: A Life of Virginia Woolf* (New York: Oxford University Press, 1978), pp. 153–173.

12. Quotations are from Virginia Woolf, *The Years* (New York: Harcourt, Brace and World, 1965).

13. For a possible connection between Delia's reaction to her mother's death and Woolf's recollection of an apparent absence of feeling at her own mother's deathbed, see Rose, *Woman of Letters,* p. 110.

14. Virginia Woolf, *A Writer's Diary* (New York: Harcourt Brace, 1954), p. 263.

3. A Long Event of Perpetual Change

1. Quotations are from D. H. Lawrence, *Women in Love* (New York: Viking Press, 1960).

2. Quotations are from James Joyce, "The Dead," *Dubliners* (New York: Viking Press, 1958), pp. 175–224; D. H. Lawrence, "The Shadow in the Rose Garden," *Complete Short Stories,* vol. 1, pp. 221–233; Virginia Woolf, "The Legacy," *The Haunted House and Other Short Stories* (New York: Harcourt, Brace and World, 1973), pp. 126–135.

3. Given his own method of juxtaposing voices and moods in *The Wasteland,* it is extraordinary that in *After Strange Gods* Eliot used this story as an illustration of Lawrence's moral obtuseness.

4. S. L. Goldberg, *The Classical Temper* (London: Chatto and Windus, 1961), p. 190.

5. Quotations are from D. H. Lawrence, *The Rainbow* (London: Penguin Books, 1975).

6. D. H. Lawrence, "Study of Thomas Hardy," *Phoenix,* p. 477.

7. Frank Kermode, *Lawrence,* p. 27.

8. Quotations are from Virginia Woolf, *Mrs. Dalloway* (New York: Harcourt, Brace and World, 1925).

4. Between Us Is This Line

1. Quotations are from James Joyce, "A Little Cloud," *Dubliners*, pp. 70–85.
2. A. Walton Litz, *James Joyce* (New York: Twayne Publishers, 1966), p. 72.
3. For a persuasive discussion of the villanelle's importance as a symbol of Stephen's development, see Robert Scholes, "Stephen Dedalus, Poet or Esthete?" *PMLA* 89 (September 1964): 484–489.
4. Quotations are from D. H. Lawrence, *The White Peacock* (London: Penguin Books, 1976).
5. *Collected Letters of D. H. Lawrence*, vol. 1, p. 25.
6. Kermode, *Romantic Image*, p. 6.
7. Ibid., pp. 1–2.
8. Though an advocate of intimate friendship, Lawrence usually spoke disapprovingly of sexual relations between men. "Sodomy only means that a man knows he is chained to the rock," *Collected Letters of D. H. Lawrence*, vol. 1, p. 319.
9. *Collected Letters of D. H. Lawrence*, vol. 1, pp. 251–252.
10. D. H. Lawrence, "Surgery for the Novel—or a Bomb," *Phoenix*, p. 520.
11. A sound commentary on this scene and the larger subject of male friendship in Lawrence can be found in Mark Spilka, *The Love Ethic of D. H. Lawrence* (Bloomington: Indiana University Press, 1955), pp. 148–168.
12. Quotations are from Virginia Woolf, *The Waves* (New York: Harcourt, Brace and World, 1959), published in a single volume with *Jacob's Room*.
13. For an excellent analysis of perspective in *The Waves*, see J. W. Graham, "Point of View in *The Waves*: Some Services of the Style," *University of Toronto Quarterly* 39 (April 1970): 193–211; reprinted in *Virginia Woolf: A Collection of Criticism*, ed. Thomas S. W. Lewis (New York: McGraw-Hill, 1975), pp. 94–112.
14. For an extended discussion of the diffusion of the narrator in the narration, see James Naremore, *The World Without a Self: Virginia Woolf and the Novel* (New Haven: Yale University Press, 1973).
15. Of the many commentaries on androgyny in Woolf's work, two of particular interest are Herbert Marder, *Feminism and Art: A Study of Virginia Woolf* (Chicago: University of Chicago Press, 1968), pp. 105–152; and Rose, *Woman of Letters*, pp. 175–193.

5. The Tendency toward Drama

1. D. H. Lawrence, "We Need One Another," *Phoenix*, p. 190.
2. Virginia Woolf, "Notes on an Elizabethan Play," *Common Reader*, p. 51.
3. As Marilyn French has observed, "Joyce's method of engaging the reader in the creation of the work here reaches its height"; *The Book as World: James Joyce's Ulysses* (Cambridge: Harvard University Press, 1976), p. 194.
4. James Joyce, "Drama and Life," *The Critical Writings*, ed. Ellsworth Mason and Richard Ellmann (New York: Viking Press, 1959), p. 45.
5. See Ellmann, *Ulysses on the Liffey*, pp. 146–147.

NOTES

6. D. H. Lawrence, "Indians and an Englishman," *Phoenix,* p. 92.

7. Quotations are from D. H. Lawrence, *The Lost Girl* (London: Penguin Books, 1976).

8. Quotations are from D. H. Lawrence, *The Plumed Serpent* (New York: Knopf, 1951).

9. For an excellent discussion of the personal, as opposed to the social and political, significance of the novel, see Jascha Kessler, "Descent in Darkness: The Myth of *The Plumed Serpent,*" in *A D. H. Lawrence Miscellany,* ed. H. T. Moore (Carbondale: Southern Illinois University Press, 1959), pp. 239–261.

10. F. R. Leavis, *Thoughts, Words and Creativity: Art and Thought in Lawrence* (New York: Oxford University Press, 1976), p. 59; William York Tindall, *D. H. Lawrence and Susan His Cow* (New York: Cooper Square, 1972), p. 178.

11. *Letters of Virginia Woolf,* ed. Nigel Nicolson and Joanne Trautmann (New York: Harcourt Brace Jovanovich, 1975), vol. 1, p. 423.

12. Ibid., p. 45.

13. Virginia Woolf, "Notes on an Elizabethan Play," *Common Reader,* p. 57.

14. Ibid., p. 56.

15. Quotations are from Virginia Woolf, *Jacob's Room* (New York: Harcourt Brace and World, 1959). Published in a single volume with *The Waves.*

16. Quotations are from Virginia Woolf, *Between the Acts* (New York: Harcourt, Brace Jovanovich, 1969).

Index

INDEX

Milton, John, 29, 33–34, 109, 118–119
Moore, Thomas, 138

Proust, Marcel, 61

Richardson, Samuel, 119

Sartre, Jean-Paul, 127
Scott, Sir Walter, 4
Shakespeare, William, 11, 31, 51–52, 57, 59, 98, 102
Shaw, George Bernard, 221
Shelley, Percy Bysshe, 17
Sidney, Sir Philip, 182

Tennyson, Alfred, 4, 17–18, 25
Thackeray, William Makepeace, 49, 189
Tindall, W. Y., 218

Woolf, Virginia
  Between the Acts, 224–235
  Jacob's Room, 222–223
  "The Legacy," 87–91
  Mrs. Dalloway, 119–129
  "Notes on an Elizabethan Play," 189, 222
  Three Guineas, 78–79
  To the Lighthouse, 6, 40–43, 68–74
  The Voyage Out, 30–34
  The Waves, 168–184
  The Years, 74–80
Wordsworth, William, 8, 47, 133

Yeats, William Butler, 53–54, 207

[244]